My Heroic Mother

My Heroic Mother

Voices from the Holocaust

Alfred Koppel

Order this book online at www.trafford.com
or email orders@trafford.com

FIRST EDITION

Most Trafford titles are also available at major online book retailers.

Printed in Victoria, BC, Canada.

ISBN: 978-1-4269-2453-8 (sc)
ISBN: 978-1-4269-2452-1 (hc)

Library of Congress Control Number: 2009913501

Our mission is to efficiently provide the world's finest, most comprehensive book publishing service, enabling every author to experience success. To find out how to publish your book, your way, and have it available worldwide, visit us online at www.trafford.com

Trafford rev. 2/4/10

 www.trafford.com

North America & international
toll-free: 1 888 232 4444 (USA & Canada)
phone: 250 383 6864 ♦ fax: 812 355 4082

Contents

Acknowledgements..vii

Family Tree..ix

Preface xi

Introduction 1

The Old Shoe Box 3

Hamburg, Germany...5

Berlin...10

Munich...14

Berlin...27

Munich...34

New York 39

Berlin...48

Spain..52

Las Palmas, Canary Islands..57

Denver, Colorado...61

Boulder, Colorado..62

Wales, Great Britain 65

Jerusalem 66

Colorado, USA 69

The Shoebox...71

Fort Collins, Colorado..72

Munich 77

Berlin 135

Lithuania 147

Munich 154

Vilnius, Lithuania 183

Munich 188

The Journey 199

Lithuania 216

Shoes 222

Epilogue 229

Afterword 241

Addendum 249

Bibliography 251

About the Author 258

Acknowledgements

The literature on the subject of the Holocaust is immense. Numerous scholars, writers and historians have done a huge amount of research and produced many books and documents. I have reviewed dozens of these documents and books and am indebted to these authors.

While I refer often to these scholars, any errors in interpretation of their material are entirely my own. A number of scholars and researchers have contributed greatly to my efforts through the written word as well as face-to-face conversations. The reviews of my manuscript has provided me with different viewpoints, corrections and perspectives of historical events. Dr. Andreas Heusler, of the Munich City Archive assisted me in much of my research and provided a number of documents relating to the memoir of my family. Robert Thomas of Llangeitho, Wales was my companion traveling to Germany and Lithuania. I could not have completed my original research trip without his thoughtful and moral support.

Mr. Juergen Sielemann of the Stadtarchiv Hamburg, by providing a number of documents for my research, enabled me to discover information about my family and relatives that I never knew.

Speaking of such support, I especially appreciate the kindness and assistance of Andreas and Claudia Böhmer who lived in the same apartment house in the 1990s where my family used to live some seventy years ago. Mr. and Mrs. Böhmer have become good friends over the last dozen years. Another person who contributed so much to my efforts was Werner Grube in Munich. He faithfully drove me all over city to the many places I used to frequent as a child. Furthermore, he drove me and stayed with me during my visit to the Dachau concentration camp, a most difficult journey for me.

In Lithuania, I am greatly indebted to Rachel Kostanian of the Jewish State Museum as well as her husband Henrich. Rachel Kostanian enlightened me about the history and great disaster that happened in this small Baltic State. Regina Kopilevich was the guide in Vilnius and Kovno, Lithuania. She is a person full of compassion.

My gratitude to my beloved wife, who departed this life after fifty years of marriage, for her support and commitment to this difficult endeavor. Jean never complained about my long absences when I undertook my lengthy research trips for the development of this book.

I want to extend my gratitude to Don Nolan, a gifted writer, for the monumental review of my book and editing the manuscript. His comments and suggestions were of immense help.

Jon Gustafson was most generous and immensely helpful with the proper layout of the many chapters of this difficult book. It took many hours to review and format the manuscript and to insert the photos and captions.

Family Tree

Samuel Koppel ....my paternal grandfather b. 1849

Jetta (Leipheimer) Koppel .... his wife b. 1859

Sons and Daughters of Samuel and Jetta Koppel

Siete Koppel...son b. 1880

Friedl Koppel... his non-Jewish wife

Lene (Koppel) Oettinger.................................daughter b. 1883

Max Oettinger.. her husband

Bernhard Koppel ....son b. 1884

Ulli (Neuwahl) Koppel .... his wife

Carl Koppel.................................... son (my father) b. 1885

Carola (Wagner) Koppel .... his wife

Lola (Koppel) Goldschmidt ....daughter b. 1887

Joseph Goldschmidt .... her husband

Hannah Koppel..daughter b. 1888

Leo Koppel ....son b. 1890

Sine (Baer) Koppel.. his wife

Edie Koppel...son b. 1894

Sons and Daughters of Carl and Carola Koppel

Günther Koppel...............................son b. 16 March 1924

Alfred Koppel.............................. son b. 13 September 1926

Walter Koppel.................................... son b. 8 January 1928

Hans Koppel.................................... son b. 9 January 1936

Ruth Koppel.............................. daughter b. 11 August 1937

Judis Koppel.............................. daughter b. 25 August 1939

Preface

*The Holocaust was a purely ideologically
motivated genocide. That makes it, despite
many other genocides, unique.*
— *Yehuda Bauer, Head of the
International Center for Holocaust
Studies at Yad Vashem, Jerusalem*

Why, almost sixty five years after the end of World War II, am I tackling the most heart wrenching task of my life? Is the reason that today, I am the only survivor of my family of that era? Is it because I feel I have a mission to tell this story? Is it a divine charge, a calling?

By all rights, I should have died on a number of occasions. It seems that divine intervention countervailed my early departure. Indeed, I have escaped death at least six to eight times in my life. Some of these experiences were so traumatic that I still have nightmares about them.

Let me relate a few of the most serious and frightful experiences. Early in my married life, my wife and child moved from a small western town across the Colorado Rocky Mountains to Denver. I had sent my wife and child ahead and was now following in a borrowed truck with all our belongings on the narrow and treacherous mountain road. Suddenly, descending the mountain pass, I lost my brakes. The truck accelerated to over 50 miles per hour in a 30 mile per hour zone.

To this day, I do not know how I missed colliding with cars or what kept me from falling off the road.

Several years later I tried to fix a leaking washing machine in the basement of our house. I prided myself being able to repair almost anything. As I opened the housing of the water pump to investigate, the metal gooseneck lamp shortened out. I had made the perfect electric circuit sitting in a pool of water.

I felt I was dying. Suddenly, the electric jolting ceased. My jerking arm had pulled the cord out of the electric receptacle. I still have horrible nightmares about this.

Other such near-death experiences have led me to believe that God has meant to keep me alive for some reason. Perhaps, I reasoned, I should write this memoir, indeed, had to write the story of my family. It would take many more years before I was able to begin the pilgrimage of memories. It would prove to be so distressing that often I could write no more than two or three pages at a time.

Slowly, I began to realize that I needed to, indeed, have to write this story, a most difficult task. I struggled with my emotions page by page. Yet, I felt compelled to begin this pilgrimage of memories.

Introduction

If one person dies, it is a tragedy. If a million die, it is a statistic.
—Unknown

This book is more than simply a memoir of my family. It will cover a long and difficult journey covering a span of almost one hundred years. It takes place in a number of different locations—Germany and other parts of Europe, America, Eastern Europe, Israel and several other countries. It will cover the travails, struggles, trials and tribulations as well as love, longing, success and failure of the protagonists of this story. Most of it is gleaned from the author's memory. Much of it is reconstruction of events through research in archives, institutes, libraries, universities, and witnesses' declarations as well as the many letters of my mother to her husband in New York.

If one concentration camp (Auschwitz) is mentioned, it is the very picture of evil and horror; if hundreds of camps are discussed, it is merely a statistic. Of all the extermination and concentration camps, Auschwitz is generally considered the icon of absolute evil. It tends to overshadow the many hundreds camps all over Europe, as Riga, in Latvia, Sachsenhausen, in Germany, Drancy, and so many others locations in Europe such as Mauthausen, Bergen-Belsen, Chelmno,

Flossenburg, Les Milles, Dachau, Eindhoven, Sobibor, Dora-Mittelbau, Arras, Belzec, Kunda, Baja, Treblinka, Novi Sad, Zagreb, Sarajevo, Maijdanek, Stutthof, Buchenwald, Tallinin, Gurs, Kaiserwald, Vught, Skopje, Siauliai, Kovno, and on and on, the majority of these locations are unknown to most people. To comprehend the immensity of these camps and years of horror, this book tells the story of one of such camp, the Ninth Fort at Kovno, Lithuania.

> "With each passing day the memory of the tragedy of European Jews, the greatest crime in the annals of mankind, recedes into history. Witnesses and survivors of the Holocaust are still alive, their memories remain vivid; yet, malicious myth about the experience keeps rising before our eyes, distorting and misinterpreting evidence, perverting history.
>
> "As new generations arise, so grows the incredible ignorance about our tragedy. Millions of men and women, Jews and Gentiles, are unaware of the basic facts of the tragedy, many have never even heard the word 'Holocaust.' This is the seed of a new disaster."
>
> −from the Holocaust Library in new York

It is important to point out that the writings in Germany then, as well as today contain many long sentences. Indeed, some sentences were so long that they took up an entire paragraph. I have emulated this style in some instances to convey the flavor of these olden times. In addition, the many letters reproduced in this story also contain long and stilted passages. This was the way people wrote letters in Germany some sixty years ago. I sincerely hope that it will not be too difficult for the reader to wade through these long sentences. Pressures, loneliness and worries weighed heavily on the minds of my family members. Consequently, some of the letters, from my mother and other relatives, seem to be jumbled, indeed even incoherent, particularly toward the latter part of 1941.

The Old Shoe Box

My father died in 1957. The end came quickly. A broken hip landed him in the hospital in New York. I lived and worked in Denver, Colorado at that time. A telephone call from my brother Walter informed me of my father's accident. I flew immediately to New York to visit him in the hospital. His mind was confused. Dad's anguish opened the curtains of his fogged mind. He seemed to relive his painful memories, trying to exorcise the ghosts of the past. The doctor's prognosis for regaining his health was poor. I remained in New York one week. His medical condition had not changed.

Having just begun a new job at Samsonite Corporation, I felt I could not stay away any longer considering the nation's economy was not healthy. Jobs were not plentiful. I returned to Denver.

Exactly one week later Walter called again. My father had died. I was fortunate that the general manager of the company was not only compassionate allowing me to leave again, but he also arranged a loan for me through the company to enable me to attend the funeral of my father.

Walter and I inherited very little, mostly items of a personal nature. Among them, I received a large brass menorah (nine arm candelabra for use during the Chanukah festival) and an old shoebox containing many letters. A quick glance at its contents revealed that my mother wrote most of these letters, written on thin fragile stationery. I did not have the courage to glance at the many letters being afraid of what I might learn of the fate of my mother and my siblings. The old shoebox ended up in the back of a closet. Subsequent moves to St. Louis, Missouri and Maplewood, New Jersey and finally, Denver, Colorado because of my promotions to Samsonite's headquarters. I always relegated that old shoebox to more closets. When I finally began to read these letters many years later, I realized that they should be the central theme of my journey into the past. Yet, forty years would pass before I had the courage to read all those letters.

Hamburg, Germany

We learn from history that people do not learn from history. —Hegel

Our family lived in Altona, Germany. Today, Altona is a district of the city of Hamburg. The Koppel family tree dates back more than 250 years to the time when Altona was still under Danish rule. The earliest entry of a family member shown in the *Stammbaum*—the family tree—was in the year of 1755. Indeed, the family tree even revealed the existence of a Rabbi Koppel in the mid 18th century.

My paternal grandfather, Samuel Koppel was born January 22, 1849 in Altona. In his earlier years he was a butcher. I remember him vividly from the time when I was a little boy. He always exhibited a stern mannerism. Eyeglasses perched on high on his aquiline nose with piercing blue eyes, he was the picture of formality. His attire was always the stiff white high collar and black tie, a gold chain dangling from his vest, together with a black suit. My most vivid memory of him was the picture of *Grosspapa*, my granddad sitting stiffly in the high back chair in the living room in my grandparents' apartment in the *Sonninstrasse*. All his eight children always catered to his every whim.

My grandfather married Jetta Leipheimer, born January 12, 1859, in *Huerben* in the State of Bavaria in southern Germany. I remember Oma, my grandmother, as a gracious and gentle woman. Her dark brown hair, always carefully made up into a pompadour style, graced her kind face. Dark brown eyes were deep set in an oval face underlined with an ever-smiling mouth. Usually, she was dressed in dark clothes adorned with a white lace bib.

My grandparents' had eight children, five boys and three girls. All of them except two lived in close proximity to my grandparents' house in Altona. It was a closely-knit family.

Even as a little boy, a sense of mystery and foreboding of castles and fortresses fascinated me. It continued all my life. Fortresses not

only fascinated me but intimidated me at the same time. My earliest exposure to a fortress occurred in the company with my older brother Günther whom I adored. I was four years old. Günther was two years older, always protective and kind to his two brothers, Walter and me. This noble quality would play an important role during crucial times later in his life.

Our parents liked to spend summer weekends in *Blankenese*, a resort town on the river Elbe, not far from Hamburg. Günther and I would hike through evocative and twisting streets from the Strand Hotel down to the sandy beach until we arrived at the strip of sand hugging the river. Huge ocean liners slowly maneuvered to the north leading to the North Sea, a picturesque scene. While our parents settled into comfortable beach chairs and played with our younger brother Walter, Günther and I ran down toward the edge of the river and began our handiwork. Both of us had brought our tin soldiers along.

Immediately we began to build our forts. I copied my fort from the picture book Papa had given to me for my birthday. The wet sand on the beach was the perfect vehicle to fashion my impressive fortress. Our forts were going to be defended by the tin soldiers. Within half an hour both of us had built mighty fortresses and began to position our soldiers around them. Before I could finish the placement of my soldiers, my big brother had his infantrymen already positioned at the bottom of my fort ready to storm its walls. Günther had a fiendish grin on his face as he placed his men inside my fortress. It was too late for my counter attack. I had lost again. But I loved my big brother dearly anyway.

The sky turned gray, the wind picked up and the temperature dropped rapidly. The waves of the river began to encroach upon the beach. It was not long before the waves started to lap at our fortresses. Soon they began to disintegrate. Both of us were disappointed. Quickly we picked up our tin soldiers and trudged back to the hotel. Tomorrow, we would build another fort.

This was the genesis of my fascination with fortresses. It would continue, on and off, the next six decades and culminate with my last exposure to a fort called the Ninth Fort. It was located in a far away country called Lithuania.

My grandparents and parents were very religious. All of us belonged to the Great Synagogue in Altona, which, in 1930, was already 250 years old. The Altona congregation received the "privilege" from the King of Denmark in 1641 to build a synagogue and vote in a rabbi to lead it. By 1930, Chief Rabbi Dr. Joseph Carlebach was heading the Altonaer synagogue. He was an imposing figure, black hair peppered with white, piercing eyes behind the horn-rimmed glasses. Even I, a little boy, was impressed when he delivered his sermons with his sonorous booming voice. Indeed, in the 1930s, when the Nazis attended every service to monitor what was being preached, those Nazis would shake Rabbi Carlebach's hand after the sermon and utter, "This was a most inspiring sermon, Rabbi." Such was his reputation not only in Altona and Hamburg but throughout Germany.

Nearly every Friday afternoon, late afternoon, all the Koppel families would meet at the synagogue in the *Papagoyenstrasse* in front of the ornate entry. Grandfather and grandmother received their offspring there.

My grandparents and their children l. to r. top row Edie, my father Carlo, Ulli and husband Bernhard, Lola, Leo, Hanna, l. to r. bottom row Lene, my grandfather, Helmut, Bernhard's son and my grandmother. (ca. 1916)

The men, the five brothers would be milling around discussing the latest gossip and news. The big war had been over more than a dozen years, yet they stood erect as though they were still in uniform. All five brothers had been in the army during the war. They had been proud of their fatherland. Like many of the men of that time, they identified with Kaiser Wilhelm by emulating the emperor's upward curled mustache. Photographs of them in uniform with their Kaiser Wilhelm mustaches gave them an appearance of determination and cockiness.

An item they discussed might very well have included news of the right wing NSDAP party (*Nationalsozialistische Deutsche Arbeiterpartei*— National Social German Worker's Party) that had been established in 1919 and whose leader was an Austrian, Adolf Hitler. This party spoke, among other things, of a greater Germany with citizenship only for Germans having pure 'German blood.' According to this definition, Jews could not be German citizens. The men decided that this was a passing phase of some radicals and that, under the democratic Weimar Republic, these right wing radicals would not last very long.

After the service, and after the greetings and exchange of gossips in front of the synagogue, all the Koppel families would slowly walk to the *Sonninstrasse* to Oma and Opa's apartment for the festive Sabbath dinner.

I was born in Hamburg in 1926. Günther was two years older and Walter one year younger. Since our apartment was situated one floor above our grandparents, we were able to visit them often. It was always a pleasure to visit because Oma would usually treat us with her sweets she had baked that day. However, we did try to avoid going into the living room where Opa would sit stiffly in his favorite high-backed wing chair. His forehead creased, he would frown through the thick lenses of his eyeglasses at anybody risking coming near him. He was already eighty years old, an ancient man in the eyes of a four year old boy.

My father worked together with his brother Bernhard in the wholesale leather goods business for a number of years. These were difficult times. Rapid inflation decimated the coffers of their business. It would be a number of years before there was a recovery. In the meantime, my father decided to relocate to Munich, the home of his wife Carla, and start a wholesale food business. Carla's uncle, Siegfried Hochfeld, was well established in the wholesale food business and would help him get started.

So, in the year 1930, my father moved his family to Munich. Anticipating this move, my parents sent me to my father's sister, Lola Goldschmidt and her husband, Joseph, in Berlin. Lola was unable to have any children. She had pleaded with my parents to send me to their home to ease my parents' move from Altona to Munich, and at the same time to enjoy a child for a while. Why was I picked from among the three boys? Out of the three children, Alfred was the suitable age who could live with his aunt and uncle in Berlin.

Berlin

In 1930, my mother hung a piece of cardboard around my neck containing my name as well as my aunt and uncle's name and address. My father took me to the railroad station in Altona and spoke to the conductor asking him to watch over me. I was thrilled to travel alone on a train just like a grown-up. That long ago trains were much slower than today and the trip took most of the day to traverse the 400 plus miles to reach Berlin. I grew very tired and fell asleep.

I was dreaming that a big black bird landed on my shoulder and jumped up and down. It was scary and I woke up suddenly. There, in front of me was the conductor tapping me on my shoulder saying, "We will arrive in Berlin in twenty minutes. You must get ready to meet your aunt and uncle."

As the train slowed down I heard the shrill whistle of the locomotive. Black smoke settled around the window of the compartment. I grew excited with anticipation of seeing my relatives soon. As I put on my jacket, the train lurched and jostled me back into the seat. I jumped up, took my suitcase dragging it to the door of the car. The train slowed down. One last whistle and the train came to a squealing halt. Our conductor opened the door. I pushed against the man in front of me anxious to see my aunt and uncle.

A tall woman was walking quickly alongside the train; her head turned to each window. I recognized Aunt Lola immediately from her many visits to our home in Altona. Our eyes met just as I stepped off the stairs from the car. I ran into her outstretched arms and hugged her tightly. She was my favorite aunt, the tallest of the three daughters of my grandparents.

Soon, Uncle Joseph appeared. A portly man always dressed immaculately in suit, tie, hat and the ever present walking stick. With a kiss on each cheek, then an appraising look, he welcomed me to the big city of Berlin.

Uncle Joseph hailed a porter for my suitcase. The three of us walked to the front of the Anhalter railway station and hailed a taxi. It was an exciting drive from the railway station through a big park, called Tiergarten. The drive seemed to take a long time. What a big city Berlin was! Finally, we crossed a river called the Spree and arrived at the apartment house of my aunt and uncle.

We entered through the front entrance of the building and walked into a *Hinterhof,* an attached building surrounding a nicely landscaped courtyard. Straight back, a flight up, and we were at the apartment of my relatives. While Uncle Joseph fidgeted with the keys, my loving aunt hugged me again and kissed me saying, "We are so happy to have you stay with us, Alfred." It was the beginning of pampering and spoiling little Alfred.

We walked down the long hallway leading into the dining room. There, in the middle of the room was a large table surrounded by six chairs. A huge lamp hung over the table and immediately impressed me. An umber colored silk shade covered the lamp, encircled by long fringes. The entire fixture could be pulled up and down. I immediately climbed on a chair and pulled the fixture up and down. What fun to play with the light fixture and no one told me to stop! I would soon learn that this dining room fixture would play a big role in the discussions of any weighty matter. The dining room table was the preferred venue for talks, arguments and discussions.

This was the beginning of a long and loving relationship with my aunt and uncle. I remained with Aunt Lola and Uncle Joseph through the summer of 1932. During those two years in Berlin I had much freedom. Since Aunt Lola could not have any children, she lavished love, affection and many gifts on me. I became a spoiled little boy to a point where I would kick my uncle if I did not receive something I wanted. I had my own room filled with many toys. I also had a healthy curiosity for what makes things work. One regrettable incident occurred after Uncle Joseph brought home a beautiful accordion for my fifth birthday. A few days after receiving the accordion and a futile effort to play a melody on it, I decided to look inside of the instrument to see what made those sounds. When I tried to put the accordion together again, I was unable to reassemble it. I do not remember what my uncle said after he saw what I did but I am certain his patience ran out at that time. He may even have given me a spanking. But such disciplining was rare. I could get away with most shenanigans.

I used to love to walk the short distance from our apartment house to the embankment of the river Spree and watch the river barges slowly pass by. At times, I would see a man in a rowboat with a fishing pole. I cannot remember ever having seen the fishermen pull in a fish.

One day while standing at the iron fence at the embankment of the river, I heard a loud staccato of noise coming from the nearby district called Alt Moabit. The Alt Moabit Street was a main thoroughfare in that district. It was lined with churches, a prison, and office buildings as well as apartment buildings. I told my experience to Uncle Joseph and Aunt Lola when I returned to the apartment. He looked at me knowingly and said, "Those Nazi hoodlums are at it again. Those shootings have been going on for weeks now." Little did we know that by January 1931, the Nazi hordes, the Brown Shirts had totally intimidated the local population. Many beatings and shootings happened in Alt Moabit and many other areas of Berlin. On January 30th, 1933, the *Deutsche Allgemeine Zeitung*, a national newspaper proclaimed in a huge headline, "*Reichspresident* Hindenburg appointed Hitler as Chancellor of Germany."

On February 28, 1933, the Reichstagsgebäude, the Parliament building in Berlin burned. It was not clear who set fire to this massive building. Hitler accused the Communists and imprisoned thousands of them. The next day he proclaimed an order to protect the population and the state. This emergency order allowed anyone under suspicion to be arrested and imprisoned. Newspapers could be censured, mail could be opened, and telephones tapped. All this took place despite the fact that the NSDAP party did not have a majority in the Parliament. In spite of all this intimidation and terror prior to the elections on March 5th, 1933, Hitler's party received only 43.9% of the votes, but was by far the biggest block. Still, it was not a majority. Hitler then decided to eliminate the Parliament legally as the organ to promulgate laws of the land and to give that power to the Chancellor, to Hitler, for the next four years. He accomplished this at a meeting of the Abgeordnete, the representatives in the new Parliament building, in the opera house. In front of the building and prior to the vote, SA and SS hoodlums screamed and intimidated the representatives with threats of killings and murder. In light of this, most of the representatives acquiesced and voted to give Hitler all the power he requested.

> *Where they burn books, they will soon burn*
> *people.* —Heinrich Heine,1820

Hitler became Chancellor of Germany on January 30, 1933. Only one hundred days later, Nazi thugs had been incited by their superiors to destroy "un-German" writings from book shops and libraries. More than 20,000 books by well known authors such as Thomas Mann, Ernest Hemingway, Sigmund Freud, Helen Keller, John Dos Passos and many more were burned in the *Opernplatz*–Opera House Square–opposite the Humboldt University in Berlin. Enthusiastic crowds watched and cheered around the bonfires of the book burnings throughout many German cities.

Munich

It was not long after the rise of Hitler to power that I moved back with my parents. Papa and Mutti, my parents had moved to Munich in 1930. I took my second major train ride as a little boy of six, no small undertaking in 1932. The trip must have taken at least ten hours so many years ago. Again, I had a placard with name and address hung around my neck. And again, the train conductor took me under his wing and watched over me. Aunt Lola had packed a huge bag with food and drink. I was well supplied with all the comforts of life. Actually, I felt a little like a grown up being able to take such a long train ride all by myself.

By mid afternoon I became tired. My eyes closed and quickly I was lulled to sleep to the clitter-clatter of the train's metal wheels.

When I opened my eyes late in the afternoon, the landscape had changed. Big expanses of pastures with many cows were framed by the compartment's window. Telegraph poles whizzed by. Here and there a farmhouse appeared with hay stacked high next to the barn. Even I, young as I was, saw the beauty of the ever-changing landscape. The conductor in his official red cap opened the door to the compartment and inquired how I was doing. "Very well, sir," I responded. "We will be arriving at Munich in about one hour," he advised me and added, "I shall tell you in time when to get ready to leave the train."

The train entered into a long curve, which enabled me to look forward. There, in all their majesty, tall mountains reached for the sky. Aunt Lola had told me about those mountains, called the Alps, which indicated that we were really close to Munich. This meant that I had to get ready to leave the train soon. I packed up the books and crayons and threw out the remnant of my sandwich.

The *Hauptbahnhof*, the main railroad station was immense. Hundreds of people were standing on the platform. I could not find my parents and brothers...too many people. Near panic, I craned my neck out of the window. Then I saw my loved ones, my family whom I had not seen for more than two years. Günther and Walter ran up to the window. I stretched out of the window to shake their hands but could not reach them. Then, Mutti and Papa saw me as well and motioned that

I should come to the door of the car. I rushed out of the compartment dragging my suitcase along the corridor to the door. There, the kind conductor helped me down the stairs and I flew into the arms of Mutti. She hugged and kissed me. Papa stroked my hair. I could tell he was full of emotion at seeing me after such a long time.

My parents had not changed since I was with them in Altona. But Günther and Walter both had grown a lot. Walter was only three years old when I left my home in Altona. Now he was a strapping boy of five. It was a delight to be with my family again.

Günther picked up my suitcase and we proceeded to leave the platform to the exit. There, my father hailed a taxi. After putting my suitcase into the trunk of the taxi, all of us piled into the automobile that immediately took off. "Where to?" asked the driver. "Maximilianstrasse 15" replied Papa.

Maximilianstrasse with the Maximilianeum in the center back. On the left are Bavarian office buildings and our apartment house is adjacent. Our family moved to the apartment building in the 1930s. Photo taken in 1890.

Maximilianstrasse was a beautiful street. Majestic chestnut trees lined both sides of the street. We approached a huge monument. Papa explained that the monument was built in the memory of King Maximilian the Second. The taxi driver drove around the monument, making a U-turn, and halted before a huge apartment house. It must have been six or eight stories tall, ornate, with fancy balconies strutting out onto the street.

Papa paid the driver and motioned for all of us to enter the wide front door to the building. It was quite a surprise when I entered the entryway. The floor had intricate designs made of little tiles…really beautiful. To the left was a spiral staircase hugging an elevator shaft. I had never been on an elevator. Günther punched a little button next to the elevator door. I perceived a humming sound growing louder and louder and soon, there appeared a cage made of glass and ornamental iron. My first ride in an elevator!

Papa took keys from his pocket and unlocked the door to the apartment. I rushed into the apartment. Immediately, I began to explore. The long hallway had a beautiful wooden parquet floor. This is an important bit of information that would haunt me later. Papa said, "Start to look at the front room and then, go through all the other rooms." The front room was the dining room. As I entered, I saw an upright piano on the left. Over the piano, in a gold frame, was a painting, a portrait of Mutti. She was attired in a lavender dress, looking directly at me with those beautiful, soulful brown eyes. In the middle of the long room was a big dining table with eight chairs around it. On the other side of the room stood a large credenza exhibiting all sorts of crystal and porcelain dishes. At the end of the room was a window looking out onto the street. From there, I could see the length of the Maximilianstrasse, a beautiful avenue lined with many huge trees and monuments. To my left stood the Maximilian II monument encircled by rails for the streetcars traveling up and down the street as well as crossing on the side street. I stood at this window for a long time watching trucks and taxis speed by, the streetcars clanging their bells and picking up passengers.

I finally turned and proceeded to the next room. This was the living room. It had a pot-bellied stove in one corner, an easy chair and several other chairs. But the most prominent piece of furniture was a huge desk and its spindle back chair. Papa told me that he used it a lot to transact his business dealings. Farther along the corridor were bedrooms. The first one belonged to my parents. The next one, Mutti explained to me, was for Walter and me. It had two iron bedsteads with fluffy down comforters. They looked very cozy. "Günther," explained

Papa, "was living with my mother's Aunt Else and Uncle Siegfried in the Schwabing district of Munich. This enabled Günther to attend a good gymnasium located in that area. "A gymnasium," explained Papa, "was an academic school which would lead to an education at a university later." Next to our bedroom was a room leading out onto a roof garden. All of us would spend many hours there playing, dining or just sitting in the sun. Around the corner, where the hallway made a right turn, was an inside bathroom. And high above the bathtub was a window facing the hallway. Although only six years old, I comprehended that the window was placed there to air out the bathroom. The last rooms were the kitchen, pantry, and a room next to the kitchen to sit down and eat informally, as well as a small room with a toilet.

Maximilianstrasse 15 today and in the 1930s was an elegant apartment.

This was a huge apartment, much larger than the one of my aunt and uncle in Berlin. Papa, who moved his family to Munich in the fall of 1930, must have built up a very successful business in the two years while I was away in Berlin.

Papa was a tough taskmaster. The first day I spent in my new home, he told me that my job would be to buff the wooden floor of the long hallway every two weeks. He showed me the long handled buffer, a heavy weighted mop at the lower end which I was supposed to push back and forth over and over again along the entire hallway. I tried it out and was nearly overwhelmed by the strenuous work it entailed. I almost cried but wanted to do my part helping out. Over the years this chore became a lot easier because I was shooting up in height and getting a lot stronger. Yet, there were many times I tried to put one over my father, skipping my duty. But he caught me every time. If I sulked and resisted, he would threaten me and even spank me on my bottom. He was quite an expert at spanking. It seems spanking was an integral part of growing up in Germany.

On the other hand, Mutti was such a gentle person. Often she would side with me. She would say, "Carlo, the boy had a hard time in school today," and add, "maybe he can buff the hallway tomorrow or the day after." That would work at times. However most of the time it did not work.

In the autumn of 1933, I was enrolled in a public school. The teacher was a strict taskmaster. No unnecessary talking or squirming in your seat was allowed. "Sit up straight and pay close attention," he would shout many times during the day. By wintertime, when the sky darkened early in the afternoon, the classroom would be lighted up with gaslights overhead. The intense yellow glow kept fascinating me. I would stare into the fixture above my head and, as a consequence, many times earned a slap across my hands from the ruler in the teacher's hand. Boys don't cry, but at times it hurt so much that tears welled up in my eyes.

A few years later my parents enrolled me in the Jewish school, which was located next to the synagogue we attended. The government had decreed that Jewish children could not attend German public schools anymore. I missed my friends from the first school and could not comprehend why I had to leave that school.

Until the early 1930s, I led an idyllic life in Munich. By the mid-thirties, it began to change. It was not very long before I learned that Jews were different from the other German citizens. I began to see more and more of brown shirted Nazis marching through the streets. All the young people wore brown uniforms that indicated that they belonged to the *Hitler Jugend*–Hitler Youth or *Bund Deutscher Mädchen*–Society of German Girls.

In the fall of 1933, after Hitler's rise to power as the Chancellor of Germany, an order was given that every apartment facing a street was required to place red glasses with a candle in all the windows. At night, the SA marched through the streets, as all the buildings facing the streets were exuding a red glow giving the impression of being in a holy place. The marching hordes would shout and sing party songs. All of us watched from our front window and shuddered. Papa hugged Mutti tightly. A depressing mood pervaded all of us. That was also the year that Karl Fiehler, a fanatic Nazi, became *Oberbürgermeister* (Lord Mayor) of Munich. He immediately issued an edict that Jews were not considered to be Germans.

I was now eight years old, too young to experience the dread that permeated all of the Jewish population. Still, earlier life in Munich seemed to be normal. I remember Papa took me on an outing to *Tegernsee*, a lake near the Alps. Just Papa and I; it made me feel very close to my father. It was an all day trip on the railroad. The rail car had an open platform where you could stand and watch the world go by. And it was a beautiful world.

At other times, we would visit the *Deutsches* Museum, a huge complex of buildings containing scientific exhibitions, railroad cars, airplanes, and the exhibit I most treasured, a replica of mining tunnels. Life-size figures with coal dust all over their faces depicted the mining of coal from deep within the earth. We would spend the whole day wandering through the many halls.

Nineteen thirty five…the newspapers' headlines screamed out "New Nuremberg Laws," laws which took away from the Jews most of the liberties enjoyed by everyone else. I was too young to comprehend what this was all about. Soon however I was exposed to hate. Christian schoolchildren started to shout insults at us as we walked to our school. Some even through rocks at us. *Verfluchte Schweinehunde*—damn bastards, they would shout at us. Others would spit in our face. We felt constantly intimidated. These were difficult times. Yet, no one at that time could even remotely imagine what would happen in later years.

"It is just a phase", Papa and Mutti would say, "and things will surely get better soon." But it did not get better. Soon, they began to talk about leaving Germany. In 1935, terror and boycotts against Jews were renewed. Jews were prevented from going to cinemas, swimming pools or resorts. Jewish businesses were paralyzed by boycott.

Then suddenly, the next year, 1936, the harassment slowed down. Only later did we find out that the government ordered this slowdown of attacks on Jews because of the Olympic Games during the summer of that year. The government did not want to upset foreign visitors or the foreign press.

The newspaper of September 13, 1937 reported that Hitler, in a speech stressed the worldwide Bolshevik menace without a doubt originated from Jewish Bolshevism in Moscow.

March 12, 1938: Hitler invades Austria—un-resisted invasion and enthusiastic welcome by its population.

By the end of 1937, tens of thousands of Jewish professionals and civil servants, actors, musicians, and journalists had lost their livelihood. On April 26, 1938, a decree was issued that all Jewish property and assets, domestic and foreign, had to be reported to the German authorities by June 30, 1938. The following month a decree dictated that all Jewish physicians were forbidden to practice medicine as of September 30, 1938. After that date, some could, with the permission from the Minister of the Interior, practice medicine on Jewish patients. In September, Jewish lawyers were forbidden to practice law as of November 30, 1938. "Voluntary" transfer of Jewish businesses to Aryans, non-Jews was in full swing. October 5, the Law of Passports of Jews was issued. Jews had to hand in their passports which would be reissued designating the holder as a Jew by stamping a big red "J" on the title page.

In late October of 1938, the "Munich Conference" took place with Prime Ministers Chamberlain, of England, Daladier, of France and the German foreign minister, von Ribbentrop. England and France desperately wanted to avert war. As a consequence of this conference, Hitler was awarded the Sudetenland, a stretch of land at the northern tip of Czechoslovakia. German troops marched into the Sudetenland on the first day of October.

Finally, the defining earthshaking event of the year occurred…the *Reichskristallnacht*, "the night of the broken glass," so called because of all the shattered windows of Jewish stores in every city throughout the country.

Alfred and brother Walter walking on the Maximilianstrasse to school.

On the morning of November 10, 1938, my younger brother Walter and I, as usual, headed out from our apartment on the *Maximilianstrasse* to walk to our school, a ten or fifteen minute walk. It was a cold morning. The fifteen-minute walk turned into a twenty-five minute walk. The huge chestnut trees had shed many leaves already and those leaves, crumpled between our fingers, served as the "tobacco" filler for our cigarettes. We rolled the crumpled leaves in a piece of paper, lighted up our "cigarettes" and pretended that it warmed us up. Lighting the cigarette was a difficult task as the wind was blowing hard. We tried repeatedly to light them again and again but the wind was too strong and blew out our matches. Finally, we succeeded. A deep puff or two and we started to cough and choke. It was an acrid tasting smoke that entered our lungs. In disgust, we threw the cigarettes away and stomped on them.

We realized that if we did not hurry up we would be late for school and be punished by Mr. Kissinger. The portly teacher Kissinger liked to use a huge ruler and would hit us on the palm of the hand for punishment. It really hurt a lot but no student would admit it.

I began to run and Walter followed after me. Only one short block to the Herzog-Rudolph-Strasse down the cobble-stone street and we would arrive at the school next to our synagogue. As we turned the corner into the Herzog-Rudolph-Strasse, we stopped in our tracks. There, in front of us was the Ohel Jakob synagogue on fire. Black smoke billowed out of the roof. It smelled strong and acrid just like those cigarettes we were trying to smoke earlier. Firemen were spraying water on the adjacent buildings but not on the synagogue or the school building. I was unable to figure out the reason for this. There were enough firemen to try to extinguish the fires in the synagogue and the school. What was wrong here? I wandered across the street opposite the school in front of the candy store where we bought candy for five Pfennig many times before school started. From this vantage point, I could watch everything. There were many firemen with shiny steel helmets moving about but doing very little. The police in their green uniforms and the peaked helmets kept the curious onlookers out of the way. Watching the scene, I became uneasy about what was happening. In fact, I started to panic. On top of this I could not see Walter. He must have wandered off.

To the synagogue - to the right from the Maximilianstrasse - on the Herzog-Rudolph-Strasse - is the burned out building, torched by the mob at night on November 10 and 11, 1938.

All of a sudden the *dicke*, the heavyset teacher of the two Kissingers appeared in front of me. "Go home quickly," he said, "there won't be any school for a while." I turned around and rushed back toward the Maximilianstrasse. Walter stood on the corner as though he was waiting for me. "Let's go home quickly," I panted breathlessly, "and tell Papa and Mutti what we saw here this morning."

This time it took only ten minutes to reach our apartment house. But a strange sight greeted us. In front of the door of the building stood a big truck with a tarp on top as well as a shiny black Mercedes automobile. I had never seen a truck parked in front of our house. Walter and I slowed down a bit and wondered what was going on. All of a sudden we saw two men in long tan overcoats emerge from the building. Papa was between them. They walked Papa behind the truck and pushed him up into it. "Papa, Papa," we screamed, "where are you going?" But no one paid any attention to us. The two men in the long overcoats then entered the big Mercedes and both truck and car drove away.

We were devastated. We rushed to the front door of the building, to the staircase ignoring the elevator, and raced up the stairs to our apartment. I banged my fist on the door. Mutti immediately opened the door and embraced both of us. "Mutti, do you know what happened at our school?" we shouted. "And what happened with Papa?"

Mutti sat us down in the living room and said, "I was so worried about you two. I don't know where these men took Papa. All they said was that Papa had to come with them. We would hear from him later."

Mutti was only thirty-six years old but was a strong person. She had to worry about her children, now increased to five, all by herself now and she did her best to assuage their fears. All the responsibility lay on her shoulders now.

Two days later the Gestapo headquarters in Munich issued a decree ordering all Jews to leave that city within forty-eight hours. Panic set in. How can a family leave their home, all the possession within two days? Yet, Mutti remained strong. The next day Mutti sent Walter and me, together with her cousin Rolf and his wife, Gerda, on to Berlin where Papa's sister lived with her husband. Mutti and the rest of the family were going to follow the next day. It would turn out to be the most fateful trip of my life.

Walter, Rolf, and his wife Gerda and I boarded the train at the main railroad station in Munich. I was now only twelve years old and it was already my third trip on a train. I liked to ride in a railroad car compartment. It gave me a grown-up feeling. Rolf, Gerda and Walter and I were the only occupants in the compartment. "All aboard," shouted the stationmaster, and the train began to move slowly out of the station. I watched the people standing on the platform waving good bye to their loved ones. No one was waving for us.

About one hour out of Munich, just as we had settled down comfortably, the compartment door was opened. There stood an SS[1] man in his black uniform and behind him was a SA storm trooper in his brown uniform. "*Ausweise bitte*—identification cards, please," the man in the black uniform said, "we must check everybody on this train because the *Reichsminister* of Information, Herr Göbbels is on this train on his way to Berlin."

It took only a minute for them to find out we were Jewish. "All Jews must leave this train at the next station," they proclaimed. "The next station is Reichenbach. We should arrive there in fifteen minutes." The SA man stayed with us until we arrived in Reichenbach. Both SS and SA men now left the train with us. We had to wait at the railroad station for the police who were summoned by the SS man. While we waited, the SS man confided to us that it might be prudent if we would all try to go over the border out of Germany because the situation in Germany would get much worse for Jews in the next several months. We did not know what to do. Within a few minutes, a police car drove up and two policemen emerged. The SS and SA men got back on the train, which then left the station.

Ten minutes later we arrived at the police prison. After checking us for weapons and any dangerous articles we were put into one cell. I had the same sinking feeling as when I saw Papa being herded into the truck a few days earlier. What will happen to all of us? Being incarcerated in a prison cell gave me a claustrophobic feeling. What to do all day long?

For some reason when I packed my suitcase for the trip to Berlin, I had decided to bring along a miniature deck of playing cards. What a

---

1   SA *Sturmabteilung* (Storm trooper or 'Brown shirts,' the original shock troops of the Nazis eclipsed politically by the SS after 1934); SS *Schutzstaffel* (Protection or guard detachment under SS Chief Heinrich Himmler was the most powerful organization of the Nazi party)

stroke of luck! They came in handy now. We played gin rummy most of the day. The only problem was the shuffling of such small cards. But we managed.

A couple of days later a Gestapo[2] agent entered the prison and took Rolf away. We had no idea where he was being taken. All of us were numb, devastated and shocked by this new event and all that happened over the last few days. Later, we found out that Rolf was put into a concentration camp with thousands other Jews who were detained all over Germany.

After several days of imprisonment, the sergeant of the Reichenbach police detachment entered our cell and told us we could continue to travel on to Berlin. Gerda, Walter and I picked up our belongings and trudged to the railroad station to catch the next train to Berlin.

---

2   *Geheime Staatspolizei* (Secret State Police)

Berlin

The thousand year history of German Jews has come to an end.
—Rabbi Leo Baeck, Berlin

Because of the edict by the Gestapo that all Jews had to leave Munich within forty-eight hours, retracted by the local Gestapo a day later, this chapter could have been headed "The Gestapo Saved Our Lives." This quirk of fate would haunt me personally the rest of my life.

This was the second time I was to live in Berlin, this time together with my brother Walter. I was heartbroken to be separated from my Mutti, my two brothers and my little sister. Aunt Lola tried and managed to make us feel welcome and at home. At any rate, Mutti had told us she and the children would follow us to Berlin in a day or two. Yet, it was already several days later and they had not arrived. "Why aren't Mutti, Günther, Hansi, and Ruth here yet," I asked Aunt Lola. "They will not be coming here," she replied, "because when I talked to her on the telephone several days ago, she told me that the Gestapo rescinded the edict to leave Munich." Moreover, she continued, "Mutti said that you and Walter should stay here because she just learned that Papa was sent to the Dachau concentration camp and it would be easier on her if you stayed with your aunt and uncle in Berlin. Mutti does not know why he is there or how long he will be there."

Aunt Lola explained to us that our Mutti had to take care of the three children all by herself, a very difficult situation without a husband. We should make ourselves at home with her and Uncle Joseph. Little did we know that making ourselves at home with our aunt and uncle would last two and a half years long. We were unable to travel back to Munich in all that time.

After "Crystal Night" as this day was called on November 10, 1938 because of all the smashed windows of Jewish shops and many apartments, my father and thousands of male Jews from all over Germany were sent to several concentration camps. My father spent six weeks in the Dachau concentration camp situated very close to Munich.

My father's brother Bernhard lived in Hamburg with his family during this fateful year in 1938. Then, early in January 1939—I remember that day well—the doorbell rang at my aunt and uncle's apartment in Berlin. I opened the front door. There in front of me stood a gaunt looking man with a shaved head. His cheeks were sunken; he looked hungry. Here stood a broken, disheveled man with tears in his eyes. I finally recognized him as my Uncle Bernhard. He, like my father and thousands of male Jews had been incarcerated in various concentration camps. Finally, in January 1939, most of them, including my father were released.

Uncle Bernhard was famished. Aunt Lola prepared a boiled egg and toast for him. Eggs were strictly rationed. That one egg for my uncle was the last one in the house. I remember to this day my ambivalent feelings about Uncle Bernhard getting this last egg. I did not have an egg for weeks and here, Uncle Bernhard arrives at my aunt and uncle's apartment and receives this delicious last egg right away. My mouth was salivating; I wanted that last egg for myself. I am still ashamed that I exhibited such jealousy.

Food ration cards issued to Jewish people only - stamped with a J.

Why did Uncle Bernhard have to appear at this time? I exhibited a child's infantile rage over a perceived injustice. Uncle Bernhard stayed in Berlin for a day to regain his composure. Then, he took a train to his home in Altona.

In August of 1939, food ration cards were issued to every person in Germany. Jews were singled out with special ration cards which had a large J stamped on it designating the bearer as a Jew. Furthermore, many specific items were disallowed for Jews and overprinted with a large red J. For example, on the first page, all coupons for marmalade and sugar were cancelled. And those precious eggs were among the many rationed food items.

The oppression of the Jews all over Germany turned progressively worse. The newest edict from the Gestapo prohibited Jews shopping for groceries during the day. It was specified that Jews could only shop in stores between four and five o'clock in the afternoon. Needless to say, by that time most of the rationed food items had been sold and Jews had to try to obtain the sold out items another day.

It became now impossible to obtain meat. One of the reasons for this was that my uncle and aunt were keeping a strictly *kosher* [1] household and kosher meat was not obtainable anymore. I remember sometime in 1940, a family we knew well emigrated from Germany. They gave us a gift of a canned jar of meat. What a delight when Aunt Lola finally decided to serve this meat at a Shabbat evening meal. Rarely had I tasted anything better than this canned meat.

Headline in the *Berliner Morgenpost*—"Russia dismisses Foreign Minister Maxim Litvinov."

Later I learned that Russia had made an overture to Germany for a better relationship to be accomplished by dismissing Foreign Minister Litvinov, a Jew. Litvinov embodied all the Germans detested—a Jew, a peace advocate, a supporter of the League of Nations, a friend of Western democracies and opponent of Nazi Germany. Vyacheslav Molotov, a complete antithesis to Litvinov, replaced him.

In May 1939, a little article on an inside page of the local newspaper described that the German Foreign Office had instructed their Moscow ambassador, "We now have decided to undertake positive negotiations for non-belligerency with the Soviet Union." This was an obvious strategic move by Germany in case of an Anglo-French

---

1   Meat slaughtered according to Jewish law

intervention on behalf of the 'aggressive' Poland. For some time now, Germany, through the press and radio, had been agitating about so-called 'aggressions' by Poland preparatory to the imminent invasion into Poland. A non-belligerency pact with Russia would protect Germany's eastern flank.

In August of 1939, Stalin said he would sign this pact with Germany. On August 23, Germany's Foreign Minister Ribbentrop arrived in Moscow. An agreement was readied and the pact was signed after midnight.

On August 25th that year, Papa telephoned us from Munich with happy news. Mutti had given birth to Baby Judis. There were now six children in the Koppel family; four in Munich and Walter and I in Berlin. Inasmuch as I was not able to leave Berlin until leaving Germany, I would not see my new little sister, a beautiful doll according to photos we saw.

Two days later, Great Britain signed a formal treaty with Poland.

September 1, 1939 6:30 in the morning. The roar of German Stuka dive bombers and fighter planes in the sky made us crane our necks as we watched the thousands of planes heading east. The next morning, the newspapers announced in big headlines that Germany was countering the "aggression" of Poland. This was a piece of fiction used by Germany to proclaim that Poland needed to be punished. It was the beginning of the Second World War. Two days later, Great Britain and France declared war on the German Reich.

Three and a half weeks later Warsaw capitulated and the Polish campaign was over. Russia had invaded Poland from the east and Germany from the west.

The German population, young and old was jubilant, celebrating all the victories of the German Army and Air Force. By this time all boys between the ages of ten and seventeen had been ordered into the Hitler Youth organization. Hitler spoke of the upbringing of the German youth: "a youth will be growing up before which the entire world will be in fright. I want a violent, imperious, unafraid, cruel youth…they must bear pain. No weakness or tenderness in them. I want my youth strong and beautiful. I want them to be athletic. That is the first and most important thing. I do not want an intellectual upbringing. With knowledge I see my youth ruined" (from high school history book *Geschichte für Morgen, Heumann and Hirschgraben*, 1987).

During this period, the persecution of Jews had gained momentum. On a more individual term, one of my own encounters was with a Hitler Youth. It happened right in front of our apartment building. I was just returning from shopping late one afternoon and was nearing the front entrance of our apartment building. All of a sudden a Hitler Youth in his brown uniform on a bicycle screeched to a halt in front of me. He seemed to be a sixteen or seventeen-year-old kid, big and husky. "You pig of a Jew", he bellowed, "what are you doing here?" I was petrified and could not even stammer an answer. He was so big and threatening. All of a sudden he laid his bicycle on the ground, took off his belt and proceeded to whip me all over my body. I was so terrified that I did not even feel the lashes from the belt buckle. To get closer to me he stepped over his bicycle and stumbled. That was my opportunity to escape. I ran the few feet to the entrance of my building, tore open the front door and raced to our apartment. In the safety of the apartment my emotions spilled over. Tears poured from my eyes. The welts on my legs and my back began to hurt. Aunt Lola tried to comfort me. She opened a can of cookies she had saved for a special occasion. I began to calm down. But since that frightening episode, I cast weary eyes up and down the street whenever and wherever I was walking.

The situation for us Jews became progressively worse. One day, while visiting Uncle Joseph's brother Mendel and several friends, I overheard a whispering of *Vergewaltigung*, the rape of acquaintance Rosa during the *Kristallnacht* violence. Only later would I learn that there was not only pillage and destruction of Jewish property during Crystal Night. The Nazis had raped Jewish women during this rampage.

Most of our evening meals now consisted of cabbage, vegetables and bread. Milk could only be obtained on rare occasions. Despite the meager rations, I grew very tall but was skinny. I was coughing a lot but did not seem to have a cold. Aunt Lola took me to the doctor who suggested the rapid growth seemed to weaken my lungs, hence the cough.

One day, in 1939, my father's brothers Leo and Edie showed up at the apartment. It seemed the Gestapo was looking for them. I never knew the reason. It was fun talking with them, talking about Werner, Leo's son and the other family members in Hamburg.

The next morning, as I was sitting on the balcony, two men in gray raincoats marched across the courtyard to the entry hall of our apartment. I became suspicious and ran to Leo and Edie to tell them about it. As I spoke with them, the doorbell rang. Immediately, Leo and Edie left the apartment through the back door.

Aunt Lola opened the door. The two men asked Aunt Lola whether Leo and Edie Koppel were at this address. She told these two men that, as far as she knew, they were in Hamburg. The men thanked her and left.

This episode left all of us with a spooky feeling.

Some time later, we learned that both had fled from Germany without any papers, and were interned in France.

After Walter and I had arrived in Berlin in November 1938, we attended the Jewish school at the Siegmundshof Street. It was located next to the synagogue my aunt and uncle attended. A large landscaped area was situated in front of both buildings. Tall chestnut trees shaded the grassy area. I went to that school from the time I arrived in Berlin until the middle of 1939. By that time, all Jewish schools ceased to exist. My formal schooling had ended.

Instead, I now went to an *Umschulungsschule,* a school in the Greifswalderstrasse that taught Jewish boys metalworking in the hope that this could be used when arriving in a new country. Five days a week, early in the morning, we would arrive at the school and do calisthenics to limber up. Then, on to learning to use tools for working with different metals basics. The first thing we had to learn was making tools in the blacksmith area. I would heat a piece of steel over a coal fire that had a foot-operated blower to fan the coals for extra heat. Once the steel piece was red hot I hammered and shaped it into a cutting tool on the anvil. This was really the fun part. I was creating something useful. After shaping it I would grind the end to a sharp cutting edge. Finally, I reheated it and then dipped it into water for a quick cooling down. To obtain a permanent sharp cutting edge, the now shaped tool had to be re-heated to a yellow color that indicated it would hold a sharp edge. Then, the final cooling process and I had a cutting tool for the lathe. My teacher now allowed me to begin work on the lathe, a large machine driven by an overhead belt. The belt could be moved on pulleys to speed up or slow down the turning of the metal peace held in the jaws of the chuck. I remember I liked this *Umschulungsschule* better than the regular school.

In the meantime, Aunt Lola had been in touch with a children's organization in New York to enable Walter and me to emigrate to the United States of America. America was everybody's dream destination. We knew that the United States had strict immigration quotas. You had to register with the United States consulate which eventually would issue an immigration quota number. With quotas in place, these numbers would take years to become effective. I know Papa had received such quota numbers for his family in Munich but was told it would probably take until 1941 before a hearing could be held at the closest American consulate, located in the city of Stuttgart. Walter's and my numbers under the children's organization quota were much lower than my parents' quota. We heard that we might be considered for a hearing as early as the fall of 1940.

There was terrible news from Munich. Mutti called us in Berlin in May and told us that Papa was taken to Munich's infamous Stadelheim prison. She did not know why. Mutti was terribly worried. What was she going to do with the four children all by herself? Perhaps she should try to move to Berlin to be with her relatives. She was a resolute and tough woman but was beginning to become desperate.

Three weeks later Mutti called again and told us that Papa had been released from the prison but was told he had to leave Germany quickly or he would be imprisoned again.

Munich

Now Papa's departure became a race against time. A number of telegrams were sent to relatives and friends in America for obtaining affidavits[1], the documents indicating that funds had been set aside, thus legally backing the necessary monetary support for obtaining the all important visas[2]. His entry visa for the United States finally came through. He could leave Germany but had to leave his entire family behind. So far, in early 1940, there was inadequate funding for entry visas for his family, his wife and the four children now to be left behind in Munich. He

My father's passport.

promised, once in America, to spend every minute to find friends and relatives to deposit support funds into the bank for the necessary affidavits to enable him to obtain entry visas for his entire family. Little did he know that this was to be an almost impossible task.

On April 16, 1940, my father received the immigration visa from the American Vice Consul in Stuttgart, Germany. Mutti sent a letter to

---

1   A written statement made on oath before a notary public indicating that sufficient funds have been set aside for obtaining a visa

2   The endorsement on a passport, showing that a person has been granted official entry into or passage through a country

us in Berlin that Papa was finally able to leave Germany in the middle of 1940. It was to be a long trip traveling from Munich east to the Baltic States, through Lithuania and its cities of Kovno and Vilnius.

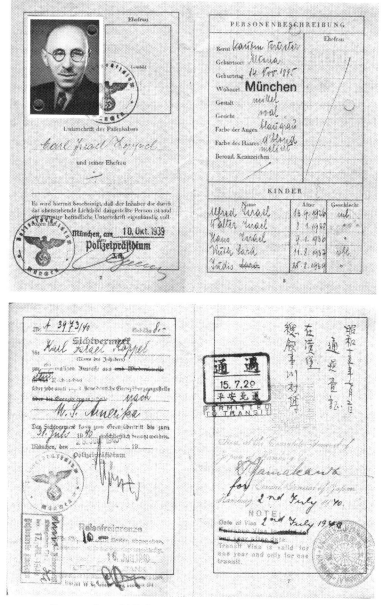

Stamped on 16 July 1940 for the long trip to America.

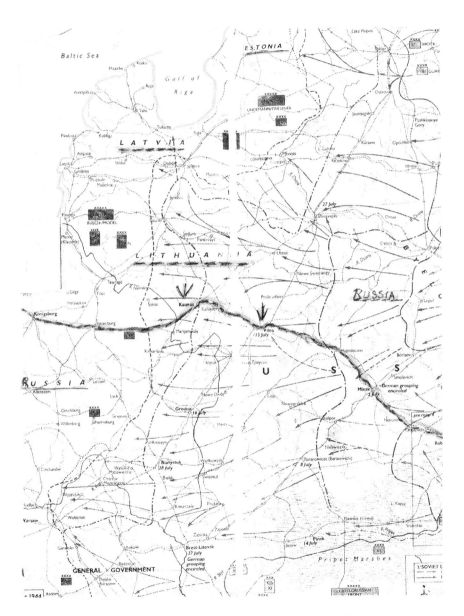

Map showing my father's long journey to the east through Lithuania, through Russia to the west coast of the USA and on to New York City.

As the train approached the city of Kovno, my father must have noticed an immense and intimidating fortress on the approach to that city. He would never know the effect this huge forbidding edifice would have on him and his family. Then his train went on into the territory of the Soviet Union and all the way east to Vladivostok. From there, he traveled to Japan and onward across the Pacific Ocean to the United States. And that was not the end of his travel. He still had to traverse the entire United States to the East Coast, to New York City. After several weeks, we received a letter that Papa had finally arrived. His sister Hannah, who had immigrated to America several years earlier, met him. We felt good that Papa was safe but very sad to be left in Germany without him.

To this day, I am unable to fathom my father's emotions and grief having to leave his entire family behind in the jaws of Nazi Germany. This traumatic experience would forever be etched on his mind and torture him the rest of his life.

Headline in the Berliner Morgenpost on May 10, 1940: "The Beginning of the Western Offense by the *Wehrmacht*, the German army."

And a small item on the back-page of the Berliner Morgenpost: "Hitler's Directive number 21: Preparation of the Invasion of the Soviet Union."

In the spring 1940, Hitler invaded Denmark and Norway. In May, he invaded the Netherlands, Belgium and France. France surrendered in June 1940. The English army became trapped at Dunkirk. The newspapers announced that Hitler has issued orders for an invasion of England in September of that year conditioned upon Germany gaining air supremacy over the British Isles.

While the newspapers triumphantly proclaimed endless victories of the *Wehrmacht*, the German army, lifting the spirits of the German population, life for the Jews became increasingly more oppressive. Since 1939, Jews could not attend theaters, movie houses, concerts, cabarets, the circus, and cultural exhibits anymore. It was a gloomy existence for the Jews living in Germany. Since my beating by the Hitler youth, I rarely dared to walk outside on the street. As the newspapers triumphantly proclaimed endless victories of the German army lifting the spirits of the German population, life for the Jews became increasingly more oppressive. Where or how would I venture for a change of scenery?

One event in September 1939 made my aunt and uncle very happy. At my thirteenth year I celebrated my Bar Mitzvah, my becoming an 'adult' in the synagogue in the Siegmundshof Street in Berlin. For many months I had studied the Torah portion for that particular week until I could chant it without any errors. On the Sabbath day of my Bar Mitzvah, I did indeed chant that portion of the Torah without any errors. That gained me laurels from our rabbi and much backslapping by the congregants after the service.

Back at our apartment that afternoon, numerous friends came to visit. Aunt Lola had saved some eggs and made a sponge cake with fruit on it. I proudly showed everybody the Chumash, the Hebrew bible inscribed by the synagogue board and presented to me as a memory of my proud achievement. This was one of the few happy events in an otherwise gloomy environment.

Now, rumors began to circulate in the German Jewish community about the establishment of numerous Jewish ghettos in Eastern Europe.

New York

My father had arrived in New York the summer of 1940. Without a job or money, he stayed with a family named Gottlieb in Brooklyn. His sister Hannah was working as a maid for this family and was also taking care of their two girls.

From: Carl Koppel
      c/o L. Gottlieb
      262 Dover Street
      Brooklyn, New York

To: Mr. N. Leipheimer (Nathan Leipheimer was my father's uncle, his mother's brother)
      New Amsterdam Casualty Co.
      P.O. Box 445
      Colorado Springs, Colorado

December 14, 1940

Dear Uncle,

We now conduct a regular correspondence with each other. This is largely caused by the development of current events. When I write to you again today, the reason for this is much deeper because I received a telegram from Carla as follows:

> Consulate wishes to receive from guarantors Leipheimer and Gundelfinger sworn documentations about precautions taken concerning insuring our livelihood in the USA for an indeterminate period of time. Only through a larger trust fund is this situation solvable.   Carola

You can imagine how this put me into a state of great anxiety. The telegram was dated the 19th of the month. By that date, my own affidavit for a money guaranty that I was able to put up was already in the hands of the consulate in Stuttgart. The consulate official said they are ready to follow through with Carla's case considering your original trust fund as well as Miss Gundelfinger's fund which are already in their possession, but they do not recognize these as sufficient.

As I wrote you a short time ago, both my boys, Alfred and Walter, are with my sister Lola in Berlin. They will be able to leave from Berlin to the USA on the strength of the Children Committee guaranty sent to the American consulate in Stuttgart. Because of this, the two boys, Alfred and Walter, who have guarantees to leave from Berlin instead of Munich now reduce the submitted affidavits at the consulate for Carla and the six children by two children. The status is now as follows. The affidavits from you, from Miss Gundelfinger and from me now cover my wife Carola, and Günther, Hansi, Ruth and Judis. Miss Gundelfinger is a cousin of Carla and employed here in New York.

You may remember that for my own visa to leave Germany, I needed then two trust funds in the amount of $700.00. From this one can figure out how much money will be needed for five people. From all we know, we need to arrange again for two trust funds at least in the amount of $2000.00. I know you will become scared by this amount but if I am to get my wife and children out before it is too late, there is no other way.

Inasmuch as I must bring my wife and children to safety and to be able to see them again, everything must be handled quickly before it is too late. When I think that one day the communication to Germany will be broken off and I will not see my wife and children until after the war, have no news from them and they will be under the yoke of the Gestapo, then my heart will stop beating because of the anxiety and anguish for my loved ones.

There was a reported "action" against Jews in Germany that will also involve Munich. Since deportations of Jews from Germany to France are now limited because there is no more room in the camps, any additional transport will now be sent to Lublin, Poland which is far worse, because from there no one can leave.

Dear Uncle, please help me. You know from experience with me that the trust funds made out to me will never be utilized by me. I have discussed this with you. In the case of Carla and children, any amount will also only be a loan. Maybe your son-in-law, in this case, can add to the trust fund so a bigger amount will be available.

The trust fund, in my opinion, must be made out for two years with monthly disbursement terms. Please write to me quickly how you can do this for me. It must absolutely be handled within six to eight days because, until everything reaches Stuttgart (the consulate), four weeks will have passed delaying their departure from Germany another month.

I underscore again that I will not claim one cent of this trust fund and it really centers on your kindness, so that the American consul will be satisfied with the funds. I hope that I will be able to put together some money here in New York, but it will be tough because all my acquaintances here immigrated to America only a short time ago and have nothing.

I hope to hear from you in the next few days via airmail, my dear Uncle, so we can follow up with the necessary correspondence and documents to the consul in Stuttgart.

Please excuse my agitation. I am sure you will understand and comprehend it.

> With best regards,
> Your nephew Carlo

In the meantime, Carlo wrote another letter trying to explain the latest situation to the officials at the American consulate in Stuttgart, Germany.

To the Honorable Consul   January 7, 1941
    American Consulate
    Stuttgart, Germany

    Honorable Sir:

With respect to the affidavits (documents of financial support) given to my wife Carola Koppel and four of my six children, Günther 17, Hans, 5, Ruth 3 1/2 and Judis 1 1/2, I wish to elaborate and make the following statement:

I immigrated legally into the United States on August 29, 1940. I was able to secure employment and my earnings at present amount to $140 per month.

It is my fervent wish to be reunited with my wife and children. Two of my children, Alfred, born September 13, 1926 and Walter, born January 8, 1928 who are now living in Berlin, have received separate affidavits through the German Jewish Children's Aid and will be able to come here soon. Inasmuch as the affidavits given by my relatives and me were originally made out for my <u>wife</u> and all <u>six children</u>, the two affidavits for Alfred and Walter will now relieve the burden of the original affidavits for my entire family. It should therefore now only cover my wife and four of the children.

In addition, my cousin, Miss Gundelfinger, whose affidavit is in your possession is also establishing a trust fund. You should receive the documents shortly.

My eldest son, Günther, is seventeen years old. He is a carpenter and would be able to increase the income of my family upon his arrival in the U.S.A.

May I request of you now, Honorable Sir, by taking into consideration all these facts, and therefore grant the visas to my wife and the four children. Your contribution would be indescribable to the happiness of my family.

    Very respectfully yours,
    Carl Koppel

WESTERN UNION TELEGRAM
20 January 1941
Cable from Munich

To: Koppel c/o Gottlieb
262 Dover Street
Brooklyn, New York

Your guarantee for us denied because of limited amount.
Consulate states too small an income, hence financial in-
sufficiency. Send swiftly essential better guarantees for us
via certified copies to the Stuttgart consul.
Carla

Papa became frantic. Nothing seemed to work out trying to obtain additional trust funds in order to obtain the visas for his wife and four
children. A letter to the daughter of his Uncle Leipheimer and her
husband describes that desperation.

To: Carl and Helen Ettinger   January 21, 1941
        Des Moines, Iowa

My Dearest,

I beg you to forgive me that I acknowledge only today the
receipt of your kind offering of affidavits. Hanna and I
send heartfelt thanks to you for it. Hopefully, the consul
will accept these without the need for more documents.
Because of the big worries about my wife and children, I
unable do anything. I had planned to move to the West, as
was my intention to begin something new there. However,
I simply can not work up to this, before my head is cleared
up and I know what will happen to my loved ones and how
I can help them.

Two weeks ago, I begged my uncle again for a trust fund.
My wife had telegraphed that the consul required this for
my wife and children. I myself put up an affidavit with a
written confirmation of my job's income. Based on this,
the consul consented to take up the case again. At the same
time the consul expressed the need, in order to issue visas,
to receive from guarantors Leipheimer and Gundelfinger

(a cousin of my wife, and working as a maid in New York) each a trust fund through which they would show an interest in their relatives. Now, if the consul does not receive the documents in a short time, then their case will be put aside because the consul will have to assume that there is no interest from these relatives. My wife and children then can not leave Germany and, therefore, will be under the yoke of the Gestapo. With $1,200, they can be saved from these beasts and save them from death through bombs.

You certainly know that I shall not use one cent from these trust funds. It will only be a loan. I shall never avail myself of the trust funds; the evidence for this lie in the fact that I never touched the trust fund for my own affidavit you made out to me. You surely know me well enough and believe me in that respect. I plead with you to help me, because here it deals with life and death. When America will be forced into the war, then all Jews will be forced out of Germany out of revenge. In addition, what that means you can surely understand, because the Camp de Gurs in southern France, where my two brothers are interned, gives enough evidence to worry about. There, daily twenty to twenty-five people die. I simply can not afford to think about this, that one day my wife with the little children will be interned at such a camp.

I repeat again, it is absolutely no risk for you and you can save an entire family, your relatives and make them happy. Please do not think about it too long or it could be too late and you surely don't want to take on such responsibility. Just imagine how you would feel if you were separated from your children and have them exposed to such terrible danger.

The cousin of my wife, Miss Gundelfinger, who is really an employee working in people's homes, will be arranging for trust fund money through a bank. In addition, she will accept the expense of the interest on the money and other costs. Therefore, you can surely see people are trying their best to help even with small amounts of money. I hope you too realize the difficulty of the situation and will help me.

I hope you and your family are all in good health. Please do not feel that my letter is unpleasant but the tremendously great pressure forced me to write about all this.

Please give me your reply quickly because I now live in continued agitation and despair until I receive your answer.

    With kind regards to all of you,

        Yours,
        Carlo

Both Uncle Leipheimer and the Ettingers gave affidavits for financial support, building up the money reservoir for the desperately needed five entry visas. Yet, despite daily efforts to solicit help from friends and acquaintances, so far he was unable to collect sufficient funds for affidavits required to issue visas by the American Consulate in Stuttgart. Therefore, he felt he needed to employ different and innovative tactics. It finally resulted, in his desperation, to turn to some of his namesakes listed in the New York City telephone book.

Koppel Industry Car & Equipment Co. January 22, 1941
230 Park Avenue
New York, New York

Dear Mr. Koppel,

I turn to you as a complete stranger. I do this because you are a "cousin-in-name" to me. It is not my intention to search for a family tie-in, but if you could help your namesake, it would be of tremendous assistance.

Permit me to put forth the following, a plea to you, about something that weighs heavily on me and how you may be able to help me.

I came to the United States approximately five months ago but had to leave my wife and six children behind in

Germany because the funds for their affidavits were not sufficient. I, myself, could not remain in Germany any longer since I was arrested and put into a concentration camp in November 1938 and again imprisoned in November 1939. I could not expose myself a third time to this danger. Furthermore, by being in this wonderful country, I hope to be able to help my family to be able to leave Germany.

Two boys of mine, ages 14 and 13 will be able to immigrate into this country, probably in January or February, through the granting of visas from the German Jewish Children's Aid Society. My big worry now is how do I accomplish to help my wife and four children to immigrate to the USA within a short time before things get even worse in Germany.

The status, at this time, is that the American Consulate in Stuttgart, Germany requires additional trust funds from both guarantors, from my uncle who is 80 years old and a cousin who is a household employee. That is the big problem. Chances are that these two guarantors will not be able to give additional monetary funds. What this means to me, you will surely understand. Because if the war will involve more countries, which I hope will not happen, then years will pass before I shall see my family again. This, I can not even think about. They will then be under the power and yoke of the Gestapo and also exposed to the danger of bomb attacks.

I plead with you to help me. I will need trust funds to support the visas. But I will give you my sworn declaration that I will not accept one cent from you. It would merely be a deposit not to be touched. This would be an extraordinary kindness of you, which, in all probability, would save the lives of my family.

It would make me happy if you would listen to me personally and I am available at any time.

Please do not look with misgiving at my writing to you. The terrible situation of my family in Germany demands extraordinary methods.

If I use the German language writing to you, I hope you will forgive me. I am not yet able to use the English language well and make myself understood correctly.

It would make me very grateful to receive a favorable reply from you soon and I remain waiting for your esteemed reply.

Respectfully,
Carl Koppel

He never received a response from the Koppel Industry Car & Equipment Company.

Berlin

The year 1941 continued to be a dreary existence and was without any diversion. I went to the *Umschulungsschule*, the Jewish trade school, to be trained in handling machinery that could fabricate items out of steel such as gears or cutting tools. It was strenuous work every day and I tired easily. But at least it was interesting and kept me busy.

While walking to the *Umschulungschule* one day, I came across many military vehicles parked in the streets. Usually many people, especially the *Hitlerjugend*, congregated around that machinery of death. I must confess that despite the oppressive atmosphere walking among the SA and SS, the brown and black uniformed men, I too was curious as I came across an armored command vehicle. I too was strangely fascinated by this show of might. Then, overcome by remorse for being interested in this monster of destruction, I quickly walked away.

Spring finally arrived after a dismal and cold winter. The sun was shining almost every day now. But we were unable to enjoy this fine weather. There was no place to go. We could not go into parks or visit the zoo. Most of the time was spent in our apartment.

Headline in the *Berliner Morgenpost*, 6 April, 1941—"Wehrmacht invades Yugoslavia and Greece." The headline ten days later—"Yugoslavia capitulates."

That same month we received a large envelope from the American Consulate. The entry visas for Walter and me were to be granted after a medical examination by a doctor. Aunt Lola immediately made an appointment with Dr. Dosmar.

Two days later she took Walter and me to the doctor. Walter passed with flying colors. But the doctor spent much more time with me. I had grown very tall and was extremely thin. I also coughed frequently. Dr. Dosmar finally decided that I had grown too fast and I had a mild case of inadequate red blood cell supply.

Dr. med. Israel L. Dosmar
Solinger Strasse 3
Berlin NW 87
Berlin, 4 April 1941

Bei den von mir untersuchten Alfred Koppel, geb. 13
September 1926, konnte ausser einer durch sein über-
massiges Längewachstum hervorgerufenen Blutarmut
mässigen Grades keine Organerkrankung oder sonstwie
ansteckende Krankheit festgestellt werden.
I. L. Dosmar

His report stated that I had no illnesses of any organs or any commu-
nicable disease. He gave both of us a clean bill of health. In retrospect,
I am sure he stretched the truth somewhat. At any rate, we received the
all-important medical documents.

Late that month we proceeded to the American consulate. After
waiting several hours, we were finally processed and the consul stamped
our passports with the stamp of liberty: Visa granted.

Now it became a waiting game. How soon were we to board the
train out of Germany? Walter and I became totally distracted, acted
nervous, and became irritable. Uncle Joseph and Aunt Lola, especially
Aunt Lola, now showered us with special love and affection. The strain
on all of us became almost unbearable.

It was almost the middle of June when we received word from
the local branch of the *Hilfsverein,* the Jewish Emigration Office, to be
ready to leave at a moment's notice. Walter and I could take along only
one suitcase each and ten Marks, the maximum amount of money allowed for the trip. Uncle Joseph and Aunt Lola were not allowed to
come along.

Then the day of departure had arrived—June 14, 1941 at 9:30
in the morning—a taxi drove up as we were waiting in front of the
apartment house. The cab was to take us to the railroad station. Uncle
Joseph and Aunt Lola were not allowed to come along. It was time to
say good bye. We shed tears, hugged and kissed our aunt and uncle
and walked up to the taxi. Before entering it, I turned around to look
at those good and kind people through my misty eyes. They had taken
good and loving care of us for all those years. I had such terribly ambivalent feelings now. On the one hand, at last we were able to leave

this oppressive land. On the other hand, it tore me up to leave my aunt and uncle behind. Instinctively I knew I would never see them again.

We arrived at the Anhalter Bahnhof, a railroad station in Berlin. A long train stood at the platform, its engine bellowing steam into the air. Walter and I were taken to a car at the end of the train. After everybody had arrived and settled in, Gestapo agents proceeded to seal the doors of the car. We could not leave the train anymore. Soon, we heard the engine's whistle announcing the departure. Slowly, the long train moved out of the station. This was the beginning of a new adventure, but I felt very sad because we had to leave all our loved ones behind. How soon would we be reunited with them again?

Aunt Lola had packed food and drink for the two of us. This was fortunate because we could not leave the sealed railroad car to go to the dining car. The train headed west toward France. It took a day and a half to reach Paris.

We opened the window of the compartment as the train was slowly entering the Paris railroad station. It was exciting to see so many people congregated on the platform. At the same time my stomach growled. We were very hungry. What would we do for food and drink? We were imprisoned in the railroad car.

All of the sudden several ladies in grey uniforms showed up at our railroad car pushing wheel-barrows stacked high with sandwiches. The taller ladies handed loads of these sandwiches through the opened windows to the imprisoned but grateful passengers. In about fifteen minutes, the train began to back out of the railroad station and was on its way to the Spanish border.

The train traveled another 400 miles before we reached the border of Spain. At the French border city of Hendaye, we had to change to a Spanish train. Another ten minutes and we would leave Germany and occupied France on the way to freedom. It was difficult to describe the feeling of the yoke lifting, of now experiencing total freedom upon entering Spain.

What strange quirk of fate enabled Walter and me to emigrate to America? An edict of the Gestapo in Munich in 1938 ordering all Jews out of that city within forty-eight hours forced Walter and me to remain in Berlin for two and a half years. In that space of time, our aunt and uncle were able to work with the local *Hilfsverein* to obtain entry visas for us for the United States through an organization in New York. Because of these fortunate circumstances, my brother Walter and I were granted the gift of life. At the same time, that left psychological scars that took years to overcome, mostly through the help of my American born wife.

Spain

Our first layover was only about forty miles from the French-Spanish border. In an hour and a half, we arrived at San Sebastian on the northern coast of Spain. Our hotel was at the water's edge of the Gulf of Biscay, a beautiful sight on our first day of freedom. Savoring this freedom made me feel like an adult. Indeed, no one was in charge of Walter and me, two boys of fourteen and twelve, who had grown up at a dizzying pace.

Walter and I had a large room at the hotel. On the first day, the next-door neighbors, a mother and her two children, came to our room. We wanted to celebrate our freedom. I reached for the one food item I had carried with me from Germany. It was a glass jar of strawberry marmalade, a precious item our loving aunt Lola gave us to enjoy on our long journey to America.

Disaster! The jar slipped out of my hand and landed broken near the window of our room. The precious marmalade was splattered all over the floor. Mumbling something about my clumsiness, I rushed to the bathroom to bring a wet towel for the clean-up job. In the minute or so it took to return to the scene of the disaster, hundreds of giant cockroaches had assembled around the broken jar for the feast of their lifetime. It was an ugly sight. We waited for about five minutes while all the marmalade disappeared and with it, the cockroaches also vanished. We were all shaken up and had to forgo our sweet moment of celebration.

Off to the railroad station the next morning for the trip to Barcelona. Traveling south from San Sebastian toward Barcelona, the train traversed along huge fields of golden stalks of wheat. Walter became bored during the six-hour train-ride. Luckily, I had my miniature deck of playing cards with me. We played gin rummy endlessly.

The landscape changed. Huge flocks of sheep and goats appeared, interspersed with quaint looking farmhouses. Finally, we reached Barcelona. A bus took us to the hotel, an old structure. It was located on a winding street. All the street signs were, of course, in Spanish which made the maze of buildings quite confusing to us. However, it was not so difficult to explore the immediate neighborhood during the day and find our way back to the hotel again.

Then again—disaster! This time it turned out to be a major one. On the evening before our departure to America, I did not find Walter in our room. It was already ten o'clock in the evening. Both of us should have been in bed by then for our departure was scheduled early in the morning. I quickly enlisted several adults to comb the interior of the hotel. There was not any trace of Walter. I began to panic. Walter had always been a free spirit. What if he decided to wander around the city to explore its sights? By now there were five or six adults who were worried as well. We started search parties of twos in several directions.

At half past eleven, we headed back to the hotel without Walter. By this time, the hotel had locked its doors. The only way to enter the hotel was to clap your hands to wake up the porter. Entering the hotel, we talked about alerting the police. After all, the ship was going to depart early in the morning. What was I going to do? Remain in Barcelona until Walter showed up? Alternatively, should I leave Barcelona without Walter? This, of course, was totally unthinkable.

It had cooled down from the daytime heat. I rushed to my room for a sweater before heading out to the police department. Entering the room, to my dismay as well as relief, I saw Walter in his bed peacefully asleep. Deep emotions exploded within me. I wanted to wake him up and shake him, but he looked so peaceful sleeping. On the one hand, I was so relieved that he had showed up safely; on the other hand, I was furious that he would wander about all by himself without telling anyone. It made me frantic, certainly inconvenienced many people, and left all of us tired for the journey in the morning.

Brilliant sunshine greeted us the next day. Soon we were to see our ship taking us to the New World. Before washing up and getting dressed, we hurriedly threw all our clothing into our suitcases. Then, I washed my face and neck, as Aunt Lola always impressed upon me. Then, my dirty feet needed to be scrubbed. Next to the wash basin was a porcelain bowl just the right height to place one foot at a time, turn on the spigot and soap them down. The rinsing was very much simplified by again turning on the spigot which shot a stream of warm water upward. As a fourteen year old boy I did not realize then that I was using a bidet. After a quick breakfast, we wandered down to the entrance of the hotel just as a bus drove up. We boarded the vehicle with about thirty other people and off we went to the harbor.

There, in front of us was what seemed to me to be a huge ocean-liner. On its side was her name, the Villa de Madrid. I had never seen such a beautiful sight, an intensely white painted ocean-liner that would carry us to the land of freedom. Later, I learned that it was a rather small ship, 9,200 tons, designed to carry only 214 passengers. I also found out later that more than 900 passengers had boarded the ship. Quickly we went up the steps onto the main deck. There, a steward directed us to the lower deck into what seemed to be a cargo hold. In this huge "room" were double deck bunks numbering in the hundreds. Walter and I were assigned upper bunks. Each of these bunks had a thin mattress and an even thinner pillow. Full of excitement, we did not care that our "beds" were made of wooden planks.

The small ocean liner Villa de Madrid, a 214 passenger ship of 9200 tons cruised at 15 knots. The freight rooms below deck were converted to hold over 900 passengers.

We rushed back on deck immediately, not wanting to miss the departure of the ship.

Two hours later the foghorn let out two long blasts, a warning that we were about to leave the pier. I leaned over the railing and watched the sailors heave the heavy ropes onto the ship. All of a sudden, I heard a rumbling emanating from deep within the bowels of the ship. The engines had started and were turning the ship's propellers. Slowly, we began to move away from the pier. The city's skyline diminished in size as we headed out to the sea.

After traveling for a day, we approached Gibraltar, the straits between the British stronghold and the African City of Tangiers. British Spitfire planes buzzed our ship. All of us were waving at the planes. It was such a happy sight to see some might of the Allied forces. Then we passed through the straits.

The next day was June 22, 1941. I will never forget that date because another enormous event occurred on that day. The ship's radio announced that Hitler attacked the Soviet Union. I could not fathom the consequences of this announcement. My heart told me that thousands of soldiers would be killed but my mind reasoned that here was a major country going to fight the Nazi hordes. England needed all the help she could get.

We were now headed straight west across the North Atlantic Ocean toward New York City. Eight or nine more days and we were going to see Papa and Aunt Hannah again. I could barely contain my happiness to be united again with Papa. This ameliorated somewhat the terrible sadness I experienced leaving behind Mutti and my brothers and sisters.

All of a sudden, the ship was turning port side. I was proud of myself having learned these naval terms. Port side meant turning to the left. I felt like a real sailor. Maybe there was a storm ahead of us and the captain wanted to skirt any turbulence. That night I curled up on the deck because it was so stuffy, hot and confining in the cargo hold where so many of us had to sleep on the hundreds of bunks.

Shouting of "There is land ahead" awoke me early the next morning. Were we approaching the United States already? I could not believe that the trip to America went by so fast. I remembered being told it would take at least one week or eight more days to arrive in New York. Again, I heard, "I can see land in the distance."

I approached an old man hanging over the railing and staring at the coastline, which appeared larger and larger as the ship sailed toward it. "Is this America?" I asked him. "No, we are headed to the Canary Islands off Africa," he replied, "and the town you see in the distance is Las Palmas. This is Spanish territory."

But why are we stopping here instead of going on to America, I asked him. He stroked his beard replying thoughtfully, "I heard from the captain's office that Spain is supposed to enter the war on the German side and the ship was ordered to the nearest Spanish port."

What a revolting turn of events! Here we were on our way to total freedom and now this horrible situation. We were probably going to be interred here for the duration of the war in this God forsaken hot country off the coast of Africa. We did not escape the tentacles of the Nazi regime after all. What was going to happen to all of us? I felt faint. Whether this from the heat or this terrible event, I did not know

Las Palmas, Canary Islands

The next morning we saw about a dozen small boats approaching the ship. They were natives selling all kinds of goods, including food and drinks. I don't know what possessed me to bargain with one vendor for a bottle of whiskey. In the back of my mind I knew I needed some of this elixir to give me energy which had been flagging ever since we started this trip from Germany. Other passengers bought the usual trinkets and even some of the native foods. This went on for several days.

A week passed and nothing had happened. The ship's food became rancid from the heat. Soon we saw barges delivering a number of huge creatures from the ocean. I suspected much of the food on board had to be dumped because of spoilage.

Now there were rumors that we were going to be interned on one of the islands. The prospect of this scared me. It was so hot here—almost unbearable. For the last week, I had slept on deck. Below the deck it was difficult to breathe.

In the meantime I had become acquainted with the bartender Enrique. In order to preserve my bottle of whiskey, I ingratiated myself with Enrique who magnanimously handed me leftovers from his mixing cup. He was either very kind or else he enjoyed seeing me somewhat tipsy. After all, a fourteen-year-old kid tottering around after a couple of big swigs of these lethal mixtures was surely a sight to behold.

We were well into the third week of our unscheduled layover when we heard the announcement over the loudspeaker: The ship will proceed on to New York City the next day after taking on more provisions. The collective sigh of relief of the more than eight hundred passengers was palpable. Shouts of joy erupted all over the various decks. We were proceeding to the land of freedom after all.

I had been hoping desperately for the continuation of our voyage. That hope as well as the whiskey kept me going. But as soon as the announcement of the imminent departure was made, my body collapsed. I felt ill and weak. There were several doctors on board. One of them examined me and pronounced that I picked up some tropical disease and needed to fight the infection. He gave me a handful of giant brown pills, which, he said, would fight the infection. Several days later I still felt miserable. Another doctor examined me. This one thought, that since I lost a lot of weight, I had tuberculosis. His diagnosis was that I was very sick and made a strong suggestion that I must see another doctor as soon as we arrive in New York. Deep down I realized this doctor knew what he was talking about for I felt very weak and sick.

I had heard of Ellis Island, the place where the American government put you if you were sick. You would not be allowed to enter the country and might be sent back to Europe. I knew I had to do something to be able to pass by the immigration officials in New York. Since I was very pale and sickly looking, I decided to sit in the sun a lot to gain a healthy look. It must have been an incongruous sight, a boy bundled up in an overcoat in the middle of the summer, soaking up sunlight. The reason I wore an overcoat despite the heat was my fever. I was shivering all the time. I was praying that a good suntan would fool the officials and get me through their entry examination.

Then came the day the ship sailed into New York harbor passing by the awesome sight of the Statue of Liberty greeting the hundreds of refugees from hell. Huge buildings framed the harbor in the background. I would never forget this sight.

We were standing in line all day to face the immigration officials and the doctors. My suntan had worked. The doctor stamped my papers "Entry allowed." Hooray, I had passed! I had made it to the land of freedom. Walter and I hurried to our bunks, picked up our suitcases and rushed back onto the deck to depart the ship which had been our home for the last four weeks.

We craned our necks to find Papa and Aunt Hannah who spent the entire day at the dock waiting for us. Finally, we saw them. After hurriedly scrambling down the staircase, we rushed to embrace and kiss Papa and Aunt Hannah. Papa then hailed a taxi and off we went to Brooklyn to my father's the small apartment. I collapsed into the seat of the taxi, totally exhausted. The fever had made me extremely weak.

We arrived at the apartment on Rogers Avenue in Brooklyn. It was a homey place. Aunt Hannah immediately heated up the vegetable soup she had prepared for our arrival. It even had meat in it…meat, which we had not had for several years. The soup tasted heavenly.

The next morning I could not get out of bed. I was totally exhausted. Papa called a doctor. After examining me, he recommended that I enter Brooklyn Jewish Hospital for further evaluation. The doctor made a phone call to the hospital and arranged for an immediate admittance. That afternoon I entered the hospital and was put into a two-bed room. The young man in the other bed was pleasant, wanted to know my name and where I came from. I was not used to such friendliness.

Meals were brought to us in the evening consisting of roast chicken, mashed potatoes and gravy, a vegetable and salad, and even a dessert, a white cake with a sauce, a heavenly smelling assortment of delicious food. I have never forgotten the sight and smells of this heavenly meal, my first in America.

"Chicken again," exclaimed my neighbor. "I can't stand the sight of it," I heard him say. I was puzzled. This food was out of this world. How could someone turn up his nose at such a wonderful meal? He kept complaining about the food every meal. I shook my head but kept silent. It was beyond my comprehension.

Two days later, after several doctors discussed my illness, we were told the truth about it. I did, indeed, have tuberculosis and not some exotic tropical disease. A hospital social worker visited us. An arrangement was made to transfer me to Denver, Colorado to a hospital called The National Jewish Hospital. I would learn later that this well-known hospital's motto then was "none may enter who can pay; none may pay who enter." There, they treated tuberculosis exclusively.

A few days later Papa and Aunt Hannah brought me to Grand Central Station in Manhattan for my journey to Denver. It took two days and one night. The train crossed the lush landscape of Pennsylvania and Ohio. Toward evening we were approaching a giant lake. Someone told me it was Lake Michigan. Wheels squealed as the train slowed down, entering the giant terminal in Chicago.

After a night's journey the landscape began to change. There were fields of tall stalk-like plants. I learned later that these stalks were ripening corn. It was the first time I had seen such plants. Then, the fields changed color. The heat of mid-America had produced a yellow vista that stretched for many miles. The nice porter on the train told me that we were in the State of Kansas.

It felt as though we were slowly climbing as the train wound its way to the west. It was nearing noon. As the train went into a curve, I saw a tall range of mountains just like the ones we had near Munich. They were really tall. Indeed, some of them even were still covered with snow despite the fact that it was the middle of the summer.

Denver, Colorado

National Jewish Hospital was a big complex of buildings. At first I was put into the Children Pavilion. A few days later I was transferred into the main building. My condition was quite serious. I was emaciated and weighed far less than I should. But the marvelous food that I devoured, as though each meal was my last delicious one, put a lot of weight on me quickly. During the first month I had actually gained a pound a day. Thirty pound in one month! I had made history. Nurses and doctors from every floor came to see me, the wonder boy who had gained so much weight in such a short time.

In the early 1940's, the treatment of tuberculosis took a long time. Much of it was complete bed-rest coupled with injection of air into the chest cavity to assure that the lung was compressed and could heal. It worked and finally a few years later I was pronounced cured. During those years I had a private tutor visiting me to teach me English and all the other subjects needed for attending high school. Later, when I was cured, I remained at the hospital as an employee in order to finish high school. I finally graduated from East High School in Denver with straight A's. That earned me a scholarship to the University of Colorado in Boulder.

Boulder, Colorado

University life was unlike anything I had ever experienced. I had freedom, freedom to come and go, freedom to express my thoughts, freedom from being harassed which I experienced in Germany. What a wonderful life! I lived in the Phi Sigma Delta fraternity house where I "hashed", that meant I waited on tables, washed dishes and helped with the cooking. It was one way to earn a roof over my head but at the same time, between working and studying, it consumed all my energy.

One day I spotted a flyer announcing a choral concert at Macky auditorium. I love music, particularly choral music. That afternoon I strode over to Macky auditorium. I sat down in the middle of the auditorium, leaned back, closed my eyes and listened to these lovely voices. I cannot remember what the choral compositions were. I was distracted because, about seven rows ahead of me, my attention became focused on a beautiful girl who was also listening attentively to the music.

Macky auditorium has many windows up high near the ceiling. That day, the sun shone through those high windows highlighting that girl's auburn hair. It was

Al's wife Jean. They met at the University of Colorado in 1944.

as though a bright halo encircled her lovely skin. "This is a girl I simply have to meet," I said to myself. How would I be able to accomplish this? I was still a shy person speaking English with a rather heavy accent. Would she talk to me? It took all my courage to do what I finally did.

I started to climb over seven rows of seats and sat down next to her. "My name is Al," I blurted out. She was so surprised that she was speechless at first. Finally she replied, "I am Jean."

"That's a lovely name," I uttered and did not know what to say next. But Jean immediately became interested in me, someone from a foreign county with, what she thought, was an attractive accent. She wanted to know everything about me. It was the beginning of a wonderful relationship that would last more than fifty years.

The chemistry was right; we became closer and closer. We fell in love. My college education now had lasted one year. Later, I took additional courses at the University of Colorado branch in Denver. Our engagement followed and about a year later, we got married in a simple wedding ceremony. Because of a shortage of apartments, we had to settle for a small studio apartment near downtown Denver. My earliest job was selling shoes at the May Company department store in Denver.

In order to visit my father and aunt in New York, I had to come up with creative ways to travel. Money was very tight. One day I learned that mortuaries in Denver occasionally needed to ship deceased persons to New York. The law stated that someone had to accompany the body to be delivered and turned over to a mortuary in New York. That earned me a free first class ticket. I was able to earn myself two trips to New York that way. It was the only way I was able to see my father and Aunt Hannah in a period of five years.

Soon Jean and I had two children, Karla and Morgan.

In the early 1950s, Papa and Aunt Hannah were finally able visit us in Denver. Papa was sick. His mind wandered and, at times, he became confused. "They are after me," he would shout. What went on in his mind? Was he reliving the times in the Dachau concentration camp and Stadelheim prison? He seemed terrified during those episodes. It broke our hearts to see this kind man tortured by memories of the past. But when we would question him about it, he either did not remember it or simply would or could not talk about it.

After selling shoes for several years, I found employment at Samsonite Corporation, the famous manufacturer of Samsonite luggage, in Denver. Our daughter Katie was born in 1958. The following year, Samsonite transferred me to Saint Louis, Missouri as a salesman of their luggage products. Our fraternal twins, Craig and Mitch arrived rounding out our family.

In 1963, I became the East Coast sales manager of a region ranging from Washington, D.C. to the Canadian border. We found a nice home in Maplewood, New Jersey, a lovely and picturesque small town. Managing such a huge sales region involved a lot of traveling, working with thirteen or fourteen salesmen. While it was a strenuous and demanding job, it gave us a good income.

My income at this stage permitted us to take longer trips, to hire baby sitters and visit far away places. For our first major vacation, a neighbor recommended a lady to watch over our brood. Little did we realize that this lady was in her mid-seventies. She certainly did not look her age. But, after returning from this first international trip, we learned that our children had been quite rowdy. They even locked this gentle old lady in a closet at one time. We considered ourselves fortunate that the house had not burned down.

This first major vacation was a trip to England for the wedding of my English cousin's son in the town of Newcastle in the northern part of England. From there, we planned to take a train to Manchester and rent a car in that city.

Wales, Great Britain

My wife's ancestry was Welsh. We spent hours researching for possible locations of her Welsh ancestry. We drove into Wales, the little country appendaged to the western part of England. We wanted to see the country and, at the same time, find relatives of hers. Winding narrow roads took us through beautiful countryside. We drove through picturesque towns with names almost impossible to pronounce—Llandudno, Caernarfon, Penmaenmawr, Penrhyndeudraeth. Some of these towns sported imposing castles and fortresses protecting them against those marauding invaders from long ago. The grandeur and beauty of these forts fascinated and impressed me. This fascination with fortresses, first ignited many, many years ago while playing with my brother Günther outside of Hamburg, remained with me throughout my life. In Caernarfon, I climbed narrow winding steps up and down in turrets, across ramparts, all the time imagining heroic defenders shooting arrows at those invaders. Some of these forts were partially ruined years ago due to wars while others majestically overlooked the countryside in perfect condition.

Our first stop was in the coastal Welsh town of Aberystwyth. The Belle Vue Royal Hotel looked inviting to us. Upon checking in at the front desk, Jean, never one to be bashful, asked the clerk if there were any people with the name of Herbert, her maiden name, in nearby towns, such as Tregaron. "I am a cheeky girl," was the receptionist's reply. "I will make some telephone calls and find out for you." Minutes late, she smiled and said, "I think I have found some of your relatives. "There is a Robert Thomas on the phone who says he is married to a Herbert."

Jean took the telephone and a lively conversation ensued. Robert Thomas' wife, Caenor was, indeed, a relative of Jean. A third cousin or a cousin thrice removed. In fact, Caenor even had a twin brother, Dr. Hugh Herbert, who lived in the nearby town of Aberaeron.

The next day resulted in meeting all these relatives of Jean. They were excited to meet American cousins. Indeed, these relatives were the most delightful people. We have remained in contact with them ever since. Years later, Caenor's husband, Robert, gave me much sustenance and support during one of my most difficult trips in the search for my family's destiny.

Jerusalem

To forget is to abandon, to forget is to
repudiate.   *—Elie Wiesel*

For our vacation in 1979, Jean and I decided to travel to Israel. It turned out to be one of the most exciting trips we ever made. Jean was a good sport, tagging along everywhere I walked and climbed on many ancient structures including some more ancient fortresses.

In 1979 Jean and Al traveled to Israel for an exciting journey. This photo shows the Wailing Wall.

One of the most impressive and deeply emotional visits was to Yad Vashem, the memorial in Jerusalem dedicated to the six million Jews killed during the Second World War. The memorial consisted of a number of halls containing photos, dioramas and artifacts depicting the loss of Jewish lives from countries throughout Europe. One large dimly lit hall, an eternal flame flickering in the center, was surrounded by signboards depicting the names of many of the infamous extermination camps.

On our way out of this memorial, we passed by a large building that housed offices and a library. "Why don't we stop here and see if they have records about what happened to your family," Jean said to me. "If any place has records, this is the one." I hesitated. Did I really want to know what happened to Mutti, my two brothers and two sisters? Did I really want to know when and how the Nazis determined their fate?

Then I said to myself, "I should do this." We had better take advantage of their research facilities and try to look up my family's record if available. We entered the building, were directed to the second floor where all the records were kept. Upon giving the lady our surname, she entered the information into the computer. Minutes passed. After all, there were millions of names in the computer. Finally, she came back to the counter with a sheet in her hand. "This is what we have," she told us, "of what seems to be your family."

I was stunned when I looked at that sheet of paper. There, in my hand, was the first thread to my vanished family. It was only one page long but had a tremendous impact on me. Tears welled up in my eyes. Everything became blurred. I finally composed myself. This is what was on that sheet of paper:

München, den 15. Nov. 1941

Geheime Staatspolizei
Staatspolizeileitstelle München

II B
EVAKUIERUNG VON JUDEN NACH
RIGA AUS DEM GESTAPOBEREICH MÜNCHEN, GERMANY

LFD. NR.	ZU UND VORNAME		GEBURTSZEIT UND ORT	WOHNUNG
270	Koppel, Karola S.	Kontoristin	18. 5. 03 München	Thierschstr. 7
271	Koppel, Günther I.	Schreiner	6. 3. 24 München	Thierschstr. 7

272	Koppel, Hans I.	o. B.	9. 1. 36 München	Antonienstr.7
273	Koppel, Ruth S.	o. B.	11. 8. 37 München	Antonienstr.7
277	Koppel, Judis	o. B	25. 8. 39 München	Antonienstr. 7

I remembered enough German to be able to identify what was on this sheet of paper. Geheime Staatspolizei is the Gestapo. The heading stated "Evacuation of Jews to Riga (Latvia) out of the Gestapo District Munich." LFD. and NR. meant successive numbers, ZU UND VORNAME was surname and first name, GEBURTSZEIT UND ORT was place of birth and the date, and finally WOHNUNG meant place of residence. The "S" and "I" after each first name stood for "Sara" and "Israel", courtesy of the Nazi regime to identify that the person was a Jew.

In a daze, I left the building. Jean held my arm and led me back to the sidewalk. According to this sheet, they were evacuated to Riga, Latvia, in November 1941. There was some puzzling information on this evacuation order. In 1941, my family lived in the Thierschstrasse 7 in what was called the Judenhaus (Jewish House) in Munich. But the three little ones had a different address, namely Antonienstrasse 7. Why?

Colorado, USA

For the next dozen or fifteen years I was busy supporting my family. In the meantime, we had moved back to Denver, Colorado again because of my promotion at Samsonite to the National Director of Sales for the Furniture Division. Raising and supporting a large family, I did not have much time to think about my family left behind in Europe. However, the real reasons for blocking out my family were the painful memories it stirred up. Many years would pass before I became again deeply involved with the destiny of my family. My pursuit of their destiny, and my own, would stir up deepest emotions and open my eyes to events unimaginable to comprehend. In 1988, I retired from Samsonite.

After retirement, in 1993, Jean and I decided to move to a smaller town and ended up in Fort Collins, Colorado, which is about 70 miles north of Denver. Our eldest daughter Karla, her husband, and two daughters had made their home in this city. We were fortunate to have two of our grandchildren so close by. Megan then was ten years old and Kendal was seven, both warm and loving children. Jean and I settled in for a slower life than in Denver. Our children visited us frequently. It was a comfortable and good life after the many years of hard work raising our family of five children. My granddaughter Kendal in particular used to love to visit us and many times would stay with us overnight. A curious child, she always explored every nook and cranny in our new home.

Jean had a real knack making a house a home, comfortable and pleasant, through innovative decorating. Plants and pictures were everywhere. She had arranged a collage of family photos in our dining room. It included Jean's mother and father, her grandfather and her great grandfather. My side of the family consisted of pictures of my parent's engagement and a grouping of my two brothers and two sisters who had been left behind in Europe.

For years, whenever I walked by those photos, guilt stabbed me in my heart. Here, I was alive and comfortable. At the same time, I did not know what happened to my family. I would always avert my eyes passing by these photos. I could not to look at my brothers and sisters or my mother for it would open a never healed wound. It was very painful to see them pictured on the wall, a painful reminder of a traumatic void in my life.

During her visits, Kendal especially liked to stand in front of the family pictures and study them thoughtfully. "Granddad," she would ask, "who are these four children?" I winced and shrunk away, not wanting to remember, not being able to talk about them. However, this precocious little girl was persistent. "Kendal, my sweetheart," I barely managed to utter, "I will tell you about them some other time." The memory was simply too painful for a discussion at this time.

Kendal's questioning happened numerous times. Each time I would avoid talking about my siblings. But by the following year, Kendal had managed to convince me to talk about those four children and my parents. It was very difficult; I choked a lot as I told her about my loved ones.

At the same time, it dawned on me that one's presence on earth is finite, that I owed my loved ones the story of what happened to my family, and to me. Thoughts went through my mind that possibly the smaller children, Hans, who would have been nine years old at the end of the war in 1945, Ruth about eight years old and Judith, six years old, might have been hidden during the war by some compassionate family. There were numerous articles in newspapers about children hidden in convents or on some farm outside the big cities. Perhaps it was time for me to to probe, do research, to look and to hope.

The Shoebox

I had stored the shoebox full of letters from Germany in the back of a closet all these years. Now, I hesitantly took this shoebox containing the many letters hidden away for such a long time, and looked at a number of them. All of them were written in German. Some of the letters were from my aunt and uncles, some from strangers. But most of them were from my mother in Munich, addressed to my father in Brooklyn, New York.

I picked out a letter from my mother at random and began to read it and then to translate it. My hands were shaking with trepidation. I began the long, long journey of translating letters, tentatively at first, then with frenzy difficult to describe.

It was fifty years after the end of World War II, in 1995, that I decided to begin this research into my family left behind in Germany. Little did I realize that it would become a long and tortuous journey. For half a century, I had repressed the memories of my loved ones, my parents and their children. I had avoided looking at their pictures but, at the same time, had contemplated what could have been a warm family life. Little did I realize the range of emotions and agonies I would experience along the path of delving into the lives of my mother, my two brothers and my two sisters. Little did I realize how my searching would involve so many more lives of other family members and strangers as well. But, I was now committed, indeed, even compelled to proceed.

Fort Collins, Colorado

The journey began in my hometown, Fort Collins, Colorado at the Colorado State University. There, at the library I devoured all the books and documents they carried on the subject of the Holocaust. One of the books I brought home was titled "Journey into Terror," by Dr. Gertrude Schneider. It dealt with the deportations of Jews to

My first cousin Werner Koppel from Altona (Hamburg) -- a terribly shocking discovery.

the Riga, Latvia concentration camp. It was obviously of interest to me because I had obtained a copy of the Gestapo edict during my visit to Yad Vashem in Jerusalem which spoke of the "Evacuation of Jews to Riga out of the Gestapo district Munich." My wife Jean was also interested in this book. While I was studying another book, she began to read "Journey into Terror."

All of a sudden, Jean emitted a shriek, like the howling of a wounded animal. I raced to her side, deeply concerned. "What's the matter?" "Here, here," she stammered, "look at this." I looked at the chapter she pointed to and began to read.

"In December, 1941, three more transports arrived at Camp Jungfernhof, near Riga, Latvia. They came from Stuttgart, Hamburg, and Vienna, bringing the population of the camp to almost 4,000. Whenever a transport from the Reich pulled in at the station of Skirotava, Latvia, Dr. Lange, who in the meantime had been promoted to the rank of *Obersturmbannführer* (equivalent to lieutenant colonel in the regular army), was there with his sidekick, *Obersturmführer* (equivalent to first lieutenant), Gerhard Maywald, to 'greet' the victims. On the day that the Hamburg transport arrived, the weather was extremely cold. Because of this, one young fellow, Werner Koppel" …

I stopped reading. This was my cousin, of my age, from Hamburg. He was the son of my Uncle Leo and his wife Sine. We played together a lot when I was a small child. My hands were shaking. I could hardly read on.

> … "Werner Koppel, was not able to open the door of the train fast enough. He paid for it with his life; Lange shot him on the spot." (From an eyewitness account and deposition of Gertrude Wasserman to the English Army in 1946 or 1947 of the train's arrival at the Skirotava Railroad Station in Riga, Latvia, from "Journey into Terror," by Dr. Gertrude Schneider.)

This happened in front of his mother. I have been trying to visualize the scene his mother screaming and crying over the sudden murder of her son. We never heard again from my Aunt Sine, the mother of her murdered son.

That same year I traveled to New York City for additional research. Two organizations were of particular importance to my effort, the YIVO Institute and the Leo Baeck Institute, both located in New York City. I obtained much information from their vast repositories of books and documents on the Holocaust. It was mind numbing, there was so much information on the subject. (YIVO Institute for Jewish Research, 15 West 16th Street, New York, NY, founded in 1925 by scholars in Berlin and Vilna, Lithuania)

Once I had returned home, I began to sift through all the materials I had accumulated in preparation for a research trip to Europe. Now I continued to read Dr. Schneider's book, "Journey into Terror," and came across a chapter which indicated that the transport originally destined for Riga, Latvia, was diverted to Kovno, Lithuania. I became confused. The official *Gestapo Befehl*—the Gestapo edict—stated that the transport was headed to Riga, Latvia. "Journey into Terror" discussed a rerouting of the train to Lithuania. Which should I believe? Inasmuch as the Nazi regime documented everything and the German mindset always dwelled on the minutest details, I leaned toward the transport heading to the camp in Riga. Only later would I find out what really happened.

My planning for the trip to Europe began in 1995. It was exhaustive work, took weeks of sifting through books and documents, indeed, it really took many months of preparations. I began my contact in Munich at the top level, with the *Oberbürgermeister*, the Lord Mayor of that city. I wrote a long letter asking many questions.

To the Honorable Mayor   27 June 1995
Christian Ude
City Hall
Munich,
Germany

Honorable Mr. Mayor,

My family lived in Munich from approximately 1931 until November 1941. In November 1938, a Gestapo edict was issued that all Jews had to leave the city within forty-eight hours. My brother Walter and I departed for Berlin to live with our aunt and uncle there. The order for all Jews to leave Munich was rescinded a day later after we had already left for Berlin. My mother and the rest of the children would remain in Munich.

Luckily, my brother and I were able to immigrate to America. We left Berlin in June 1941. My father was forced to leave Germany a year earlier, in 1940. Regrettably, my mother, brothers and sisters had to remain in Munich.

I have begun research for a book about my family. My initial work began by translating letters and telegrams from my mother, my aunts and uncles into English. All these letters had been sent to my father who now resided in New York City. It deals with about 50 letters and messages from 1940 and 1941, until my mother and four children were banished to Riga, Latvia about November 15, 1941. The last letter from my mother from Munich was dated November 10, 1941, addressed to my father. And the last letter from my father in Brooklyn, New York to my mother had a postmark of December 10, 1941. That letter was returned to him as undeliverable.

The reason of my letter to you is the following: I require all possible assistance for research for my book. It is exceedingly important to paint a picture about individuals, a story about the history of these five people—my mother and four children, rather than something so difficult to comprehend, the story of six million Jews having been murdered.

The death of six million has to be, for most people, completely beyond comprehension and, as a consequence, becomes an abstraction. But, one can surely identify with the personal destiny of one family.

I was born in Hamburg in 1926, lived a few years in Altona. Later, my family moved on to Munich. We lived on the Maximilianstrasse by the Max II monument. In 1938, my brother Walter and I left for Berlin to live with our aunt and uncle. We remained in Berlin until June 1941 when we were able to leave for America.

My father and mother had to give up the beautiful apartment in the Maximilianstrasse in 1939. My parents then had to move with the four children into the Thierschstrasse, a Judenhaus (a Jewish house).

I have to do much research in Munich as well as Hamburg-Altona and Berlin. Therefore, I would be grateful for all the help that can be offered when I shall visit Munich.

Please forgive my poor usage of German. I have rarely used the German language during the last 50 years.

I shall be pleased to receive a response from you soon.

Most cordially,
Alfred Koppel

The Lord Mayor did not respond to me himself. Rather, some time later I received a letter from an archivist of the City of Munich. In his letter he offered assistance to me in my quest for information.

The year 1996 had arrived. I was ready to prepare for my trip to Europe. It would turn out to be a torturous four-week long trip. I made many telephone calls and wrote numerous letters before I finally was ready to construct a detailed itinerary. Based on the letter I had received from Dr. Heusler of the City Archive of Munich, I felt I had to travel to Lithuania as well as to Germany.

One of these telephone calls was with the husband of my wife's third cousin, Robert Thomas, whom we met years earlier in Wales. In fact, Robert and his wife Caenor had just visited us in Fort Collins the year before at our family reunion. Upon learning of my exhaustive journey into the unknown, he promptly offered to accompany me for companionship and, above all, to support me during this emotional journey. I accepted his kind offer. Little did I realize how much I would need his support especially during the latter phase of my agonizing journey. We agreed to meet in Berlin after I had already visited Hamburg and Munich.

Munich

I had landed at Frankfurt airport. From there, I took a train to Munich. The train was one of those marvelous modern, high-speed IC trains, called Intercity train. Settled in the comfortable seat, I had much time to reflect as to what I wanted to accomplish.

This trip was not my first one to Germany. My work at the Samsonite Corporation involved visiting many countries in Europe on business trips. This included several trips to Munich. Germany was, in fact, my most important country in terms of sales volume. Yet, every time I visited Germany on business, it was with great trepidation. Despite the fact that I could converse reasonably well in German with my customers, I did not let on that I had been born in Germany. I would tell my German business associates, as well as customers, that I had learned German in school and had been practicing it during my extensive travels during the '80's. I simply did not, could not, talk about my family's destiny or my own background.

Shortly after I settled down in the Hotel Regent one block from the Munich main railroad station, I received a telephone call. "This is Werner Grube," a voice said, "and can come to see you in about forty five minutes." Who was this Werner Grube?

Werner Grube arrived promptly in 45 minutes. Both of us settled down in the two comfortable chairs. Werner, a gregarious person, and I were already on a first name basis. Werner explained: "Frau Ruth Steinführer from the *Israelitische Kultusgemeinde* called me a few days ago," he stated, "and told me to help you around the city." I strained my memory. Yes, I had written to the Jewish community headquarter asking for a meeting with this Mrs. Steinführer and received a reply.

Israelitische Kultusgemeinde München
Sozialreferat
Reichenbachstrasse 22
80469 München

Mr. Al Koppel
17. January 1996
1219 Ticonderoga Drive
Fort Collins, Colorado

Dear Mr. Koppel,

We acknowledge, with thanks, the contents of your letter of 2. January 1996, which we received the 15th of January 1996. We can convey to you that the streets addresses you mentioned in your letter are valid ones (I had asked for names of several Munich locations in order to be able to write to people there) but, regrettably, we are unable to tell you who currently lives at those addresses.

Please convey to us when you will be in Munich inasmuch as the undersigned knows some children (formerly children) who were in the Antonienheim in Schwabingen. The Antonienheim does not exist anymore.

Please direct your correspondence to me.

With kind regards,
Ruth Steinführer
Director

Obviously, she had telephoned this Werner Grube asking him to contact me. The strange message in her letter was the mentioning of an Antonienheim, probably in the Antonienstrasse, the same address shown on the order of "Evacuation of Jews from Munich to Riga, Latvia."

While I was still unpacking my suitcase, this earnest looking man with sparkling eyes and a pale complexion said again, "Frau Steinführer asked me to help you out during your entire stay in Munich." A no-nonsense person, he immediately related his story to me. "I was in Munich all the time during the war years until almost the end. Toward the end we were taken to Theresienstadt where my brother Ernst and Sister Ruth and I were liberated by the Red Army in May 1945. Tell me all about yourself," Werner asked. "Why did you come to Munich?"

I settled into the comfortable chair at the desk and began my story in a much-abbreviated version. "After fifty some years I finally came to the realization that I needed to find out the fate of my family and write a book about it," I replied. "I have had many conflicting statements and records about what happened to my family. As a consequence, I decided to do all the research necessary in the three cities we used to live in Germany prior to the war namely Hamburg, Munich and Berlin"

"I will be glad to help you while you are in Munich," Werner stated, "and drive you anywhere you need to go."

"That is so kind of you. As difficult as I think it will be, I need to visit the Dachau concentration camp where my father was taken on Kristallnacht. I also must meet a Dr. Heusler from the Munich city archives."

"That's no problem. We can drive to Dachau tomorrow," he said. "It will be best if I leave now so you can get rested for tomorrow's trip"

We said good bye and he left. What a nice man to offer so much help. Although I remembered a lot about the city where I lived some fifty-five years ago, it would have been very difficult to travel around the city by myself, certainly on public transportation. I was thankful to have met Werner and was looking forward with anxiety to our trip to Dachau.

The next morning Werner appeared punctually at eight o'clock. We had a quick breakfast together in the dining room. Then, we left the hotel, walked a short block around the corner, where Werner had parked his giant vintage Mercedes station wagon.

Werner and I talked during the trip. I mentioned that my father never once spoke about his incarceration at the Dachau concentration camp.

As we drove in a northwesterly direction, my mind raced, memories overwhelmed me. How would I react when we arrived at the camp? My chest tightened. I began to sweat although it was early spring and still cool. To take my mind off these horrible images, I pulled out and studied the map of Munich and surrounding areas. Dachau seemed to be about 15 miles northwest of Munich. It should take us thirty to forty minutes to arrive at the camp. I had read that this concentration camp opened in 1933, and had been the first one to be established in Germany.

We arrived at the parking lot at Dachau. Several tour buses and many cars were already parked there. Approaching the camp, I saw a moat now without water. Barbed wire, once electrified, surrounded the entire facility. Images of prisoners having thrown themselves onto electrified barbed wire, like a fly in a spider's nest, materialized in my mind. At intervals were watchtowers which, obviously, had held guards, searchlights and machine guns. Escape would have been impossible. Now, we entered freely through the gate with the inscription above it: *Arbeit macht frei*—Work makes you free.

This concentration camp was originally built to hold 5,000 prisoners, but during the war years, it actually held as many as 12,000 prisoners at a time. 200,000 prisoners had been incarcerated there between 1938 and 1945. Approximately 32,000 were killed here.

One building had been converted into a museum, holding all sorts of instruments of torture and horrible pictures of medical experiments. There, I picked up a brochure describing the layout of the camp. Only one barrack was still in existence. The other twenty-nine barracks housing the prisoners had been razed. In their place were large concrete slabs indicating a former presence of those barracks. There had been another four barracks containing an infirmary, library and other administrative facilities. In front of these barracks were two *Appell* areas—roll-call areas.

I am quoting from a statement of an eye witness text, an Oskar Groebel, who wrote the following about the Dachau concentration camp and its prisoners aged sixteen to sixty who described all the prisoners had to stand at attention before being assigned to various barracks of this notorious concentration camp:

> 10th of November 1941 to Dachau. It had snowed—had to stand in rows for roll call many, many hours. We could not move, could not empty our bladders, and the next day had to stand hour after hour again. We were told that we would be shot in case we would fall down. Finally, we were assigned to the barracks.

> The first day, many died of pneumonia. Heavy work—several men were hanged. We were in Dachau nearly two months. We had to sign a paper that we would never talk about what we saw in Dachau.

As Werner and I walked about the camp exploring every corner of it, we came upon the ovens of the crematorium. People shot or having died from disease or torture were burned in these ovens. I experienced an overwhelming feeling of terror and the need to get out of the building.

This concentration camp had been sanitized after the war. Everything now looked neat and clean, quite orderly. Still, visions of my father incarcerated here in 1938 floated before my eyes. I was overwhelmed visualizing that my father spent six to seven week in this place.

The next day promptly at 9:00 o'clock in the morning, Herr Doctor Andreas Heusler of the Munich City Archive arrived at my hotel. A tall young man, very friendly but rather serious in his mannerism, he offered to help me in any way he could during my visit in Munich. I had written to him in January 1996.

He suggested that I visit the Institute *für Zeitgeschichte*, the Institute for Contemporary History. There, I found a number of important documents helping me to piece together lose ends, the voids, in the search of the destiny of my family

The numerous times I had been in Munich on business afforded me the opportunity to walk by the apartment house, our old home on the Maximilianstrasse, where we had lived before the war. However, I never had the courage to ring the bell of what used to be our apartment on the second floor.

Our apartment building, next to the large Bavarian government building and opposite the memorial to King Maximilian II, had not changed in the nearly sixty years since we lived there. It was beautiful building.

Although I was anxious to see our old apartment again, first I wanted to visit the street where both the synagogue and the Jewish school stood next to each other more than half a century ago. The school was next door to the Ohel Jakob synagogue, which our family had attended. Both edifices are not in existence anymore. The synagogue was burned and torn down in 1938. The school was destroyed a number of years later.

When I turned into the Herzog-Rudolf Street where both the synagogue and school buildings stood before the war, memories quelled up in me. I saw the same cobbled street that existed so many years ago. Indeed, even the little candy store from across the school was still there. Many a day, we, the students would spend our little allowance to buy some sweets before or after school. Pictures of our teachers appeared in my mind—the "*dicke*" and the "*dünne*" Kissingers, the fat one and the thin one, also Fraulein Hellman. I remembered one student, Hans, fighting with me in front of the class just as the "dicke," the heavy Kissinger entered the classroom. Immediately, the "dicke" would request that we would have to get up from the floor and extend our right hands. While holding my wrist with his left hand, he whacked my open hand with a thick stick in his right hand. That really hurt a lot. After hitting me five times, tears would well up in my eyes. But, I never cried out aloud. Memories!

I had to use much imagination to visualize the former synagogue and school building. In their place now were bland looking modern apartment houses. One of them had a plaque, way on high that, if you did not know it was there, you would certainly overlook it. The inscription reads in Hebrew and German:

"Here stood the synagogue Ohel Jakob which was destroyed on November 9, 1938 by the hands of the Nazis."

That day, I remembered, I stood at the corner of the little candy store and looked at the burning synagogue. I still remember vividly that the firemen did nothing to extinguish the flames, merely stood and watched the building burn.

The visit to the Herzog-Rudolph Street took a while. By this time, it was already mid-afternoon. My next destination was a short, fifteen-minute walk to the apartment house where we lived for so many years. Actually, it was a very pleasant walk on the Maximilianstrasse, a magnificent street beautifully landscaped on each side of the main traffic lanes. These grassy areas contained stately chestnut trees. Interspersed among the trees were a number of monuments of historical figures, some even on horses. The street is lined with many exclusive shops and government buildings.

Our apartment building, next to the Bavarian government building and opposite the memorial to King Maximilian II, had not changed in the nearly sixty years since we lived there. It was a beautiful building. It looked exactly as it did some sixty-five years ago, still majestic and ornate, a stately dowager despite its age of about one hundred years. Would I dare ring the bell of the second floor apartment? I hesitated fearing my emotions might get the best of me.

I rang the bell. A female voice came through the little speaker, "Hallo, wer ist da?"

In my limited German, I responded to the "who is there?" with, "I am Al Koppel visiting Munich, my home town of more than sixty years ago. My family lived in your apartment and I would like to see it again."

I heard a gasp and the quick reply, "Please come up. I will buzz the door so you can enter."

I entered through the double doors of the entry hall that still had, as I vividly recalled, those small intricate tiles on the floor. I turned left and walked to the elevator. It was the same ornate iron cage, slowly descending to the main level. Now, it was too late to turn around and flee from the memories awaiting me.

The elevator stopped at the second floor. The entry door to the apartment looked exactly as it did sixty years ago. A tall lady stood in the doorway to the apartment, inviting me with a warm smile into the apartment. "I am Claudia Böhmer," she told me, "and this is my husband Andreas Böhmer."

It was a modern apartment, completely different from what I expected to see. Invited into their living room, Mrs. Böhmer offered me small cakes and asked if I preferred tea or coffee. They were a friendly couple, easy to talk to. Both showed great interest in my visit. I told them why I was visiting Munich and what I was prepared to do, the research and the visiting of all the places I remembered from my childhood.

Despite my limited German, the conversation went quite well. Only later would I learn that both spoke excellent English.

"Ist da eine Terrasse in dieser Wohnung"? I questioned them. Is there a terrace, somewhere in the back of the apartment I had asked them?

"No, there is not," both replied, "but there is a roof terrace at the apartment on the third floor." After walking all over their apartment, it turned out that this was not where we had lived so long ago. Our home had to have been the apartment on the third floor. They mentioned to me that the floors were renumbered and, in all probability, the third floor apartment was the correct one. A Mr. Schreyer, a lawyer and accountant, they told me, had his office on that floor.

After a one-hour conversation, I left these lovely people. Little did I realize then how close a relationship we would develop over the many years.

The next day I telephoned the office of Herr Schreyer. A lady by the name of Laux answered the telephone and told me she would be pleased to show me the rooms on the third floor. I showed up early in the afternoon, rang the bell and again took the ornate elevator, this time to the third floor.

I had stepped back some fifty years in time. It was our old apartment! I was absolutely amazed. Nothing in it had changed except that the apartment now contained office furniture. Everything looked the same as it had so many years ago. Nothing had been modernized. Visions of the living room with its pot-bellied stove for heating in the winter appeared before me. The bedroom where Walter and I had slept and had our many pillow fights still had the ornate door with the old brass hardware. It was easy to conjure up the images of the big dining room table, the credenza holding my mother's entire beautiful china collection and crystal, the upright piano over which the delicate color portrait of my mother hung. This was the room, because it faced the important Maximilianstrasse, where we had been forced to place lighted candles in red plastic containers in the windows to celebrate Hitler's election in January 1933. By edict, every apartment facing the street had to place these lighted containers in the windows transforming the entire street into a semblance of holiness.

By now, three young ladies and the office manager working in this office had assembled around me, hanging on every word I uttered. They were fascinated by the appearance of someone out of the distant past.

"There should be a roof terrace in this apartment," I told the group, "which had heavy iron doors for protection." "Yes, there is such a terrace," they replied, "but we are not allowed out there because of safety problems." Sure enough, as we walked through the

last room that used to be a bedroom, I saw the terrace. I walked
out to look around. Our family
had spent many happy hours out
there. We sometimes had friends
on that terrace enjoying dinner
with us. The little children would
play out there. I still have photos of these happy times. Now
I turned around to reenter the
apartment. Lo and behold, the
two iron doors, somewhat rusty
now, were facing me. Again, disbelief showed up in the faces of
the four ladies accompanying
me. It was as though they were
transported back in history.

My family had lived in the
Maximilianstrasse until 1939.
That fateful year produced an order by the Gestapo that all Jews
had to move into *Judenhäuser*—
Jewish houses, where Jews were
concentrated together. This

Stepping back some 50 years in time,
visiting our former beautiful apartment
on the Maximilianstrasse in Munich
on the large terrace. Top to bottom:
Walter, Alfred and Günther.

freed the Jewish apartments and houses for Nazi party members. At
the same time, it enabled the Gestapo to keep an eye on all the Jews
of Munich.

That year, as Walter and I lived in Berlin with my aunt and uncle,
the order to move into a *Judenhaus* was issued to my family in Munich.
My family had to move to the Thierschstrasse 7 not very far from our
home on the Maximilianstrasse, which was a small apartment building
consisting of three floors and a street level floor that contained the offices of Jewish dentists.

The next day I went to that *Judenhaus* in the Thierschstrasse. There,
I met the family Zrenner the current owners of this apartment house.
I explained to Mrs. Zrenner that my family had lived here on the third
floor some fifty-five years ago. Upon asking to see my family's apart-

ment on the third floor, Mrs. Zrenner told me that the occupant was not at home, but she would ask the elderly lady on the second floor if I could view her apartment. That apartment, she said, was identical to the one on the third floor. First, she showed me the *Erdgeschoss*, the street floor, which now consisted of a bedding store and the Zrenner's small grocery store. In 1939 and until 1941, these quarters were the offices of Jewish dentists. Next, Mrs. Zrenner took me to the apartment on the second floor, the one identical to the third floor apartment. Frau Zrenner was very kind and let me explore every room in the apartment. The entry had the original double doors, opening into the hall that led to all the other rooms. To the left was a long and narrow room, the toilet. Immediately next to it was a narrow, windowless chamber. Next to it was the kitchen which, according to Mrs. Zrenner, in the '40's had a coal stove that was used for cooking as well as for heating the apartment. In the summer, a gas stove was used instead. The single kitchen window had an iron guard attached to it but the narrow space was not usable. There were some cabinets in the kitchen, a sink, and a small table and chairs.

In the center of the entry hall, directly opposite the entry doors, was a bathroom. It contained a long bathtub sitting on decorative curved legs. To take a bath, Mrs. Zrenner stated, one had to heat water on the stove and pour it into the bathtub. Mrs. Zrenner told me it could possibly also have contained a tiled stove for heating. On the other side of the entry hall were a living room and one bedroom. Both the living room and the bedroom each had one window opening upon the Thierschstrasse.

I tried to visualize how my family—father, mother, two sons and two daughters—were able to live in this tiny, cramped apartment. It was beyond my comprehension. Undoubtedly, the narrow chamber was used as a sleeping quarter. The living room must have held two people and the bedroom, my parents and the new baby, Judith.

All the apartments in Jewish houses were crowded with people thrown out of the living quarters they had occupied for so many years. I shook my head in disbelief. While Walter and I had lived in Berlin in relative comfort, my family in Munich was squeezed into this unbelievably small apartment. My research had produced a *Hausbogen*—a register of the occupants of the building (courtesy of the City of

Munich archives). An entry of June 1, 1939 indicated that my family had been forced to move here in 1939.

I tried to visualize my mother writing many letters, including those long ones to her husband in New York after he had to leave Germany in the mid-1940s. Undoubtedly she composed those long letters in the kitchen, the only place of privacy after the children were put to bed. Those many long letters from my coura-geous mother, written in loneliness, expressed all her hopes and fears.

My father Carlo and mother Carola. In 1939 they had to give up their apartment in the Maximilianstrasse and relocate into a small apartment in a Judenhaus.

My mother was a gutsy lady. She tried every available means to obtain help for her family to be able to immigrate to the United States or any other country. A letter to her uncle in America was typical of her many efforts.

> From Carola Koppel
> Thierschstrasse 7
> München   the 22nd Oktober 1940
> To Herrn. Charles Wagner
> Staten Island, New York
>
> Dear Uncle Charlie,
>
> Although you did not respond personally to my last letter, I shall write to you today again. In the meantime, my dear husband immigrated to the U.S.A. and, I assume, that you

have already gotten to know him. It was very difficult for my husband to leave me defenseless behind with six children which you undoubtedly can imagine. Now that you have surely had conversation with my husband and he reported everything to you, you will no longer hesitate to help the children and me. How you can do this you can best discuss with my husband. With God's help, your assistance will not be too late. You can imagine that for me here it is an extremely difficult time until it will be possible for me to accomplish our emigration. This is my urgent plea to you to fulfill the clearly human obligation and help the only daughter of your brother (Albert Wagner, my mother's father) who died at such an early age. I remember your last visit to Germany at which time you told me I could count on your help if I would find myself in serious difficulties such as life and death. Now the time has arrived to fulfill this promise.

Now, I wish you and your dear family all the best. My heartiest regards to all and, again, your help is needed as quickly as possible.

With everlasting love,

Your Niece
Carla

My mother, alone now in Munich with four children, had written this letter to her uncle in Staten Island, New York and, apparently, never received a reply. This was substantiated through a letter from my father, writing desperately to the niece of Charles Wagner.

Carlo Koppel c/o Max Morrison
1160 President Street
Brooklyn, New York   December 29, 1940

To Miss Mohr,
New York, New York

Dear Miss Mohr,

Undoubtedly, you have already been informed through your Uncle Charles Wagner of my arrival in New York. If

I turn to you today in writing, it is not to ask anything of you. It is merely to relate to you what is on my mind and in my heart for which you surely have compassion.

After I arrived in the United States I wrote to Charles Wagner but received no reply. Only after my third letter to him did I receive a signed letter wherein he stated that he could not receive me in his house and, so to speak, he left it to chance that we might meet perhaps somehow in the huge city of New York.

I must admit that this turning me away without any reason made me ill. After all, if the United States lets me immigrate into this country after verifying my irreproachable reputation, that a man like Charles Wagner, regardless as to reason for his earlier denials to see me, will not receive the husband of his niece in his house is incomprehensible to me.

My visit, after all, does not commit him to anything, but he surely could listen to me. My pleading to you, dear Miss Mohr, is to accomplish through you a meeting with your uncle and me in the next few days, regardless as to place of meeting. It would please me at the same time to get to know you personally.

Many thanks in advance for your help. I send you my best regards and remain,

> Most cordially yours,
> Carlo Koppel

Nowhere was I able to find any letter or documentation that Charles Wagner, uncle of my mother, ever lifted a finger to help her and the four children living in Munich to escape from Germany.

The National Refugee Service in Brooklyn, New York had suggested that my father move away from that city in order to find a better job more readily. But with my father's limited knowledge of the English language, his efforts to bring his wife and children to the United States, he felt it best to remain in New York. Here he had friends who might be able help him. Most of them spoke German as well as English. Everything concerning immigration to America transpired in this city.

From: Carl Koppel, c/o Max Morrison
1160 President Street
Brooklyn, New York   March 17, 1941

To: National Refugee Service, Inc.
Brooklyn District
80 Willoughby Street
Brooklyn, New York

Dear Mr. Perlman,

I refer you to our conversation this past Friday. After careful consideration and reasons that I will enumerate below, I arrived at the conclusion to turn down your friendly offer to send me to Buffalo.

You know that since five months I have been claiming from your organization support for my livelihood. During that time, I was sick for one month and there was left four months to look for employment. Regrettably, I was unsuccessful during that time to find anything. Perhaps it was too short a time, especially since the employment market is very tight. In addition, my age probably has something to do with it. Obviously, I shall endeavor to continue to find a job and hope that the day will come where I shall find employment.

The main reason for turning down the offer to move to Buffalo is that I must be able to achieve independence in order to sustain such a large family once they arrive in the United States. With the current uncertainty of the job situation here, the support of my family is put into question. I must add that on Saturdays and Jewish holidays I do not engage in any work. If such a holiday falls on a weekday, then there is the danger that I will lose my job and it would result in a continuous change of jobs, especially since I am a refugee.

I have explained previously to Mr. Filler and recently to you that I will receive from friends some money that will help me to become independent. And this sum of money was promised to me by the beginning of May or the 15th of May. Therefore, it will be only a short time until my plan can be executed and I hope you would assist me with advice.

I am convinced that you have an understanding for this. I can not let this chance escape me because it means everything to me. Inasmuch as I had been involved in food distribution, I would like to work in this field again. When my wife and the children will arrive here, and with her knowledge of baking of all sorts, there will be additional earnings capability.

You can believe me, I have not sat still. I have observed the activities in the area of grocery distribution here and collected much information.

In closing, I beg you to let me have the announced portion of continued support for which I will be very thankful to you.

Most respectfully,
Carl Koppel

In 1941, my father was fifty-six years old. The United States had barely come out of The Great Depression. Unemployment was still at high levels. It was extremely difficult for an older refugee with little knowledge of English to obtain a job. Indeed, there prevailed a deep resentment toward foreigners entering the United States and taking away scarce jobs from the 'natives'. This was also the prevailing attitude of the State Department, which issued many rulings obstructing the issuance of visas to the desperate Jews of Europe. In fact, it was learned that in many instances, quotas for German visas had not even been filled.[1]

---

1 On June 16, 1940, Breckenridge Long determined to obstruct granting visas to Jews seeking to immigrate into the United States. He sought to "delay and effectively stop" such immigration by ordering American Consuls

In 1940, President Franklin Roosevelt put the question of Jewish immigration into the United States into the hands of Assistant Secretary of State Breckenridge Long, a known anti-Semite and his associates in the State Department. Breckenridge Long, a xenophobe, was particularly distressed at the prospect of more Jews entering the United States.

During 1941, my mother's situation became more desperate by the day. A single light bulb at the kitchen table illuminated her efforts to be close to her husband through numerous letters she composed to him. This was an almost a weekly ritual, the only contact with her husband in New York. The following is a portion of a letter from my mother to my father in New York. The main portion of the letter must have gotten lost and there is no date shown. It was probably written in the summer of 1941.

> Had mail yesterday from Lola and Lene (both sisters of my father living in Berlin and Frankfurt). They are counting on eventually visiting the ill Selma Herz. Many people have been visiting her. Lola had mail from Leo and Edie (brothers of my father. Both escaped from Germany to France in 1939 where they were eventually caught and imprisoned). They write about the need for money all the time but, after all, money is very tight.

> There is an extreme time constraint for our application to emigrate. Help is needed and one can not wait until such help becomes meaningless. The Americans think only about themselves. It is simply unbelievable how heartless they are. When it is too late, all the nice words and all the remorse will not help anymore. You can tell that to the ones it applies to.

> So, I will close for now. Günther is still in the trade school.

> My very best and regards to all the loved ones and to you, my most affectionate beloved Carlo, most heartiest regards

---

to "put every obstacle in the way to postpone the granting of visas. He was quite successful at that over the next few years.–From *The Holocaust Chronicle*, 2000.

and many kisses from your very much loving you and longing for you little wife,
    Carla

Thus began my mothers numerous letters throughout the summer and
fall of 1941, a kaleidoscope of pent up emotions expressed through
the written word.

From Carola Koppel
Thierschstrasse 7, 3rd floor, Munich
23. July 1941

My dear, dear Carlo!

Many heartfelt thanks for your dear letter of the 3rd of this
month which I received yesterday. I was very pleased with
your detailed report. I wrote you in my last letter already
that I received a communiqué from the embassy in Berlin
concerning the transfer of the documents to Switzerland.
In the meantime, Dr. Baer wanted to inform himself what
could be done here. When Günther comes home, I shall
visit him this afternoon. The *Israelitische Kultusgemeinde* here
in Munich (The Jewish Community Administration) sent
out a letter requesting forms to be filled out. I personally took these forms to Dr. Schaeler at the Israelitische
Kultusgemeinde and filled them out myself there yesterday because of lack of personnel there. I also took over
the responsibility to fill out the forms for all that live in
our apartment house and have certification from the AC
(American Consulate). The letter sent to us stated: Based
on the just received notification from the *Reichsvereinigung
der Juden* in Deutschland, (the Federal Organization of
Jews in Germany), we are conveying to you the following:
Applications for American immigration visas can only,
since July 1 (1941) be secured by a citizen of the USA
in Washington, DC. Whether, in what circumstances and
under which assumptions such applications can be considered, and especially since the closing of all consulates in
Germany which could issue such visas, one can not specu-

late at this time. One has to count on a substantial contraction of issuance of visas.

On July 1, 1941, all American consulates in Germany were closed. This, in effect, greatly diminished the possibility that German Jews could escape the scourge of Nazism. If there had been a lack of hope earlier, the notice sent out to the Jews in Munich and, obviously in all of Germany, changed the situation to utter hopelessness. My mother's letter continues:

> Nevertheless, the Federal Organization of Jews in Germany, Division of Emigration, will attempt, for those who already have a substantiated possibility for an issuance of a visa from their American relatives, to obtain support for such applications through the Hilfsverein, (Assistance Organization for German Jewry to provide information about emigration).

> Based on these circumstances, all Jewish people who already were invited this year to the American Consulate or at least had received an American Consulate certification, are asked to fill out a questionnaire in the Counseling Center, Emigration Department, and bring along all documentation received from the Consulate.

> Dr. Schaeler (a director of the Israelitische Kultusgemeinde München, Branch of the Reichsvereinigung der Juden in Deutschland) tells me that these forms are being collected in Berlin and from there will be sent to the Joint Distribution Committee and the HIAS (Hebrew Immigrant Aid Society) for both organizations in America. You or your attorney can without hesitation, therefore, turn to both these organizations in New York for assistance in your efforts. Inasmuch as Dr. Loewenstein is still sick, I correspond at this time with Professor Dr. Cora Sara Berliner (both in Berlin) and asked her in my correspondence of today to let me know the new booking information which you then can deliver to Washington. I hope she will do this. She has been writing very nice letters to me, shows an interest in me, and will probably follow through if it

is possible. The current booking information for August 15 went to the Consulate in Stuttgart and is incorporated with all the documents. Our registration number is put on the AC (American Consulate) file which I sent to you and which you must have received in the meantime. I received the registration number twice, on April 8 and April 9 so that I could dispense with one of the certificates. I feel this certificate will be of great help to you in Washington. I will make a photocopy of the number and send it to you in my next letter. You are doing everything possible and I hope the attorney will be successful.

It is a pity how much everything costs and one has to wonder where Hannah (father's sister in New York) obtains all the money. Leo and Edie (brothers of my father who were imprisoned in France) are costing you and Hannah so much money and now I am costing you so much more. That is painful for me. One does not know how one can repay all this some day.

I hope that you have at least some advantage in Washington through the timely handling of our case, and have a lead so that our case will still be handled. In addition, don't forget always to mention that we are a Second Preference Case and, therefore, in any case should proceed separately, apart from our otherwise desperate urgency.

My mother showed a spark of hope that her case could be effectively handled in Washington, DC through lawyers and their contacts. However, the State Department was moving at snail's pace and, indeed, pigeon holed the paperwork of the thousands of desperate people ready to depart Germany.

My father had been working with attorneys as far back as June 1941. A letter from a Herman Judell, (a friend of my father in New York) to my father speaks of his efforts to work directly with the State Department in Washington. It also contains some veiled remarks that everything else "I will convey to you verbally."

Hotel Continental   June 30ᵗʰ 1941
Washington, D.C.

Dear Mr. Koppel,

Regrettably, I did not have any success. Senator Chandler
introduced me to the State Department and to my surprise
there were several dozen lawyers from New York waiting
to be called up. Through my appointment made earlier, I
was immediately introduced to Mr. Sanderhoff. After I presented your case, several other officials were called upon
and telephone calls were made to the highest place. The last
telegram out of Munich was presented to a Mr. Warren and
it was determined that your wife until now did not receive
the visa. The confirmation from the American Consulate
in Germany is not recognized at the governmental agency
here in Washington.

In a letter to her superiors, Margaret Jones, an American Quaker who
was working with European Jews, alluded to a Consul in Zurich who
related to her recent orders from Washington. This order would greatly
limit the number of visas usually issued each month from the various
consulates. Margaret Jones' letter to her superiors underscored the following communication from Mr. Judell.

> Documents were shown to me that a secret agreement is in
> existence with the German government, that no more visas
> would be distributed. The reason for this I can only convey
> to you verbally.

I could not find any documentation of the verbal comments of Mr.
Judell that he alluded to in my any of my father's letters he saved from
this period. However, having done a lot of research pertaining to this,
the following situations might very well apply here.

David Wyman is a historian who has written several books in
which he related official American sentiments about the Holocaust.
At a conference of a number of people discussing America's involve-
ment, Wyman stated that in American consulates in Europe, anti-
Semitism was widespread. He further stated that there is clear evidence of this. June 16, 1940, Breckenridge Long, Assistant Secretary

of State, determined to obstruct granting visas to Jews trying to obtain permission to enter the United States. Breckenridge attempted to delay and thereby effectively stop their immigration by ordering American consuls "to put every obstacle in the way to slow down granting of visas." His strategy was quite successful for the next few years. Wyman also stated that in his twenty years of research, the most disgraceful document he discovered was a memorandum written by Breckenridge Long, Assistant Secretary of State, in June 1940. This document outlines the means by which consuls in Europe could secretly and illegally cut back sharply into immigration. It resulted in requirements of more documentation, additional regulations and any number of other obstacles. "Long opposed 'excessive humanitarianism' in regards to the Jews. Long seemed to be particularly distressed at the prospect of more Jews entering the United States." (from *The Holocaust Chronicle*, page 188, Lincolnwood, Illinois: Publications International, 2000)

On June 24, 1941, U.S. Secretary of State Hull issued a memorandum advising all consular and diplomatic officials to tighten regulations on foreigners applying for entry visas. This resulted in a drastic reduction in the number of visas issued.

> Cases were shown to me where firm ship's bookings were reserved for the 9th, 14th and 20th of July but visas were not issued. It was suggested to me to introduce steps that your wife and children immigrate into Switzerland and obtain from the American Consul the permission to search a way to enter the United States. You have to obtain all new affidavits, which must be submitted here in Washington. It was promised to me in your case to do everything possible and eventually to give preference. But, it is necessary that your wife applies at once for permission to immigrate to Switzerland. If that is possible, she could, according to the officials here, still board the ship on 15th of August.

> I am terribly sorry that I could not achieve anything, but at least I have been able to do more than a dozen lawyers who were all turned away with the same advice that, by order of

the Secretary of State, no telegrams are allowed to be sent to Germany anymore.

Everything else I shall tell you personally. Please telephone me.

Best regards,
Herman Judell

With this information from Mr. Judell alluding to the existence of the secret agreement, the desperation, but also the courage of my mother, had a huge impact on my father. This came to the surface in the continuation of my mother's letter from July 23rd, 1941

In the forms, one must declare the exact addresses of all the givers of affidavits, the ones who are on record at the American Consulate in Stuttgart. All blood relatives have to be declared. We only have you, Alfred and Walter overseas and have no blood relatives in Germany. We are, therefore, completely alone here and for this reason a preferential case for emigration.

The matter with Switzerland is not so simple. According to my thinking, if a general regulation comes into existence for this, meaning if eventually through the intervention from Washington, a way could be found for this way to emigrate. I had already, at the behest of your telegram, made inquiry at the Swiss Consulate. They told me that the consul feels that the Federal Republic will eventually renounce the need for an end-visa (the final visa for entry into the United States) if a verification from the American Consul is deposited at the Swiss consulate. In that case, a visa would be issued. However, in any case, they require French and Spanish transit visas to traverse those countries for departure to America. Those are very difficult to obtain and it takes weeks to accomplish this. A general ruling would have to be found for this in order to overcome all these difficulties.

Now I sit here anxiously waiting for your telegram that should announce your success with Washington. I hope I won't have to wait very long for it. As fast as you believed things would work out, it has not worked out yet because I certainly would have heard something by now. I addition, therefore, it is good that the ship's booking was only on a pro-forma basis and not the final booking.

I hope to God that we have some luck this time.

Apparently, all the paperwork of my mother and the children seemed to be almost ready for passage to the United States except for some endless details. For that reason, the statement of my mother that "it is a good thing that the ship's booking was only on a pro-forma basis and not a pre-paid basis because of the potential loss of the tickets if the date of departure could not be met."

> Today, Mrs. Schaeffer and Mr. Gross have changed their residence. I have not spoken to Gertrude as yet. They are all single people, alone in this world and I hope it will remain so.

This seems to be a 'between the lines' comment indicating Mrs. Schaeffer and Mr. Gross had to leave their apartments and were put into Judenhäuser, the exclusive Jewish buildings.

> Just now Anna (Anna was the household help during my parent's better times) was here and she is taking a walk with Muschi (Ruth) and Hansi. The baby is still sleeping. She will be coming back next week.

> Leo (Dad's brother interned in France) requests all sort of things from you. Surely, he gets many French francs for $45.00 you sent him. If he can afford an excursion to Marseille twice in one week, as he writes, then he can not have too difficult a time. After all, it costs a lot of money. He also receives something from Switzerland.

Leo and Edie, were both imprisoned in France. Actually, their internment in the camps in France was not very pleasant. Indeed, many internees died at these camps before they were finally deported to the East. Gurs was a terrible place. Streets, if you could call them streets, were full of mud literally reaching up to the ankles. There was little food, mostly cabbage or turnips and some bread. But my mother did not know of any of these terrible conditions. Leo and Edie would perish somewhere in Poland or Russia.

I have not turned in my packing lists because permission to pack would expire. One can do this on short notice and can get it expedited.

I am already very curious until I receive the first report from you and also from the two children (arrival of Walter and Al in the USA), but have to be patient and realize I have to wait at least ten more days. *Heilbuths* (friends) are at Lola's (my father's sister in Berlin) at this time and I have sent pictures of all of us there quickly. They will bring them along for you when they leave Germany. My picture, as usual, is hideous. Also Günther looks very serious and thin. The short pants he is wearing give that impression. He looks much better in dress pants.

I hope you have received the forms from Washington in the meantime. As a precaution, I will enumerate all the affidavits that are on file in Stuttgart (at the consulate) so that you are covered when you turn in new documents. They are from Uncle Nathan (Nathan Leipheimer, brother of my paternal grandmother), besides trust funds and letters from Ettingers, Fenchels, and from Lilly. Also trust fund only for our Baby Judith from Hannah (father's sister in New York). In addition, trust funds from Rolf and Manfred for all of us not yet forwarded to the American consulate in Stuttgart.

In the enclosure are four parts of Rolf's affidavit and one part of Manfred's affidavit. If I wrote in a mixed up way, you will probably understand since you know how upset I am.

Now, my dearest Carlo, my heartiest regards and intimate kisses from your infinitely longing little wife,
 Carla

Herman Judell, who had written to my father about his trip to Washington on June 30, 1941, apparently had also written to the State

Department in Washington trying to facilitate the issuance of visas for my mother and the four children. Finally, in August of that year he received a reply from A. M. Warren, Chief of the Visa Division of the State Department.

The Secretary of State
Department of State
Washington

In reply, refer to
VD 811.111 WR Judell, Herman
August, 1941

Mr. Herman Judell
256 East One Hundred and Sixty-sixth Street
New York, New York

Sir:

With reference to your letter of July 9, 1941 you are advised that all agencies interested in obtaining forms and instructions for the documentation of visa cases under the new procedure effective July 1, 1941, should address their inquiries to The President's Advisory Committee on Political Refugees, 122 East Twenty-Second Street, New York, New York.

This organization is acting in a liaison capacity between the Department of State and interested immigrant agencies, and will be pleased to furnish detailed advice regarding the preparation and presentation of the prescribed forms.

Very truly yours,
M. Warren
Chief, Visa Division

Visa Form K-2

The letter from A. M. Warren to Mr. Judell was posted 6–8 weeks after Mr. Judell's letter to my father, which was dated June 30, 1941. Undoubtedly, Mr. Warren already knew that no more visas were to be issued. The State Department had effectively shut down all emmigration for the desperate Jews of Germany. My mother had no inkling of this. Hope was still a strong motivator as shown in her next letter to my father in New York.

From Carola Koppel
München 22
Thierschstrasse 7/III   München, the 4th August 1941

My dear, dear Carlo,

Regrettably, also this week I have no mail from you, which makes me very sad. Your last letter was from July 3rd and, for example, the Mendle's have already received a letter from their daughter dated July 18. I can't believe that you wouldn't have written to me in all that time. By the way, the young Mendle is not in New York anymore. Instead, he is in a small place nearby. The place is called Hartford, I believe. He got such a good position there that he could get his wife out of Germany and she does not have to work in Hartford. They have, I believe, a small garden for their own use and feel very well situated. They are the only immigrants in this town and are courted and attended to by everyone. People are always inviting them out for a Friday evening dinner.

In the meantime, Heilbuths have departed from Germany and have the pictures of the children with them. With the receipt of this letter, you surely will have received them. I have had a postcard size enlargements made of two pictures and will give them to Sally Gutmann who will leave here the end of the week. She will travel to Chicago and will either call you from New York if there is time or will send them to you by letter.

This week I had a terrible disappointment. You can well imagine how I have been longing to receive your telegram from you advising me of your success in Washington. Last Friday a telegram came with the mail. I was so excited that, first I had to sit down. I couldn't even open the telegram right away. When I finally opened it, it was a telegram from Bernhard (brother of my father in Hamburg), that he sent me an express package which we should pick up. I can not even tell you how disappointed I was. I could not even be very happy about the package. By the way, it contained, among other things, wonderful plaice (fish) and, therefore, we had something really nice to eat.

Do you have all the new papers together and has the lawyer turned them in to the proper authorities in Washington? That it does not go so speedily as you thought it would, I had this figured out. We could never have made the ship's departure on the 15th of August. But now, I fear, it will take even longer than I had anticipated. Do you still have any hope at all? I am terribly depressed. I hope my depression will get better when I receive mail from you again. A letter from Alfred and Walter describing their trip to America should really be coming soon. I hope they wrote a detailed description of their entire long trip.

Lola (father's sister in Berlin) wrote that she will travel to Altona (a district of Hamburg) from today until this coming Friday. Bernhard and Ulli, if nothing comes up, are planning to visit us in Munich for 3 days. They felt that Günther should come to Altona during his vacation from 15th to 30th May. But this is not possible. One can not make a decision of this sort from one day to the next. Besides, I don't want to be here alone with the three little children. Who knows what might happen?

Günther had turned seventeen years old in March. In the absence of my father, he became the head of the household, a great support to my mother. The three little children loved him and looked upon him not only as their big brother but also as a father figure.

We would have liked so much to make our Sunday excursion to you in New York! If we could have taken the ship's passage on the 15th of August, then it would have been possible. Instead, if the weather is nice, maybe we shall go to Grünthal with the children. (Grünthal was a beautiful expanse on both sides of the river Isar). I can take the baby carriage on the streetcar. That is, however, some big difference from visiting you.

Baby (Judith, two years old) alerted me the other day that Hansi took something away. She said, "Look at this!" I replied, "What is the wicked Hansi doing?" and she said promptly, "Spank him." And yesterday, Günther asked me what time it is? I told him, "it is a quarter past seven," whereby Judith shouted out, "it's high time!" You can see, she already understands everything at age two. She turned out to be a real flatterer and has grown a lot as you can see from the pictures.

I heard here that a few visas were supposed to arrive from Washington. However, it dealt with visas that had expired and an extension had been given by telegram. Those visas came in time to cover the ship departure dates.

Visas for us from Washington would be far more practical than trying to immigrate to Switzerland because it is so terribly difficult to receive permission to enter Switzerland. A practical alternative, I believe, would be that the visas were to be issued to enter Barcelona, Spain. Then, when we receive new reservations for the ship, we can surely all leave from Barcelona to America. Try to obtain information about this. Portugal is not so favorable because at this time it is very difficult to receive Portuguese visas.

My mother was under the assumption that the visas for entry into the United States were ready to be issued from Washington hence her statement, "the practical alternative" of visas for entry to Barcelona, Spain.

One more point I am worried about. How is it with the moneys from the Joint (Joint Distribution Organization, New York) for the ship's passage? Or are their moneys also blocked?

Many people now travel by way of Cuba but that way is very expensive. Dr. Schaeler (of the Jewish Community Administration) told me one has to figure it costs $3,000.00

per person. $2,000.00 have to be deposited which one will get back when leaving Cuba again. $500.00 is necessary for entry and ship's passage between $500.00 and $800.00. Günther and I would probably be full price and the three little ones may be the equivalent amount of one adult person. But this would be an amount which will be impossible for you to obtain and the Reichsvereinigung, (the Federal Organization of Jews in Germany), has no influence. All this has to be worked out from America. It would only be possible if one can find a patron with a big heart, which I feel, is impossible. I think and ponder about all this all the time, day and night how all this could be accomplished.

Now, I must close. Should a letter arrive from you this afternoon, then I will add on to this letter. My best regards to all loved ones, especially Hannah. To you, my dearest Carlo, take my dearest regards and infinite many kisses from

Your very much longing for you little wife,
Carla

My mother kept on fighting and hoping. She tried to provide a near normal life for the children, a difficult situation given the fact that they all had to wear the yellow Jewish star. People would stare and whisper when they saw my mother and the children but the outing to Grünthal (green valley), not very far from their house, would certainly have lifted the spirits of the children. My mother tried to make certain that the three little ones not be burdened by all the restrictions imposed on the Jews.

My mother's safe harbor was the tiny apartment and the letters she received from her husband were her sustenance enabling her to hang on and not give up the daily struggle. It was also comforting to her to receive letters from the brothers and sisters of my father who were still confined in the hell of what was their fatherland. Unable to escape from the tyranny, the oppression manifested itself into a feeling of abandonment. A terrible loneliness as was now evidenced by the fact that my mother felt compelled to write another letter to my father only two days after the last one.

From Carola Koppel
München 22
Thierschstrasse 7/III   München, the 6th August 1941

My dear, dear Carlo!

Today, finally, your dear letter No. 42 of the 16th of July arrived which made me very happy. I was already very impatient that I had no mail from you for such a long time and had big worries because of this. I plead with you to adhere to regular times of sending me letters because you know that your letters are my only hope. And if those letters don't arrive promptly, then I become very ill. My nerves, after all, are now stretched so far that I can hardly function anymore.

Concerning emigration out of Germany I want to tell you that Mr. Walter Weiss of the board of the local Jewish Community Administration here in Munich received approval from Spain for a stay there for 25 days in order to wait for the approval of the American visa through Washington. I doubt very much that he would return if it were not possible to accomplish the receipt of the visa within the allotted time. There are rumors that his American relatives have been able to achieve this. They have friends in Spain who dealt with the necessary formalities. I am constantly thinking things over in case we are able to get into Spain. It would be the best solution inasmuch as in such a case, one can obtain transportation from Berlin to Barcelona and one would not need all the different transit visas. Please check this out if you can manage to do this.

Perhaps the Joint (Joint Distribution Committee) can, through the Reichsvereinigung (Federal Organization for Jews in Germany) which is involved with things like this, contact their branch in Barcelona so that the limited entry permission into Spain can be achieved. I have also thought about Sweden, but first of all one can not receive permission to enter and if yes, I wouldn't know how one gets to America from there.

With the arrival of the boys (Alfred and Walter) in New York early in the morning, you must have had tremendous patience standing all day waiting to have them cleared by the immigration personnel.

I remember we were standing in long lines on deck of the ship while immigration officials and doctors inspected all the immigrants very carefully. When my turn came, I was actually shaking and hoped the doctor would not notice. Having stood in line hour after hour, I became very weak from my illness. My legs almost buckled under me. Still, even at the tender age of fourteen, I realized I needed to look healthy and strong. So the last three to four days of the voyage, I had sat in the sun most of the day and acquired a healthy looking tan. I was surprised how easily I passed the scrutiny of the doctor.

I knew all along that Alfred is very independent. He exhibited that independence even here already, such as changing money or working on visas, and so forth. It had to be an astonishing sight when the ship arrived and you saw your loved ones suddenly.

Don't you have the lawyer anymore for Washington? When your application arrives among the huge number of other applications, then you can wait a long time until it will be handled. We did not have much luck in this respect in the past.

I am very much afraid that we will be forced to remain here and only be able to leave Germany when normal times are here again. Miss Gutman, sister of Mrs. Walz has been informed that she will travel via Cuba, but $2,000 has to be deposited per person, which would be returned upon departure. In addition, there has to be $500 at arrival and about $700–800 for the voyage. That, of course, would make this way of departing impossible for us.

What all the boys must have related to you! I would have loved to listen in on it. You did not write how you found the boys looked, nothing about the height of Alfred, and so forth. Do they have to attend school? What will they do now? How is your apartment? Do you have a room with other people or is it a separate apartment? It is certainly practical to live so close to your suppliers.

Little did my mother know how difficult it was to make a living in America in 1941. My father had hoped to start a wholesale business in canned grocery goods as he did so successfully in Germany. But it was not to be. Indeed, he never confided this disappointment to his wife. He then looked for any type of a job, a difficult proposition since he was already 56 years old. Finally, he landed a job in a fountain pen factory.

After all, you know how I am interested in everything, even the smallest details. Can Hannah always cook for all of you? Does she live near you? It seems Walter is very capable, going shopping all by himself already. He will surely cultivate someone somewhere soon; he understands this very well.

I haven't heard anything from my Uncle Charlie (Charles Wagner in Staten Island) despite the inquiry to him from the Joint Distribution Committee.

I kept the crystal plates, the red goblet and the small crystal plates, painted fruit plates as well as several smaller pieces. All other pieces I sold. Besides, I really have no room with only a living room, kitchen, one bedroom and a chamber.

I had three suitcases made for me by the Schoeber Company in the prescribed acceptable sizes. I also ordered larger items from Bernhard since he was in the suitcase business. Now I own six large suitcases 80 centimeter, four suitcases 75 centimeter for our travel cases. For the smaller hand baggage I have two 60 centimeter sizes and perhaps I will obtain one in 50 centimeters. Besides all this, I have a large travel pouch that is currently so modern here and holds as much as a small suitcase. All those items should suffice for the eventual trip to New York. On top of all this, I have several large bags for holding food items while traveling. Furthermore, I have three ship trunks that I am certain I can not use unless the emigration situation should change. Well, we shall see.

My heartiest thanks to the boys for their informative letters. Walter wrote very nice describing the trip. He made a few mistakes. I am happy to learn that the English with the boys is working out pretty well. How are you coming along with English, Carlo?

Two suitcases per person are the most anyone person can take and perhaps a small one for a hand suitcase. One has to pack at home. I have already sorted out our things and made up temporary lists. I will not submit those lists yet until I know it makes sense. Otherwise, everything will be for nothing.

When will the new forms be distributed from Washington? I am afraid that one will say in Washington that, for people living in Germany, that there is no point in letting them have those forms because the American consulates in Germany are all closed. That, however, would be unthinkable. Our separation is already too long. I am convinced being alone here is hurting me health wise.

Why do you need the medical documents for Alfred and Walter? I don't have any here and asked Lola in Berlin if she has copies. After all, they were again examined shortly before their appointment at the consulate. Perhaps the doctor will give duplicate exam papers.

I am sending you a photocopy of our emigration number at the Stuttgart Consulate. You have to hold it up to the light and it will be easier to read. I was unable to obtain a better copy. I still have the original.

Lola is in Altona until Friday. After that it is back to Berlin. Is your new apartment near Hannah and the synagogue? What did the people say about your big sons?

What you tell me about your various wishes is simply impossible. One can tell from your letters that you have been away from here a long time already and are unable to empathize with today's conditions. Friedl (wife of Siete, our father's elder brother) and Lotte (Friedl's sister) speak with each other very seldom now. After all, they are unable to do so anymore.

This was a "between the lines" way of saying that Lotte who was not Jewish, could not take the risk anymore of conversing with her sister who was married to a Jewish man. It was far too dangerous.

> You need to let me handle things that have to be handled here. I do the best I can under the present difficult conditions. When, with God's help, we shall be together again, we will build a new life as modest as it will undoubtedly be. You will have to excuse Günther writing you so seldom. Since today, he has to work until 6:00 in the evening and comes, therefore, home as late as 7:00 o'clock. It looks as though, he will have to work also on Saturday and Sunday as well, beginning this week. The workshop is extremely busy and they have huge orders for delivery.

It seems that between his *Arbeitseinsatz*—forced labor and lack of nourishing food—he had lost weight, looking very gaunt. In a photos I have in my possession of my elder brother, Günther looks exhausted and emaciated.

> There is nothing one can change and, once in America, we shall then with God's help do things differently. Yesterday, I spoke with Mrs. Schaeffer for a long time. She is in pretty good shape considering the conditions. Inasmuch as she is in forced labor, she has, after all, enough mobility to get along. Mrs. Katzenstein is bringing me bread today because I have no one to go shopping for me anymore and I am unable to leave our tiny apartment. How I will handle this over a longer period, I will have to think very much about.
>
> Give the boys a big kiss and my heartiest regards to Hannah. I thank her that she takes such good care of you.
>
> For you, my fervently beloved Carlo, my heartiest regards and many, many kisses.
>
> With unending longing,
>> Your very much loving you little wife,
>>> Carla

PS I have a question about Hochfelds (mother's aunt and her husband). A few years ago, acquaintances of theirs, a family Blau, the wife's name was Cilly Jakob, immigrated into Spain. Perhaps you can find out about them and make a connection. You can accomplish this much better from New York, although I don't know if they are still in Spain. Also, you have to make absolutely certain that Günther's emigration will be accomplished before he will be eighteen years old. Otherwise, he will not be able to leave here!

Else Hochfeld was the sister of Selma Wagner, my mother's mother. Else lived in Munich with her husband prior to their emigration to America. A special bond had formed between the Hochfelds and my parents due to the fact that Günther had lived with them in Schwabingen (a northern district in Munich). The reason that Günther lived with them rather than at home was to facilitate his enrollment into a classical *Gymnasium*, a high school located in Schwabingen. Günther lived with them until he was thrown out of the Gymnasium in the latter 1930s although he was one of their star athletes. Indeed, he even had received a sport medal emblazoned with a swastika that he had to return when forced out of the school.

March 16, 1942 was a critical date. At that time, Günther would be eighteen years old. All males eighteen years old had to report for forced labor. This effectively ended any possibility to leave Germany. My mother was frantic. That crucial date was a short six months away. Her mind was racing. If it took another six to eight month to be able to leave the country, only she and the three little children would be allowed to leave. Leaving Günther would be unthinkable. Having her oldest son with her was a great comfort.

Communication was what kept up my mother's strength. There were almost weekly letters from my father to his wife in Munich to which his wife responded eagerly. As the noose tightened, all those letters from her husband and to her husband were her only sustenance.

From Carola Koppel
Thierschstrasse 7/III   München, the 25. August 1941

My dear, dearest Carlo!

Your dear letter No. 45 of 8. August arrived this past Friday. I was so pleased to receive mail from you so quickly. I am terribly worried what you write to me about Alfred. Had his condition worsened from the strenuous voyage? After all, the doctor in Berlin said that everything seemed to be all right and he should be examined every three months only for the sake of monitoring him. Please write me about this honestly. I hope he was able to get into this sanatorium in Denver to regain his health. Who will be paying those expenses? How long must he remain there? I had a premonition and was terribly worried that he had not sent any mail to me. Being in Denver, he is only one hour's time away from Uncle Nathan (Leipheimer, brother of my father's mother) in Colorado Springs. I wonder if he will take notice and care about the boy. Alfred, after all, is unable to visit him since he must not interrupt his cure. With God's help will he be cured in Denver.

Have Uncle Nathan and Ettingers (Uncle Nathan Leipheimer's daughter and son-in-law) actually offered affidavits again for me? I have requested and received forms for transit visas from the Spanish Consulate. It is so difficult to fill in everything in Spanish and also give references. It is said that one would have to have this eventually accomplished at the Spanish Consulate, but I can manage this only if I receive a positive information from you about receiving our visas from America. I hope my telegram was of great help with your petition in Washington. Surely, you are working this with the help of a lawyer.

Bernhard and Ulli (father's brother and wife from Hamburg-Altona) are at this time at Lene in Frankfurt (father's sister and her husband in Frankfurt)) and will arrive here in Munich this coming Friday. I shall hold off with the matter of Spain and talk it over with Bernhard as to what to do.

Perhaps he will even go with me to the Spanish Consulate and the Portuguese Consulate. Dr. Schaeler is of the opinion that I can visit the Spanish Consulate only when I receive from you positive news from Washington (receiving visas for entry to the U.S.A.). You know he is quite pedantic and, therefore if possible, I would like to prepare things in advance. Three forms have to be filled out per passport with a number of photos. That means fifteen photos for us. Tomorrow, I shall speak with Dr. Schaeler regarding the reservations for the ship's passage. However, I believe I will not receive such booking because the Reichsvereinigung in Berlin, (the Federal Organization of Jews in Germany in Berlin) wrote that Washington, contrary to the previous custom, does not require a booking. This is logical because one can not pin down a firm date since, in any case, no one really knows how long dealing with the matter of emigration will take. I am not pinning my hopes on another pleading.

You have really decked Alfred out in fine clothes. Did he have so few things with him when he arrived in New York?

What will you do in terms of work when we arrive in New York? With Günther it looks very bad because he is nearing his eighteenth birthday early next year. I am very happy for you that you have such a nice and comfortable apartment, something one can not say anymore about ours here. When does Walter have to start school? Does he mean he will have to enter a lower class in the primary school?

Today is my little baby's birthday. I bought a roll of pretty Scottish tartan cloth and sewed a lovely dress for her. I did it all by hand. Something like it would have cost at least DM25.00 to 30.00 at the Boll's store and I was able to make it for DM6.00. One must use ideas and handiwork nowadays.

Bernhard and Ulli, who will be coming from Altona soon, can sleep in the chamber where Günther usually sleeps. It is not as elegant as the 'Kaiserhof Hotel' in Altona but, after all, more pleasant for all because we can be together longer in the evenings to talk. Hansi will then sleep on the sofa and Günther on the folding bed in the kitchen. I am already very happy in anticipation that we can thoroughly discuss things. Bernhard will undoubtedly relish the peace here.

Last week, lightning struck our water pipes in the kitchen; made a huge noise. Günther happened to be in the kitchen and saw the lightning hit. Even the people across the street saw it hitting the roof. It really scared Günther and I was happy that he did not get hurt. Two days later, we had a heavy rain shower and our kitchen was flooded from the rain coming through the hole in the roof. And so, one can not escape so many frightful scares, sometimes this and sometimes that, and one is always relieved when things turn out all right.

I assume that, in the meantime our friends Heilbuths have arrived in New York and you received the photos of the children. Regrettably, they are not totally in focus but, nonetheless very sweet. Eventually, you will receive more pictures from Sally Gutman. I am going to try to obtain another roll of film so I can send you more pictures.

Did the boys have their suitcases with them and did they contain all the items I wrote in my letter?

At this time, I still have some hope that our matter can still work out all right. I do hope that I will not be disappointed.

How are you coming along with the English language? I, myself, have now quit altogether; I am, at this time, far too nervous and can not memorize a single word.

My heart becomes heavy when I read of your longing in your letters and I can do nothing to alleviate your longing. I don't even want to write you how dejected and despondent I am because I don't want to put any more strain on your heart. Nothing seems to help; we have to take it all as it comes, even when one at times feels, one can not go on anymore. Ulli will surely wonder how grey my hair has become and how, at thirty-eight, I look like an old woman. I hope you will accept me the way I am now.

Now I will have to close. It is already midnight; where you are it is still 6:00 o'clock in the evening and you probably have just sat down to dinner. Oh, how I wish I could be there for it!

Hansi is counting the days until Uncle Bernhard will arrive here and is very excited. His little mind is in overdrive and he thinks 'Surely, Uncle Bernhard wrote he would show up on Friday, but he will surprise us and come earlier; and what things he will bring with him!' This will surely be of crucial importance to him and the other children. I am curious what Bernhard and Ulli have to say about our children.

My best regards to Hannah, and Alfred and Walter. Many kisses from your little wife having an unending longing and much love for you.

Carla

The enclosed letter is for Alfred in Denver

The tone of my mother's letter is growing more desperate and dejected. What little spark of hope that existed is slowly beginning to disappear. Total desperation had affected my mother. My efficient mother would not normally repeat herself. I can not imagine how she kept her sanity under all this pressure. Then on top of this, she worried very much about me, her Alfred, who was sick in America recuperating in a hospital.

From Carola Koppel
München 22
Thierschstrasse 7/III   München, the 27. August 1941

My dear, dear Carlo!

It has been only two days since I wrote you the last letter. But I have such heavy loads weighing on me, that I must open my heart to you. I am afraid that all the efforts you are expending on our leaving Germany will be in vain and we will have to have much patience until we see each other again. As much patience as Jacob with Rachel. (In the bible, Jacob told Laban, Rachel's father he would serve seven years for Rachel, Laban's younger daughter). You do know when my 45th birthday is (in 1948) and that's how long we will have to wait.

This was my mother's outpouring of her heart. In the Bible it says, Jacob served Rachel's father seven years to be able to marry her. In addition, my mother underscores this by alluding to her 45th birthday, which was seven years away. What a heart rending cry for help!

You can imagine my present mood; yet, I still hope for a miracle that we shall still be able to emigrate. Günther has to be away from here before his next birthday when he turns eighteen. In my desperation I have already debated to have Günther and the children emigrate alone. However, the children would not receive the American visas if they leave blood relations here, which, in this case, mean their mother. Yesterday, I spoke with Dr. Schaeler about all this in detail and he promised to write to Berlin at once. I still hope that, since you are already in America with two children, an exception will be made since this situation deals with a separated family. I know nothing definitive about this. It is only hope on my part. In any case, you must do everything in your power to accomplish our emigration. Maybe you can carry it out.

It is difficult for me to visualize the hopelessness and desperation my father must have felt. Time seemed to have run out for a resolution. Were all his efforts already too late? Where could he turn to help his loved ones.

Bernhard and Ulli are now at Lene and Max in Frankfurt. They will arrive here on Friday. I will discuss everything with them thoroughly as to what one can eventually still accomplish. You know that I will attempt everything possible; whether it will work out or not, does not slow me down. I had mail from Hochfelds (Else Hochfeld was the sister of my mother's mother) from the eighth of August and will probably write to them today. We are so pleased about the visit of Bernhard and Ulli. The children are counting the days how often they still have to go to bed until they arrive. We will then probably write to you together on Sunday.

I have discussed the matter to request a firm booking on a ship and Dr. Schaeler said he is willing to write Berlin about it. Admittedly, he does not know if he can accomplish anything because of the new conditions. I gave him miscellaneous items to include in his letter. So, I hope it works out. Actually, he could have used a telegram from you stating that Washington requires the ship's booking.

It seems to me that various such telegrams are already there. In the meantime, if you don't hear anything from me about this, send me another such telegram for that reason.

I don't dare to leave the house now in order to be here when a telegram arrives from you mentioning that Washington will give the visas. Then and only then can things still continue to be worked out. Perhaps I will be able to succeed, in the meantime, to find out which office in the United States you need to turn to where our permission to leave Germany (the Ausreise) will be granted. I shall see.

Thank God, the children are well. I am supposed to send you special regards from Koronczek (one of the directors of the Jewish Community Administration); I try to visit him now and then in order to have conversations with him. He is well disposed towards me and in several matters can provide influence. Yesterday, he comforted me, I should not lose my courage; everything will eventually turn out all right. He would assist me wherever he can. Those on the first floor of the building could use that as an example!

For today, I will close now. I am somewhat nervous and will write to you in detail when my nerves have quieted down somewhat. I hope all goes well with Alfred and I receive from him some lines soon.

The best regards for Hannah and the children. And you, my beloved Carlo, many, many regards and kisses from your loving you and always thinking of you little wife,
Carla

Later on, after much research, I would learn that the warm hearted Mr. Koronczek was a *Spitzel,* an informer for the Gestapo.

From Carola Koppel
Thierschstrasse 7/III   München, the 4th September 1941

My dear, dearest Carlo!

This week I am a little late writing to you. Bernhard and Ulli arrived last Friday and you can imagine the busy times we are having. I am unable to accomplish anything since your brother and his wife are here, but have been very happy about it. We were going to discuss everything regarding our emigration and go over all the new regulations. When Bernhard will travel to Berlin again, he should go to the Reichsvereinigung der Juden in Deutschland, but he will probably not be able to accomplish very much. I had hoped, as long as the loved ones are here, we would receive a letter from you where we could see something new or the long expected telegram, but until today I am waiting in vain and tomorrow they will leave. Concerning the permission for our departure, I have inquired repeatedly but could not learn any particulars. I believe it would be prudent if you would attempt to visit the German embassy in Washington that they would take care of the permission that departure from Munich would be granted. You should clarify exactly our condition, the long separation, some of the children are here and some are in New York, our terribly unpleasant conditions, and so forth. Because three of the children are very small, I don't have to report for work and until now I have not been requested to work. You need to emphasize this. That, I feel, is the right thing to do. Think about this and, eventually, discuss this with your attorney. Maybe he will travel to Washington and could represent you in this. In any case, you must work further with the greatest possible urgency regarding our affair.

If the order to report for forced work were to be issued to my mother, it would be a complete disaster. What would she do with the three little children? There was no money to have someone take care of them all day long, every day. The worries and pressures had become almost unbearable.

In any case, first of all the confirmation for traveling through Spain has to be made in Washington for the American Consulate in Spain so that they will work up the entry permit for America from there. Maybe Mr. Hechinger of the Israelitische Kultusgemeinde can help me. He is currently out of commission with a serious appendix operation.

That I am doing everything possible you can well imagine. Dr. Schaeler asked Berlin regarding the ship's booking, but so far have not received any news. Tuesday the latest I shall complain.

The day before yesterday in the afternoon, all of us were in Grünewald, the forest here in Munich. Yesterday we went to Starnberg which is, as you know, a little ways out of Munich. Günther could not take off longer although Bernhard went to the workplace to plead for extra time. Bernhard and Ulli went to the well known Tegernsee with Hansi and Ruth, our little Muschi; they left at eleven in the morning and came back on time in the evening. There is great enthusiasm with the children because of the visit of Bernhard and Ulli. I can not go along on any of these outings because of the baby. However, this enables me to write to you in total peace.

I am afraid Uncle Joseph will not be able much longer to send anything to us. As far as I know he has the best types of investments. When exchanging them for money, he is loosing much in the transaction.

I hope you can read my scribbling; you have to get used to it since I can not write otherwise anymore.

This is the first letter of my mother not written on her typewriter. As I would learn later, the Gestapo had confiscated most personal things including her typewriter. It was a continued effort by the Gestapo to isolate the Jews and further place indignities upon them. By confiscating typewriters, radios and so on, Jews were placed in a position where they had great difficulties communicating in learning what was going on in the world, and, specifically, what was going on in their own city.

Olm (their former household help) is very decent about helping out. It was good that I sold things in time, otherwise I would have nothing, as is the case with so many others. Why don't you buy a used typewriter on time in New York. Surely you can afford it and you really need it for your business.

I worry about Alfred that I have not heard from him. I hope it all goes well for him. Send us the address where he is in Denver; there are two sanatoriums there.

How did my mother know that there were two sanatoriums in Denver? This was another example of her great ability to probe, to do research, to find out about things. She was very business oriented and could have been so much help to my father in New York if only the family could leave Germany.

How are you getting along with your household? Is Walter much help? Has he already started with his schooling? He should work diligently in school so that soon he will be in the proper class.

Bernhard and Ulli slept in the small chamber and were happy that it was so quiet without any disturbance. Until today, it has not been very peaceful around here; you know, after all, what it can be like.

I am disquieted that I don't have any mail from you. My last mail from you is from August 8. Someone had a letter from America dated August 17 and received it already eight days ago! If you could at all, you must write regularly and always at the same time. I always wait for the mail anxiously and lack of any mail from you make me extremely nervous. After all, it is the only thing I can look forward to.

Günther has to go to his place of employment tonight for some training at the sports field; Sunday they have a big competition there. If baby wakes up, I will go out with her because right now the weather here is beautiful. One has to take advantage of this even if other tasks have to be delayed for a while.

Write to me very soon and discuss everything in detail. Bernhard seems to be pretty well judging by his appearance. My best regards for Hannah and the boys.

To you my most beloved Carlo, much regard and many, many kisses from your infinitely longing thinking of you daily, little wife,

Carla

The children had not been to a movie house, the circus, and the zoo for a long time. It was a way to intimidate, to isolate the Jews. Yet, at this time Uncle Bernhard and Aunt Ulli could still take the children to Grunewald, the wooded area along the banks of the Isar River. What a thrill it must have been for the little one to go on this excursion with the uncle who was always so happy and full of surprises.

The next letter I translated into English was again written by hand. It made it quite difficult to decipher some of my mother's and other people's letters because the authors were still using old German script. Indeed, my mother's next letter, the second hand written, took much longer to decipher than the earlier typed ones.

> From Carola Koppel
> München 22
> Thierschstrasse 7/III   the 7th September 1941

> My dear, dearest Carlo!

Many heartiest thanks for your detailed letter of 18th August for which I had been painfully waiting. In the meantime, Bernhard and Ulli visited here and I was tremendously happy with their visit. I now have a fountain pen and must first try out with some handwriting, inasmuch as I am still somewhat unaccustomed to write by hand.

I had put such big hopes on Washington and now you disappointed me so much. I wonder if it would be prudent if you yourself would travel to Washington to explain the urgency. They surely will then come to the realization of our difficult situation and put more emphasis on our case. The way as described in my several telegrams would, after all, be workable. Washington has the guarantee that we can receive the Spanish transit visa once Washington will issue our visas at the American Consulate in Madrid or Barcelona. There is no risk for Spain or for America. Our health is so, that we will not have any difficulties to be able to receive our visas. In case all this can be accomplished, I would have no difficulties to obtain ship's bookings at once. Could you work with the Spanish Consulate in America beforehand to assist the procedure to receive the transit visas, perhaps even before the American visas.

Further, what is it with the matter of Cuba? Could you perhaps, through some connections, get us those visas? In that case, the Cuban Consulate advises the Spanish Consulate about the issuance of their visas. In that case, I shall be able to get permission to travel to Spain so long as you arrange for the American visas in Washington. Those visas would have to be conveyed by telegram to Spain in order to be there on time. As soon as I have the visas in hand, the Cuban visas could be given back whereby the money deposited for Cuba will be freed. At most a small amount might be withheld. Think about this scheme; perhaps you can arrange for this somehow.

It was amazing how my mother was able to delve into the most complicated schemes to try to obtain those various visas.

Yesterday I heard that possibly there is a way via Argentina. I don't know any more about this avenue at this time. Perhaps you can obtain information about this. After all, one has to find some sort of solution for us. It would be impossible to remain here with all the children until the end of the war and even then, emigration would not be available right away. I have also begged Bernhard to speak for me in Berlin; will again remind him in a letter to him.

When you find a solution somehow or a way, I am convinced I can receive ship's booking right away. You can readily put that into the equation when you try to find a way. I am also convinced that, in our case, once our departure has been secured and in some manner the emigration permission will have been granted.

With four children at home, I would not be suitable to report for forced labor. Therefore I would certainly fight for the emigration permission because to have to wait for seven more years would be an impossible situation.

Tuesday I shall speak with Dr. Schaeler again to see what can be done. I approached him again the last time I saw him, with the subject, that the Reichsvereinigung ruined everything for us and that they unconditionally must find a way to make amends. He did not deny any of this.

Bernhard and Ulli departed this morning. Baby said, "They went to America!"

I am very happy that Alfred is now at a place where he can rest and recover. The wonderful food should be very good for him. Does he receive any schooling there? Please write his address to me. Is Walter going to a school and can he help you a little with your business? You have not yet written to me what you earn in your business. Let me know, even if it is a small amount. Everything interests me. How much rent do you pay for your apartment? And what does it cost in Denver for Alfred and who pays for it?

Write to Uncle Nathan in Colorado Springs that he should send me a few lines. I would be pleased. He can add his lines to one of your letters.

To immigrate into Switzerland is impossible, even if one had parents or children there. Should you travel to

Washington, you really should have someone along to help you with your English and help translate. Write everything down ahead of time in terms of what you need to ask so you won't forget anything you need to ask.

The following is from Ulli and Bernhard. They write: 'My Dears, Naturally, shortly after our departure, we find some time to write a letter to you together. Those few days went by very fast but it was very gemütlich, comfortable, and was good for us. The children are charming, alert and lively. The little one is a darling. I wish that a way would be found that all of you could be together again in America. Günther is a fine boy; he works hard. Too bad, he can not visit us in Altona. It was very nice at sister Lene in Frankfurt. It was also so nice that we were able to talk together again. For today, I must close.

Best regards,
Ulli.

Now, Bernhard continues:

'The children are all nice and sweet. Hansi is a logical thinker. The time went far too quickly. The provisions were good and tasty. Also, the Munich beer tasted so good. Should I travel to Berlin soon, I will go to the Hilfsverein, the organization for emigration, for Carla. I have already spoken to Mr. Loewenstein. We had mail from our son Kurt (Their son is in Canada) He has a new address.

Yours, Bernhard

Carla continues her letter to her husband.

Dear Carlo, can you not work for your own account as for example, when you get certain goods directly from California through help from Hochfelds?

Before one realizes, the Rosh Hashana (the Jewish New Year) is here. I would not have thought that we would still be here. In any case, I wish all the best for the boys and Hannah. Good fasting for the High Holidays. We hope very much that we find something good as we pray, plead, and hope to hear from you very soon and receive some favorable news. Regards and kisses for the boys, and Hannah.

Heartiest regards and most affectionately loving you,

Carla

PS Just now had mail from Lola. She writes: Regarding deposits for Cuba, banks in New York work this up, since this is merely a pro-forma matter. Carlo will surely have knowledge of this and perhaps can open a new trust fund deposit at such a bank.

My mother was becoming increasingly disheartened and despondent. Her moods swung from high hopes to despair. Her responsibilities were overwhelming her. How was she going to make life and death decisions which she talks about in her next letter. In desperation, she was now writing her husband every couple of days now.

From Carola Koppel
München 22
Thierschstrasse 7/III   the 9th September 1941

My most affectionate dearest Carlo!

Many thanks for your letter that was postmarked the 26th of August. I was so happy with it, especially since it arrived fairly quickly. The content was, regrettably, not very pleasing. I did not think that all matters would be denied. Regarding my leaving here, I don't believe in it anymore and you can now figure out when we will see each other again, if indeed we would even be the case at all. Do the officials in Washington have no understanding whatsoever and no pity; it is really an inhuman cruelty when one is condemned to remain here with four children. How can one separate a family with so many children for so many years? I was at Dr. Schaeler today for more than one hour and made strong accusations to him with respect to the Reichsvereinigung. But what good does that do? It won't get us out of Germany. The Spanish as well as the Portuguese Consulate insist that they receive official advice that we would receive the American visas as soon as we arrive in their country. Without such assurances about this, they will not issue any transit visas as I have already let you know with my telegram. Washington must, after all, have compassion and feeling about us; otherwise, the consequences are unthinkable. Dr. Schaeler thought you should, with the help of a bank, try for visas for Cuba and probably they should be tourist visas. However, he is of the opinion that one would first have to travel to Havana, Cuba and then to America.

One can now again obtain the Cuban visas in Germany. It would need to be obtained from the Cuban mission in Berlin. One would have to send a notarized photocopy of this to the U.S.A. for presentation in Washington. Washington would then have to send our visas to Havana before our arrival there. Dr. Schaeler believes this is the only way at this time. Nothing can be done for this from here. You can accomplish this only from the U.S.A. Don't forget that Günther has barely five months to be able to emigrate. He will then be eighteen years old!

With me, the difficulty is my age. I don't know if I would receive the booking for the ship from the *Hilfsverein* (Jewish Relief Organization). I have already written to Joseph in Berlin and Bernhard in Altona that they should put this question to the organization. But I think if all the difficulties were cleared over in America, then one could overcome these difficulties here as well. If nothing can be accomplished, you must see to it that at least Günther or Günther and Hansi will get out, even if I don't know what will happen to me and the little ones. However, this must not hold one back to saving one or two children. Whoever gets to you will have life. Whatever is in your power to accomplish is more important for us than for your brother Leo in France.

Family Herrmann's are giving up their apartment and are extremely discontent. Most recently, Bernhard has no more opportunity to visit Lola in Berlin. I am not sure if it is still possible to travel next week. I would very much like it if he would be able to appear before the *Hilfsverein* in Berlin. Joseph, regrettably is not the right person for this. Even Lola writes he is not forceful enough.

At this time Jews were now forbidden to use the railroad hence, the inability of Bernhard to travel now from his home in Altona to Berlin.

I reworked all our dresses in order to update them. There was a sweater in a nice color that will look good on me.

I was just now thinking if I should write the American Consulate in Barcelona. They should request my papers from the American Embassy in Berlin. Maybe they will do this. One clings to the smallest thread of hope. I hope to receive a telegram from you that you were able to happily solve everything.

I am pleased that Alfred has recovered some already. He certainly must have been sicker than you wrote me. Hannah sent him fine presents. He must feel like a big shot.

The Spanish consul can't be seen anymore, he is so independent. Nevertheless, I shall try again to see him. My mood was so bad yesterday and today like I never experienced before. It is no wonder when one considers how much the people at the consulate are inundated and how it is almost impossible to see anyone there. Nevertheless, one can't afford to think about these difficulties.

I am so happy that all of you were together so comfortably. If only I could be there with all of you. It is so late that I can not hold my eyes open anymore.

All the children send you their love. Sunday I will continue to write this letter. Heartiest regards to the boys. My little ones and Günther greet you in English and send you their kisses.

From me, my deeply beloved Carlo, take many regards and unending kisses from your forever-longing little wife,

Carla

PS I have written a very urgent letter to Loewenstein in Berlin; also a pressing letter to the American Consulate in Barcelona. I gave them your address in case they have questions for you and also that they can request from you telegrams and photocopies since I can't add anything further from here. Friedl told me that she could not send you her regards (to America) inasmuch as it would not be accepted by the post office. When she will be traveling again, she will try some other way to send it to you; otherwise, only I shall receive regards from our families in Germany.

Mail during those times was very slow. Partially, this is because the mail had to be shipped by ocean vessels and also because the German censors took their time reading the letters and finally giving authorization to send them on to the recipients. The following letter from my mother was dated September 17, 1941 and was received by my father in New York on October 14, 1941. For critical information, my father and mother used telegrams to expedite information. Regrettably, most letters were delayed and caused a lot of heartache to them.

> From Carola Koppel
> München 22
> Thierschstrasse 7/III   the 17th September 1941

> My deeply beloved Carlo!

> I had counted very much on receiving mail from you today, but in vain; therefore, hope to hear from you tomorrow. I just had mail from Aunt Else and Siegfried Hochfeld from Los Angeles, dated 31st of August. Their son Rolf seems to have an outstanding job. Aunt Else wrote that Rolf composed a letter for me until late into the night. I hope that it will be useful. In my last letter, I told you that I wrote a detailed letter to Berlin with pressure on Lowenstein for which I have not received a reply yet. I begged him that he should turn to the *Hilfsverein* in Spain in order that they can secure the entry permit into Spain. At the same time, I talked about the question of a booking for the ship, if it would be at our disposal on short notice. In case it is possible for you somehow to obtain visas for Cuba that one

can receive them at their mission in Berlin. It was written in the Jewish newspaper that one can obtain visas for Cuba through bank loans. If nothing else falls into place, then try it that way. If you can accomplish all this in America and we can receive visas, then there still exists the possibility that we can overcome the hurdles and we can leave here.

She did not realize that the State Department of the United States would not issue visas anymore. Somehow, this was tied to the message of a secret agreement between America and Germany, as noted in Mr. Judell's letter to my father. Carla continuing her letter:

If all these hurdles can be overcome is questionable. Therefore, don't celebrate too soon. I wrote a detailed letter to the American Consulate in Barcelona. I hope they will reply. I spelled everything out in detail and wrote that we could not obtain the visas here anymore because of the closure of the American Consulates, but that we had a written confirmation and booking already. I begged them to request all our papers from the embassy in Berlin and then issue us the visas. They should be willing to inform the Spanish Consulate in Munich that the American visas are already in Barcelona, thus enabling them to issue the transit visas. I hope they will do this. I added your address in case they need to ask questions or there are costs involved which, of course, I am unable to handle. I hope you received my holiday wishes on time. I received the beautiful gift from you and will wear it proudly and with dignity. I moved Hansi's birthday ahead since Günther has to work that day and both days of the coming week. We wanted to have all the children together for his birthday. We can not do anything about Günther's work schedule.

How much we think about you, you can well imagine. I wish it were already eight weeks later, then I would be somewhat calmer. If I receive mail from you, I will write to you again. Now I am very nervous and fidgety. Bernhard had to break off his trip since he had to be back in his house because of the new travel restrictions for Jews. I had begged him to travel to Berlin for me to discuss my matter energetically with the *Hilfsverein*. Regrettably, this is not possible anymore. Joseph is not energetic enough and lets himself be pushed away. Now, Lola will speak with Mr. Adler in Berlin, but I have not heard anything about it. I shall report to you right away if I hear anything.

I sent Günther to the barber today that he would look good for a little while. Yesterday, I had a permanent done; they keep for five to six months and then we will see what happens. Please write to me often and in detail; you are the only contact that I have now.

Warmest regards to all the loved ones and especially the boys.

To you, my beloved Carlo, I send the most affectionate regards and never-ending sweet kisses from your ever-yearning little wife,

Carla

The situation for Jews in Munich and all of Germany worsened daily. Pressure on my mother was enormous. She continued with hidden meanings between the lines. Bernhard could not travel by train anymore, eliminating any personal contact with any of the relatives in other cities. The isolation of Jews by now is almost absolute. The cries for help were becoming louder.

From Carola Koppel
München 22
Thierschstrasse 7/III   the 24th September 1941

My dearest beloved Carlo!

Today, I have to respond to a lot of mail from you and was very happy with it. Your Rosh Hashana mail came very much on time on the 18th of this month. I hope that our mutual wishes will come to fruition and will be the opportunity to be together again. In the meantime, you must have received my telegram. You can believe me it was a call for help. If you find no way to get us out from here, then I don't know what will happen. It is now, at most, a question of four weeks until we have to travel like Leo.

Leo and Edie, my father's brothers had fled from Germany to France where they were finally imprisoned at Camp Gurs.

You can imagine what this means to us, especially since all of us will be separated. People have already come by and looked at our apartment a number of times. The apartments of van Wien and Isaak here have already been rented.

I had pleaded with Joseph to meet with Professor Berliner or Dr. Braun (in Berlin) who are authorities in these matters, but naturally, he was unable to accomplish this. He spoke, however, with a Dr. Freitag who said that if Günther and I and, I assume, the children would receive from America a granting of visas through the American Consul in Spain, then and only then can the Hilfsoverein do something for me. As soon as I have those papers, I will have to be examined by a doctor and can, based on this, get out. It is especially important to speed things up for Günther because there will be no possibility to leave after his next birthday.

I thank you very much for your telegram. You were right, I had hoped for a more favorable message. I hope that Washington will give an answer soon. Some place will have to have an understanding, compassion and pity. Might it not be important if you yourself would travel to Washington with all my telegrams and letters? I would even attempt to make contact with God but don't know where I would have to go for this.

I have had no response from the American Consulate in Barcelona. Dr. Schaeler said today one could obtain visas from a Central-American state, I believe Trinidad. Then receive, within two days, the transit visas from Spain that is good for 20 days. When I told him that I would be willing to travel that way, he explained to me that the *Hilfsverein* does not help with this scheme where there is a responsibility for four children. The problem, they contend, could be that we might not be able to travel on from Spain and remain there. This would mean we would eventually be deported from there. I simply could not talk him into letting us do it. If one had documents in hand from Washington, one could risk that complicated route. One would have to assume that we could get the end visa that is to America, within that time. I would also have to give an official document to the Spanish Consulate that our livelihood, while in Spain, would be taken care of. Please see to it that you can send this information to me certified. I will again detail in writing our entire situation to the Spanish Consul; otherwise, he won't even consider speaking with me. It can drive you crazy.

Dr Schaeler is of the belief that the safest way for us is using tourist visas via Cuba. It is, of course, also the most expensive way. All moneys will be paid back with the exception of a small amount. It deals with the fact that you have to borrow the money and that costs interest. For that reason, you should contact a bank. He feels that maybe with committees in America something could be done in our case. Maybe my cousin Rolf and Gerda (son of Hochfeld's and his wife who were on the train from Munich to Berlin and were put into prison in Reichenbach, Germany in 1938) could accomplish something from America with their rich relatives. Any monies would be borrowed and not be a gift; it would merely be deposited in a bank. Please, put everything into play so that you can help us.

Günther is working outside this week. It should be a better type of work and will start Friday.

Maybe Rolf can accomplish something with his relatives.

What you write about Alfred has me very excited. I did not realize that he was so sick. Joseph admitted that the boys were sick a long time last summer and had high fever. Typhus was prevalent but it was not typhus. Maybe Alfred's lungs became weak because of this. Well, the important thing is that he is gaining weight and will be cured. His gaining of 30 pounds in only one short month, in any case, is a good sign.

If we are unable to find ways <u>ourselves</u> to emigrate, depending on the *Hilfsverein* will be absolutely useless.

I am pleased that you were happy with the pictures I sent you. I am unable to have my picture taken anymore. How is Walter doing in school? Friedl is now unable to go where Mrs. Jacobsohn lives. Therefore, she could not send the promised greetings anymore. (So much euphemism! Was Mrs. Jacobsohn put into a *Judenhaus* or a holding camp prior to her deportation?). By the way, Günther is still not home. Your business will surely improve with time. One has to have patience.

I am afraid that if you have to wait for my arrival, it will take a long, long time. I know of one case, where Washington approved the immigration of two children left behind when both parents were in America. That tells me if we are not here, then at least the children would get to leave. I am so very happy with Alfred's letter. Now I have to hurry that we can get into Spain. Miss Goldschmidt from the congregation died. Cancer of the liver. Otherwise this week already seven are dead. You can well imagine why. (Here again, my mother is writing between the lines, letting us know there have been many suicides). I will write again soon.

Many regards to from the four children and kisses, also for Hannah. And to you, my beloved Carlo, the most affectionate regards and many, many kisses from,

> Your endlessly longing little wife,
> Carla

My mother's letter at this time sounded almost incoherent because of the enormous pressures. She was totally hopeless at this stage and yet, she kept on trying desperately.

In 1996 I spent a week in Munich reflecting about the number of years I had lived in Munich with my family. I recalled so many memories from my early childhood in Munich. The early years living in Munich were happy ones with all my family. I remember one year my father took me, his second oldest child, on a day's excursion into the mountain south of Munich. It was a real privilege that my father extended to his son Alfred. Soon, however, that happiness deteriorated rapidly beginning in the fall of 1936. That year Germany held the Summer Olympics that were relatively peaceful. However in the autumn of that year the Nazi hordes commenced to attack Jewish people, their homes and their businesses.

Stark images reminded me of these increasing attacks during this period of my childhood in Munich. So many vivid impressions! Memories and images were overwhelming in those terrible years.

Berlin

*The concept of 'Holocaust' is implicit in
an almost sacred uniqueness of the horrible
events. It stands for the absolute evil.*
—Ian Kershaw, The NS-State, 1988

A taxi took me from the Hotel Concorde to the Munich Hauptbahnhof, the main railroad station. My next stop would be Berlin where I was to meet Robert Thomas. Robert traveled from his home in Wales to meet me in Berlin. The City of Berlin had invited a group of former residents of the city, including me and a companion. Robert became this companion.

I had spent two years with my aunt and uncle in Berlin when I was four years old and later another two and a half years when I was twelve years old. For a number of years, the city of Berlin invited former Jewish residents to visit the city of their youth. Robert was so kind as to offer me his companionship for this very difficult trip ahead of me. Indeed, without his support for the next two weeks, I would probably have broken down completely having had to face the most difficult part of my journey alone.

In the early nineteen thirties, about 160,000 Jews lived in Berlin, the capital city of Germany, by far the largest Jewish population of any German city. There, Jews had contributed much to the German culture, in literature, music, arts and commerce. Now, officials of the city government hosted these former residents, many in their seventies, eighties and even nineties.

The trip from Munich to Berlin took six hours by train. I enjoyed traveling by train because, unlike by plane, I could take in the ever changing landscapes of cities and the countryside. I was alone in the compartment with a man who looked to be about fifty years old. Neither of us spoke. I was reading a newspaper and the man across from me was reading a book. I could not stand the silence. Inasmuch as I was doing research on this journey to Germany, I tried to think of an opening for a conversation with that man.

I finally started the conversation with, "This is a fine spring day we are having."

The man put down his book and replied, "Yes, it's a great spring day, quite unusual for this time of the year."

"Are you going to Berlin?" I questioned him.

"No, I am traveling to Dessau."

I looked closer at the man. His dark hair had streaks of gray; deep blue eyes showed a sparkle. He was dressed in a grey suit, probably a traveling salesman. It seemed my opening remarks struck a cord and he asked me, "You must be going to Berlin, am I right?"

"Yes," was my reply, "I will be in Berlin for some meetings." I did hesitate to go into the details of the reasons for my trip.

"Your German is very good," he continued, "but you are not from Germany. Am I right?"

He seemed to want to strike up a conversation and this was all right with me. I continued, "I am from the United States and am here to do research about the fate of my family."

"You must be Jewish then," was his reply.

Immediately, my defenses were up. Here was another anti-Semite and I did not wish to have anything to do with him. I clammed up but he continued, "When the war started, I was only six years old. In those days, one grew up fast. By 1943 or 1944, I had learned of the fate of many of my neighbors, all Jews. They simply disappeared. No one told me where they went. I did not find out what happened until the end of the war. Then, during the war criminal trials, I learned that my father was involved in the shootings of Jews, men, women and little children. A year later, they hanged my father and I am glad."

I was stunned at his openness and did not know what to say. I murmured something to the effect that I hoped he felt relieved and did not feel that he was guilty because of his father's sins. The rest of the trip, until he left the train at the Dessau station, we completed in silence for I was unable to talk about my family's fate with a German citizen.

Bahnhof Zoo, the railroad station called Zoo for the Zoological Park next to it, was noisy and crowded. I took a taxi to the Hilton Hotel, which was located in what used to be the East Berlin sector. It was a cool and cloudy day, April 16, 1996, which, incidentally, was my wife's birthday.

The reason I mention the cold and cloudy day was an incident that happened before I had left on this trip. A Mr. Ruediger Nemitz of the Berlin *Senatskanzlei*, the Senate Chambers of the City of Berlin (the City of Berlin is governed by a City Council and is also a state of Germany as well) arranged all the details of the visit. We faxed each other information a number of times. In one fax I jokingly requested that he should make certain that the weather in April should be nice and warm by contacting the 'higher power' above. Generally, in April the weather in Berlin was not too pleasant. Mr. Nemitz promptly returned a fax to me in which he stated he would be delighted to contact the 'higher power' above if I would send him the appropriate 'area code' immediately. I was delighted with his response, his sense of humor, and looked forward to meeting him in Berlin.

Next, I checked the front desk to find out if Robert had arrived. He had, indeed, checked into the hotel already. I immediately called his room to announce my arrival. The dear man was delighted to hear from me and suggested that we have a cocktail and talk over old times. I was immensely pleased that he would be my companion for the rest of my trip. This last portion of my pilgrimage would be the most difficult one. I would need his support, his uplifting humor, and, above all, his companionship.

The city had prepared an extensive program for the contingent of about 120 former residents of Berlin. One of the earliest events was a visit to the *Rote Rathaus*, the red brick city hall. As we entered the large building, a children's choir consisting of about twenty five to thirty boys and girls ten to twelve years old greeted us. They sang like angels, indeed, even sang some Hebrew songs. It was so touching that tears welled up in my eyes. Then, as I was listening to these children, disquieting thoughts swept over me. Such small children could have given a similar concert during the Weimar Republic times, say around 1926. Only seven years later, these innocent looking children, the Erwin's, the Juergen's and Ludwig's and the Irmgard's, the Helga's, and Irmtraud's would have been in the Hitler Jugend and the Bund Deutscher Mädchen. They would have been ecstatic and loyal to their Führer, Adolph Hitler, all the while shouting 'Heil Hitler.' A frightening thought. Could something like this happen again? Surely not, but then, preceding the rise of Hitler, people thought a madman like Hitler would never be able to ascend to the leadership of Germany.

On another day, Robert and I visited the huge department store of Berlin, KaDeWe (Kaufhaus des Westens, Department Store of the West). It is a magnificent store, originally built and run by a Jewish family. Then it was called the Herman Tietz Department Store. This huge store, occupying a whole city block carried large assortments of every type of merchandise. In the food department, there may have been a couple of hundred different types of cheeses from all over the world. This store ranked with the likes of Harrods of London, and Saks Fifth Avenue in New York. Walking all over the store tired us out. I suggested to Robert we should find a café and rest a while.

As we left the department store and began to cross the Wittenberg Platz, we passed the entrance of a subway station. Next to that entrance on a pole was a tablet with the inscription, "Never forget these places of horror" and below that, a listing of all the major extermination and concentration camps. I was stunned. This memorial was located next to one of the busiest corners in Berlin. Robert and I stood there for at least twenty minutes and watched people passing by. Not a single person stopped to look at this plaque. Disappointed, we crossed the large square and found an outdoor café. Pulling up the wicker chairs, we sat down and began to relax.

Just then the *Kellner*, the waiter passed by. "Two Pils please," I told him.

"With pleasure," he replied.

A few minutes later he brought two tall glasses of the local beer. Sipping the cool drink, I looked around. Next to us sat a young couple, perhaps around forty years old. They too were drinking refreshing beer.

Since this trip was a research trip for me, I usually spoke to people at most venues, at cafes, railroad stations, in hotels, and many more places. I greeted the man and woman at the next table. Through conversation back and forth, they learned that I had traveled from the United States to learn about the fate of my family during the Holocaust. They were friendly and commiserated with me.

"The Holocaust happened some fifty-five years ago and today, there is a need to balance those events in terms of time elapsed. If too much is made of this subject, it becomes counter-productive," the man said. "People don't want to hear about this anymore." He intimated that it might even produce some sort of anti-Semitism. I did not know what to say. I was discouraged.

Turning to Robert, I said, "let's walk to the synagogue where my aunt, uncle and I used to walk to on the Sabbath." He and I walked along the bank of the River Spree, as my aunt, uncle and I had done so many years ago. It was a rather pleasant walk. There were wooded areas along the river, tall trees interspersed with patches of planted flowers. Fifteen minutes later we arrived at the Siegmundshof Strasse where the synagogue and the adjacent school once stood. No more. Again, as at most former destroyed synagogues, in its place stood a large apartment house obviously built after the war. Memories overwhelmed me. I went to this school for about one year after leaving Munich in November 1938 for Berlin until all Jewish schools in Germany were shut down. Teachers and friends from that school were long forgotten. We walked closer to the site. There, in front of the building on the sidewalk stood a concrete structure about five feet tall, eight feet long, and two and a half feet wide. The structure consisted of arches and columns on which were inscriptions. Upon closer inspection, we saw names and dates of what used to be rabbis, teachers and probably the leadership of the synagogue.

All of a sudden, we heard, "Hey, what are you guys doing?"

We looked up and saw a young man leaning on a bicycle. He repeated, "What are you looking at?"

He must have been about thirty years old. I replied, "We are studying the names of people who used to be part of the synagogue and the school which were located on this spot some sixty years ago." "Indeed," I continued, "I went to the school in 1939 until the Nazis closed the school for Jews."

"What a terrible time that was," he replied. "I am fairly new in Berlin, have a job not far from here," he continued, "and pass by here every day. In the morning, I cycle in this direction and in the evening, I return in the other direction. You know what? In all those years I have never taken notice of this little monument."

This was such a revelation. I recalled the sign at the Wittenberg Platz near the department store, at the entrance to the subway. No one took notice of it. Now here, this young man passed a larger concrete memorial at eye level, no less, and never noticed it in several years passing by it every day. What would it take to call attention to the physical destruction of Jewish facilities, of remembrances of the millions of Jews killed during the vicious reign of the Hitler area? These thoughts remained with me for days and were again propelled to the forefront a few days later.

The organizers of our visit to Berlin had worked up a full menu of events. I chose one from that menu, a *Meinungsaustausch*, an exchange of views with the *Abgeordnete of the Parliament*. Abgeordnete are members of the State and City of Berlin Parliament consisting of three different parties. I signed Robert and myself up fort his discussion. A bus took us to the Parliament Building, old, stately and ornate. We then went to a huge room and sat at tables lining both sides. Members of the three parties as well as the president of the Parliament were sitting at the head table. One was a member of the SPD, the *Sozialdemokratische Partei Deutschlands,* a rather liberal party. Another was from the CDU, the *Christlich-Demokratische Union*, much more conservative. And the third one was from the Green Party. Listening to the president's recitation of some history and a lengthy oratory citing many statistics, I became impatient. I raised my hand and was recognized by the president.

"For more than ten years," I started out, "there have been discussions, deliberations and delays for the national memorial to be built here in Berlin for the victims of the Holocaust. It was meant to be a national memorial to the six million Jews brutally murdered, gassed, starved, and shot. When will this memorial finally be built?"

The SPD member stood up and said that the final debate would be forthcoming in the near future. "The design by Peter Eisenman seems to have been accepted," he stated. A huge memorial was to be built, located on five acres behind the rebuilt prestigious Hotel Adlon near the Brandenburger Tor.

The Abgeordnete of the CDU party stood up and suggested that there were enough memorials all over the city already and such a large monument would not be necessary. "Even the mayor of Berlin, Eberhard Diepgen," he stated, "questioned whether Germany should go ahead with plans to build a national Holocaust memorial. Diepgen," he added, "had commented that it might not be possible to deal with this horror artistically."

I listened to the CDU man's reasoning why no national memorial needs to be built. My blood pressure was rising, I was seething with indignation. I finally regained control and responded with the description of my experiences at the entrance to the subway and our encounter with the young man at the Siegmundshof Street.

"Indeed," I said, "such a memorial is absolutely needed. After all, memorials and monuments of all sorts are found in every city in Germany, most of them commemorating far lesser events than the Holocaust." He and other members of the visitor contingent encouraged me to continue.

"A large memorial such as the Eisenman proposal is very much necessary or it will also be overlooked the same way the small memorial at the Siegmundshof synagogue and school and others are being overlooked. Size is very important. A major visual impact is of paramount importance. It is the only way to make an impression on visitors to remember the "Holocaust: the murder of six million Jews."

"Indeed, a large size in an important location will attract many visitors as well students from schools throughout Germany to Berlin. A museum or research center attached to this memorial will alert everyone to the dark history of the dozen years of the Hitler regime and, hopefully, be a warning to future generations."

I am not certain if my outburst had made an impact on the three members of the Parliament. Perhaps I convinced the SPD and Green Representatives but I certainly did not change the mind of the CDU representative.

After this meeting I was told by one of the invitees about a deeply moving memorial at the location where the Levetzow Street synagogue once stood. Robert and I took a taxi to Levetzow Street, not far from where my aunt and uncle lived at the Thomasius Street. There, in front of us was one of the more impressive memorials to the destruction of the six million Jews. A replica of a cattle car made of granite, a ramp leading up to its door greeted us. And on the ramp were figures hewn of granite, hunched over, being herded into this cattle car. Behind this large granite memorial was a huge metal tablet reaching for the sky listing all the deportations of Jews from Berlin engraved upon it. Here is a sampling of the sixty-three deportations:

24 October	1941	Unknown number of Jews to Lodz
13 January	1942	1,037 Jews to Riga
9 December	1942	997 Jews to Auschwitz
2 March	1943	1,758 Jews to Auschwitz
19 April	1943	688 Jews to Auschwitz
5 March	1944	32 Jews to Auschwitz
6 September	1944	39 Jews to Auschwitz
April	1945	24 Jews to Ravensbrueck/ Sachsenhausen

I have taken only a representative sampling of dates of the sixty-three deportations between 1941 and 1945. This site was the collection point for Jews who were deported to the East. One of those transports to the East, to the killing camps, held my dear Aunt Lola and Uncle Joseph. With bowed heads, we stood a long time before this huge tablet containing the death records of many thousands Jews from Berlin.

At the base of this giant tablet on the ground were brass plaques enumerating the many synagogues destroyed during Crystal Night in November 1938. For example, the plaque indicated the Levetzow Street synagogue, the location of this memorial, had 2,120 seats, was built 1912–1914, damaged in the Second World War and was finally torn down in the 1950s. The synagogue Uncle Joseph and Aunt Lola attended, Siegmundshof, had 320 seats, was built in 1924, destroyed in the Second World War and finally torn down after 1945. An inscription of another brass plaque stated in part: "…in the Pogrom night of the 9th of November 1938 the synagogues of Berlin were damaged, burnt down, destroyed by the National Socialists." As symbol of an extensive Jewish tradition of culture, they were the most significant targets of the actions of the state terror. Besides the synagogues shown on the many brass plaques, there were in Berlin more than eighty private Jewish prayer houses. All of these were also devastated the night of November 9, 1938, or were closed a short time later, sold or expropriated.

After my brother Walter and I had departed Berlin in June 1941 for New York, my aunt Lola responded to a letter Walter had sent to her from New York. Lola's letter, too, spelled out euphemistically between the lines the restrictions dealt against the Jews.

> From Joseph and Lola Goldschmidt
> Thomasiusstrasse 14
> Berlin   the 25th September 1941
>
> My dear Walter,
>
> Your Mutti enclosed your dear letter with hers. We were especially pleased with it. The content is well written, but the handwriting should be better. Well, you will soon become a praiseworthy student in school. So, first of all many thanks for your detailed description of the trip to the United States and arriving in the big city of New York. This was very interesting for us. You really lived very elegantly in San Sebastian, Spain. Your room with bath and everything to go with it must have been beautiful. Because of this, you must have felt like grown-ups.

The 'everything' my aunt alluded to included a bidet in the bathroom. Both Walter and I did not know what this contraption was meant for and decided it was meant to wash your feet, being just the right height. It worked out well, indeed.

> That was really something for Alfred, don't you think? The swim in the ocean must have been something special. However, the main thing is that you weathered everything. Well, I see where you really helped out on the ship. There were, undoubtedly some extra delicacies, which you would scrounge up. The cook was probably pleased that he had such a good assistant. With all that extra food, you must finally have looked like a well-fed pig.
>
> Have you played the game of *Mensch Ärgere Dich Nicht* (Man, don't get mad) sometime? Now I have to tell you something, dear Walter, about which you will laugh. Your

teacher, Miss Lipsky, got married recently and is now called Mrs. Buttermilk. What do you think of that name?

The High Holidays have already passed and I have sorely missed my boys, you and Alfred. It was too quiet during the holidays. To be sure, you are far better off in New York than here. I do not have to enumerate all the names of your friends who send you their regards and are happy that all is well with you. You have, undoubtedly, very good meals over there. How does it feel finally to be able to eat meat again? Today, we do not have any meat, or better put, we had our "favorite" specialty namely, spinach.

After a poor summer, the weather here is finally very nice this fall. I certainly hope it will remain so for a while. How are you taking the heat in New York, dear Walter? I wrote a long letter to Alfred recently; hopefully, he will be cured soon. It is good that he feels well in the hospital in Denver, Colorado and Uncle Nathan will surely visit him. After all, Colorado Springs is not very far from Denver. How do you find your way around in the big city? You must have been astounded and gotten dizzy with all those skyscrapers around you.

How were your High Holidays in the synagogue there? We now have services in the Levetzowstrasse synagogue instead of the one on Siegmundshof; that is, the men for themselves and then the women for themselves. There is room for only twelve women. On Yom Kipur I went from seven in the morning until half past eleven; then the other women come from half past eleven. The men stay there until one o'clock.

If only Mutti with all the children could be with you in America! Here it is said, one can achieve something only through America, which means, instructions must emanate from Washington that visas are at the American Consulate in Spain. Only then can something be accomplished here. Maybe it is still possible for your father to accomplish something from New York. One does not know anymore what one should do.

Uncle Bernhard writes what darlings the little ones are. Günther has had much pressure and had to work during the High Holidays. The littlest one, the baby girl, is so lovely. It is better with your cousin Werner in Altona. He wanted to visit us here in Berlin, as mentioned already, but this is not possible anymore. (No more travel by railroads). The three of you (Alfred, Walter and our cousin Werner) were together here happily some time ago. No more! Dear Walter, have Papa take a picture of you sometime because we have no photo of you. We would very much like to have a picture of you about the time you were with us.

I did not find a continuation or a signature.

With Robert from Wales and me, visiting in Berlin, my home for two and a half years just before my leaving Germany, nostalgia set in. I had to see the apartment building where we used to live. I remembered it as being very attractive, in close proximity to the river Spree. Many a day I would watch barges traversing up and down the river. It was a large apartment. Two or three bedrooms, living room, a large dining room, where I used to play with the old-fashioned light fixture over the dining room table. I would pull the large ochre-colored shade up and down all the time.

"Stop this," my aunt would shout, "or you will break the lamp."

Adjacent to the dining room was a veranda. Many times I would sit there reading a book and at the same time watch people walk through the apartment complex's courtyard. My aunt and uncle, unable to have children, loved having Walter and me in their home. They were that: like second parents to us. Now, a visit to that apartment house proved to be disappointing. In place of the attractive, ornate building I shared with my relatives a long time ago, there stood a modern, non-descriptive apartment house. An inquiry of the owner of the new building produced the history of the old apartment house. It had been damaged during the war and was torn down in the 1950s to make room for this modern box of a building.

Aunt Lola, like my mother, felt a desperate need to communicate with her relatives. Forbidden to travel, none of the brothers and sisters remaining in Germany could see one another. The isolation proved to be devastating. Here, Lola is trying to keep up the communication with her sister Hannah in New York.

The spaces between the lines divulge more than the letter itself. The noose around the necks of the Jews is tightening. What else was written "between the lines?" It was forbidden for Jews to use the railroads hence, visits of all the brothers and sister was not possible anymore, causing total isolation. Lola writes, "The circle of acquaintances is getting ever smaller." Most people by now were herded into *Judenhäuser*—Jewish Houses—and had to double up in their apartments. Aunt Lola wrote, she "sold" her dining room that was converted to extra space for non-family Jews. This concentration of Jews into fewer and fewer apartments enabled the Gestapo to keep close track of all Jews.

Lithuania

Holocaust memory is terrifying because it
does not disappear but always poses more
questions than it is capable of answering.
— Bjorn Oberdorfer, from Remembrance
and Reconciliation.

On April 23, 1996, Robert and I headed to the railroad station for the trip to Frankfurt. From Frankfurt, we were going to fly to Vilnius, Lithuania.

The train ride took several hours giving me time to discuss events with my companion Robert. I was also reflecting on the letters my mother wrote during the month of October 1941. Those letters conveyed the heavy weight of responsibility imposed upon her. Only thirty-eight years old at the time, she showed a brave face to her four children while nearly collapsing from all the worries and pressures.

I had prepared myself for the trip to Lithuania. Someone had told me that a former university president traveled to Lithuania quite frequently. Ed Jakubauskas and wife Ruth, live in Fort Collins, Colorado. One day, before my departure to Europe in April 1996, I visited them and asked for information about Lithuania. It was a fortunate meeting for Mrs. Jakubauskas had worked with an official of the Jewish museum in Vilnius, the capital of Lithuania. Mrs. Jakubauskas had assisted a Mrs. Rachel Kostanian in various activities of the Jewish museum.

Mrs. Rachel Kostanian of the Jewish State Museum in Vilnius, Lithuania.

Rachel Kostanian was to be my contact in Lithuania. I had written a letter advising her of my arrival with Robert and the need of a hotel for us.

To Ms. Rachel Kostanian   13 December 1995
Lithuanian State Jewish Museum
Lietuvos valstybinis zydu muziejus
Pamenkalnio 12
Vilnius, Lithuania

Dear Ms. Kostanian,

I was fortunate to be able to obtain your name through Ruth and Ed Jakubauskas who live very close to our home here in Fort Collins, Colorado.

The reason for my contacting you is to obtain information and names of people who could help me. I left Germany in June 1941 but had to leave my mother, two brothers and two sisters behind. They were deported from Munich (München) on November 20, 1941.

I plan to write a book about my family, have done a lot of research so far, and will travel to Europe in April 1996. I should arrive in Vilnius about 24 April 1996.

Mr. Jakubauskas suggested that I stay at the Turistas Hotel in Vilnius and travel by bus or train to Kovno. I would appreciate your thoughts about this—should I stay in Vilnius or should I get a hotel room in Kovno? How many days do you recommend that I stay in Lithuania (I was planning on two days).

The Jakubauskas gave me an old "Vilnius in your Pocket" guide. I assume there is also a city guide about Kovno.

The Jakubauskas have been very helpful but suggested I contact you for more details.

Thank you for your assistance and additional names or contacts you can give me. I would appreciate this very much.

Sincerely yours,
Al Koppel

Ms. Kostanian replied promptly with the following letter:

> To Mr. Alfred Koppel
> Ft. Collins, Colorado, USA   15 January 1996
>
> Dear Mr. Koppel,
>
> I received your letter of 13 December 1995 and will try to answer your questions.
>
> As for your visit here, when you come such a long way and plan to write a book about these places, I would suggest that you stay in Vilnius at least two days to see our Jewish museum which exposes a lot of materials on the Holocaust. You should also see the place of massacre of the Vilnius Jewry at Paneriai. I would also recommend the Ghetto area and other historical sites. It will take two to three days depending on what you choose. You may visit all these places by yourself or with the Jakubauskas. If you want a professional tour, you may have a guide for $50 a day, without a car.
>
> As for Kovno, you can do it in one day; visit the Ghetto, the 9th Fort and some other sites of Jewish interest. I would also recommend having a guide. The same guide may take you to Kovno.
>
> I should know beforehand, at least a month, as to whether you want us to arrange for a guide and hotels.
>
> As for the hotel, I would recommend the Hotel Neringa in the center of Vilnius, then you would not need transportation to come to certain places. Somebody has to book it for you. If you have a guide, he may do it. A double bedroom costs about $80 a night. There are also cheaper hotels.
>
> With best regards,
> Yours,
> Rachel Kostanian

Although I had traveled all over Europe many times, I had never been to any of the Baltic States. I felt it would be prudent to obtain all the help I could get. I assumed that most of the people in Lithuania did not speak English as well as Mrs. Kostanian.

I was very glad I would have Robert with me because the journey to Lithuania would turn out to be overwhelming and deeply emotional for me. I answered Mrs. Kostanian's letter quickly giving her the dates of my travel and indicating that I would have someone accompany me. She again replied immediately.

To Alfred Koppel   15 February 1996
Ft. Collins, Colorado, USA

Dear Mr. Koppel

I got your letter of February 4. You did not write if I have to do anything for you, such as to book the hotel, a guide, etc.

It is a pity you do not want a guide for Jewish Vilnius, but it is not my business. Please let me know exactly.

Yours,
Rachel Kostanian

P.S. Bringing anything here makes no sense to "shlep" (haul) as with local money you can acquire anything needed. Thanks for your offer to bring things. Call me when you arrive, if you do not want to be met. Is it one or two rooms you need? If you look for a cheaper hotel, let me also know.

I immediately sent a message to her.

FAX MESSAGE

To Ms. Rachel Kostanian   25 February 1996
Lietuvos Valstybinis Zydu Muziejus
Palmenkalnio 12
2001 Vilnius, Lithuania

Dear Ms. Kostanian,

Thank you so much for your letter of 15. February 1996.

In response to your question if 'I can do anything for you,' I want to thank you in advance for your kind offer. <u>Of course</u>

150

I shall be guided by your recommendations. Therefore, I should also get a guide for the Jewish Vilnius as well as Kovno—one day each (perhaps for Kovno on Thursday, 25. April and for Vilnius on Friday, 26. April, if possible).

Inasmuch as my wife's cousin will be accompanying me, it is probably best if we book two single rooms (I snore!) rather than one with two beds. The Vilnius City Guide Mr. Ed Jakubauskas gave me indicates that the Zaliasis Tiltas Hotel has singles between 60 Litas and 250 Litas. If you think this hotel would be all right, we would like to get two single rooms at about 150 Litas each. I shall defer to your knowledge—I am sure you know what will be best for us. If you pick out another hotel it is OK. And yes, please either you or the guide should make the hotel reservation for our arrival Wednesday, 24. April. Our departure will be 29 April on Lithuanian Airlines Nr. 460. Would you please let me know which hotel it will be and if they need a deposit?

As you can see, I have taken your advice and will be staying in Lithuania about four days instead of only two or three days. Thank you very much for all the trouble in helping me. I really appreciate it a lot inasmuch as my visit is so important.

Most sincerely,

Al Koppel

I was much surprised to receive Mrs. Kostanian's latest reply so quickly. Despite her lengthy correspondences, she turned out to be most accommodating and a lovely person. We developed a rather close relationship after I had met and worked with her. We exchanged numerous letters subsequent to my visit to Lithuania which concerned her love and efforts for the Jewish Museum in Vilnius she was involved in as a director. Mrs. Kostanian continued her letter writing with me.

To Al Koppel   6. March 1996
Ft. Collins, Colorado, USA

Dear Mr. Koppel

For someone who lives in Vilnius and travel toKovno, you will have to pay for his train tickets between Vilnius and Kovno too. Then you would have to hire a taxi to get around. The taxi would have to wait every time you make a stop. What I want to say is that it is more convenient and not much more expensive to hire a car from Vilnius to Kovno. But again, it is your choice.

Now what about the other days? In Vilnius you need another day to visit Paneriai, the site of the massacre. It is out of town, so a car is needed, as well as the Jewish cemetery with the tomb of the famous rabbi, the Great Gaon (genius). But you may try to do all this yourself. Maybe you know some Russian or Lithuanian. Then it is simple. You did not tell me if you need to be met at the airport, or will you manage to take a taxi to the hotel by yourself?

A guide will come to your hotel on the 25th of April at 9 o'clock in the morning.

Hope to hear from you soon.

Truly yours,

Rachel Kostanian.

She followed up this letter with another one finalizing all the details.

To Mr. Al Koppel
Ft. Collins, Colorado, USA

Dear Mr. Koppel,

I got your letter.

You will probably have a different guide, a Miss Regina Kopilevitch. We shall book the hotel for you—two rooms. The guide will call you the 24th, and guide you with a car the 25th and 26th of the month.

I will probably go to a conference in Warsaw the same day.

You are welcome to Vilnius and I hope you will enjoy your trip.

With best wishes,

Yours,

Rachel Kostanian

Surely, the last line of Mrs. Kostanian's letter, and I hope you will enjoy your trip, was simply a usual polite closing of a letter. My trip through Lithuania was to be the most difficult portion of my journey into a nightmare.

Munich

The world's history is the world's Judgment.
—Friedrich von Schiller, 26 May 1789

In the fall of 1941, my mother was still trying to pull together all the necessary documents to leave Germany or at least to have some of the children leave that country. It was desperation at its highest level.

From Carola Koppel   2nd October 1941
Thierschstrasse 7/III
München Munich

My dear, dearest Carlo!

Because of the holidays, today's letter is leaving a little late. Today, I want to tell you that Günther and I, for the important holidays, fasted well despite all the problems. Günther could only go to the synagogue for the Yom Kipur prayers at 6 o'clock in the evening inasmuch as he only arrived home from work at 5:45 in the evening, as did most of his coworkers. Many of Günther's friends, as Shmuel Rothschild, Stark and others were at forced labor for the first time yesterday. Günther now works outside through the workshop. He has to get up at 5 o'clock in the morning as he has to leave the house before six. Then, he has to use the streetcar for more than one hour. Then, he still has to walk for twenty minutes. His job starts at 7 o'clock. Until he returns home in the evening, it is already half past six and he is then terribly tired and hungry. He goes to bed immediately after eating. Therefore, you can not be angry with him if he does not write.

I did not go to the synagogue to be on the safe side because there is always visiting and I don't want to make new acquaintances. Sunday, I wrote again a very detailed letter to the Spanish Consulate and received a reply yesterday. The consul wrote that he would meet with me today at noon and I should bring along all the necessary documents in my possession. So I went there today with great hope, but was greatly disappointed. The consul would not speak with me personally; I could only speak with a Count Rassenheim who was, after all, very amiable. I "talked the blueness away from the sky" but could not accomplish what I wanted to achieve. The only thing I did accomplish was that Count Rassenheim, after he spoke with the consul himself, said that I should write at once to the consul here in Munich and send him a request, that would say, they are ready to grant the visas for a temporary entry into Spain. This is contingent upon the Spanish Consulate receiving from the American Consulate in Barcelona the news that we shall receive the end visas as soon as we arrive in Spain. I am going to send you all the materials at once via registered mail, so that you can, based on Count Rassenheim's opinion, personally present all of it in Washington.

He said further, when it comes to issuing the Spanish visas based on a written authorization from the American Consulate before having that end visa, you would have to be able to" accomplish" that in America hoping that the State Department gives this type of assurance. You need to have a letter from the Spanish Consulate in München, that the consulate will issue the visas as soon as they have the confirmation of the American Consulate. Perhaps you will have to travel personally to Washington after all. Would it be possible that my cousin Rolf meets you in Washington and both of you go together?

The Spanish consulate in Washington would then have to wire their consulate in Barcelona. Further, I feel it is important that Washington also wire the confirmation to the Spanish Consulate in Munich. I am sure I don't have to beg you to send me a telegram about this. The Spanish Consulate requires from me original firm ship bookings acknowledgements before issuing the visas. I shall have to scrounge around for this at Loewenstein's office in Berlin as he is still very sick. I still have had no reply from him to my letter of 10ᵗʰ September date. To be sure, I begged Joseph in Berlin to speak to him for me but, regrettably, he is not the right person for this task. The people who have influence are Mrs. Professor Berliner and Dr. Braun, but Joseph was unable to see either one of them. He spoke only with a Dr. Freitag who stated we had to produce the commitments for visas from Washington. Only then could the *Hilfsverein* (Jewish Relief Organization) be of help.

Rolf knows this Dr. Freitag. Perhaps he can write to him appropriately. By the way, Count Rassenheim said if we had any relatives or acquaintances in Madrid who could appeal to the Interior Department in Madrid, it would be a great help. It might not be impossible that an exception would be made. Dr. Schaeler said recently that the Joint (the Joint Distribution Committee) has a representative in Madrid who handles their affairs and is entrusted to handle travel via Spain with such a transit visa. Maybe you can discuss this with the Joint in New York that they cause the officials of the Spanish Interior Ministerium in Madrid to listen. Maybe they can even accomplish an earlier entry. I have not been able to ascertain this Joint representative's address in Madrid, which prevents me from explaining everything to him. But you should be able to find it out in New York and could write him more easily. Try everything and remember that Günther will have his eighteenth birthday soon.

The van Wiens had the lease of their apartment in our building cancelled as of the 15ᵗʰ of November. The people actually wanted our apartment, but since I have small children, I received consideration this time. Undoubtedly, I have to count on that the next people interested in our apartment will get it. Then, the only logical conclusion will be the same as what happened to Edie; there is nothing else. (Edie, her brother-in-law was deported to a camp in France)

By the way, the newest item is that Dr. Schaeler here has visas for Cuba and will surely depart soon. Then I have no one who will be worrying about me anymore. It is odd that for those who are running things, everything always falls into place. No one knows who will replace him. Maybe no one, inasmuch as the *Hilfsverein*, after all, seems to be asleep.

When one now asks Baby Judis, what is your name, she says nicely, "Judis Koppel is my name." This, from a 2 year old baby! She understands every word one speaks to her. The children are now in the courtyard and Baby is at the kitchen window. People are, largely, very decent, but one feels embarrassed when people stare at you with the Yellow Star on your garment. That's why I do not leave the house very much anymore and the children play always in the courtyard. As soon as I have news from the consulate, I shall write again. I am already waiting for mail from you. Just now, the management of our building was here and told me that it could be that the cancellation of leases might be delayed for half a year. That would also include the van Wiens downstairs.

The address of the Spanish Consulate here in Munich is Wiedenmayerstrasse 22, München 46/I.

Heartiest regards to the children and Hannah.

To you, my most beloved Carlo, heartfelt regards and many, many kisses.

Your loving little wife,
Carla

Less than one week later, my mother frantically wrote another letter. The need for communication, some word from her husband became overpowering. She was clutching on to those letters and when one was late, she became despondent.

From Carola Koppel
Thierschstrasse 7/III
München 22   the 8th October 1941

My dear, dearest Carlo!

This time my patience is being sorely tried because it is already the third week that I have no mail from you. In the meantime, I received the promised communication from the Spanish Consulate. Due to the holidays, I could send it to you only today and, of course, I sent it via registered mail. As a precaution, I had three copies made and had those notarized by the police. This morning I showed their letter to Dr. Schaeler who was very enthusiastic about it. It promises to have implicit success. By the way, he also told me that this week a lady here received the confirmation which she had received from the Spanish Consulate. You will now have to send this communication with a corresponding cover letter to Washington, maybe if you feel it is necessary, bring it to Washington yourself. With God's help, you will, to be sure, have success. Everything else required can be secured here.

The biggest difficulty with it will be the question if I can leave here. Well, if we have come along this far, then maybe it can be achieved. In any case, Dr. Schaeler, based on this communication, instilled in me much hope. From Loewenstein in Berlin I received a reply to my letter dated the 10th of September. He responded already on the 15th of September, but because of his illness, it was delayed. Mrs. Loewenstein wrote her husband sent the necessary application to the State Department in Washington already. She received the usual news that the only way the visas can be issued, if it can be proved that, via notarized communication, they have received the Spanish transit visas. Then, one can pick up the American visas in Barcelona.

This information is nowadays generally known and the *Hilfsverein* here is attempting, through their American branch, that the American consul in Barcelona should be empowered to issue preliminary visas. That, mean, they would declare that the emigrants can call for the visas in Barcelona. Based on such a preliminary visa, we hope for sure to receive the necessary Spanish transit visas. We hope our attempts come to fruition in the near future.

So many contradictions and so many lies! The American State Department could only issue visas if they received a notarized confirmation for Spanish transit visas. In addition, the Spanish Consulate would only issue those transit visas if they had confirmation from the State Department that American entry visas were issued. Why did the American State Department issue such misleading information? There were secret understandings within the State Department relating to holding up the issuing of visas. Slowing the processing by withholding information and disallowing the paperwork submitted which then would have to be started all over again, made it impossible for the desperate Jewish people to escape the hell that existed in Germany.

> It does not matter if, in the meantime, we now receive a Cuban visa, so we travel to Cuba and from there, perhaps to America.

> But, to receive the Cuban visas, it is necessary to spend roughly $1,000 for each member of the family; for children, less is required, Mrs. Loewenstein wrote. She wrote that she is writing this merely for information's sake because Carla will probably not be able to raise such monies.

> She further stated, the question is, if Carla can leave Germany, considering her age, is still not solved. Carla is healthy and, therefore, in principle I am able to work, although one may not expect that with four children I would have to report for actual forced labor. When you have a visa, can one attempt to put forth the application for the children to leave, despite their youthful ages? We would have to wait and see if this could be successful. The *Hilfsverein* generally is not allowed to work such requests. Perhaps your husband can achieve something, at least for the son who will be eighteen years old soon, to obtain a Spanish tourist visa.

> In this respect, one will have to get in touch in New York with a reliable mediating concern as for example:

>   1.   Herbert Seeliger, c/o American Lloyd, Inc.
>   West 42nd Street, New York

2.   Ignatz Rosenack
     233 Broadway, Woolworth Building
     New York

Regrettably, the letter was delayed because of my illness.

With friendly regards,
Loewenstein

Dr. Schaeler, though, told me he felt it would be a mistake to bring Günther alone to Cuba inasmuch as he does not believe that he will be able to obtain the American visa there if he leaves me and the three children, as blood relations, behind in Germany. In any case, you can discuss this at those two addresses and I hope they do not charge much for this advice. However, the best and simplest way would be if the matter with Washington would materialize. Do everything possible and quickly because of Günther's upcoming eighteenth birthday. Since today, Günther was sent from his workshop to an Aryan boss; maybe he will even get some pay for it.

Today, I received an invitation from Aunt Melocke for this Friday. Only I don't know what I will do with the children. Well, I will first have to go there and see what I can accomplish with regards to our emigration. I have spoken with Koronczek; he may be able to employ me eventually half days, if I can put this arrangement through the employment bureau or perhaps I will be totally excused to report for work. In the next letter to you I should be able to report about this in more detail. I am very disquieted about Alfred. Send me mail from him with yours.

The children, thank God, are all well. So I want to put the letter in the mailbox now. Today, Mrs. Gold is here and so I can leave right now. I also want to go shopping with our Hansi. On Sunday, with God's help, I will write more. Until then, I hope to have mail from you. My best regards for the children and Hannah. Your brother Siete in Hamburg has a birthday on the 10th this month.

To you, my dearest beloved Carlo, take my most heartfelt regards and many, many kisses. Your very much loving and having endless longing for you little wife,

Carla

Enclosure: Letter of the Spanish Consulate

My very efficient mother kept on daily exploring ways and means to save the children. Only two days later, my mother must have breathed a sigh of relief. A letter had arrived from her husband and she responded immediately to it with her own letter. My mother had written nearly twice as many letters as her husband did from New York, underscoring her desperate need to have some contact with the outside world, with her loving husband.

From Carola Koppel
Thierschstrasse 7/III
Munich 22   the 10th October 1941

My dear, dearest Carlo!

This letter was shorter than most my mother sent to her husband in New York; yet, it affected me more than I realized at the time of my reading it. The innocuous little sentence about my sister Ruth needing eyeglasses would affect me deeply later and haunt me for the rest of my life.

On October 15, 1941, my mother sent a Western Union cable to my father in Brooklyn, New York as follows:

KINDERAUSREISE 20/V UNMOEGLICH
ENDGUELTIGE AUSREISE WIRD GEKABELT

CAROLA

Children's departure 20/V impossible. Final departure will be wired

Carola

I am not certain what my mother meant with this telegram. Was she going to send the children by themselves? It seemed she knew that there was a restriction because of her age. Yet, she was a woman with determination not ready to give up the fight. Eternal hope made her hang on to the very last moment and keep on fighting.

From Carola Koppel
Thierschstrasse 7/III
München   the 20th October 1941

My dear, dearest Carlo,

You are probably wondering why I did not write for such a
long time (it was really only ten days) but I simply could not
get to it. The decision of the Jewish Community Office for
my hiring has been delayed. Another authority delayed the
decision. Today, I had to go there again and the matter was
handled after all. Mr. Koronczek supported me to the best
of his ability. Officially, I shall work there in an honorary
capacity, will further receive some support and probably
will receive a performance increase in the future. In any
case, I like this much better than factory work because I
understand this type of work and I am happy with it.

The most difficult part is always that one has to walk such
a long way to go to work. I have to walk almost one hour in
the morning and again in the evening. The office hours are
from eight in the morning until half past six in the evening
with a thirty-minute lunch break. So you can see, I am out
of the house twelve and half-hours every day. This walking so far every day is very bad for my legs but I can not
change this.

By this time Jews were not allowed to use streetcars anymore.

Fortunately, on Thursday, I was able to place the three little
ones into the Antonien home. This is the well known children's home, as you may remember, in Munich. They are
well provided for there. I looked everything over in the
home and, for today's conditions, it looks quite comfortable. Sunday, I visited them by walking the long distance
to the home. The children's happiness was great. Naturally,
Baby cried when I left but calmed down some when she
did not see me anymore. The children are, thank God, well;
you don't have to worry about them.

You undoubtedly received my letter in which I gave you the addresses of the firms for arranging emigration to Cuba. To be on the safe side, I am repeating them here.

1. Herbert Seeliger c/o American Lloyd, Inc.
    55 West 42nd Street, New York
2. Ignatz Rosenack
    233 Broadway, Woolworth Building

I am very eager to receive your next letter in order to hear what you have undertaken. It is now really highest time! It is a fact that we shall not get to go to Edie's place in France. We will in all probability be sent to the East instead. The same possibility exists with your sister Lola and Leo's wife Sine.

I sent the notarized photocopies from the Spanish Consulate to Loewenstein in Berlin and Lola writes me the following: "I have to tell you first of all that you are the most competent of all of us. Just now, Joseph returned from Loewenstein with whom he had a conversation. When he received your letter this morning, he immediately conveyed the matter to Professor Berliner for further handling. Professor Berliner is quite confident and said maybe things will fall in place with the two boys. I hope the correspondence will not be delayed since, at this moment, one does not know how and what will happen. Mr. Loewenstein was very clear and inquired about everybody—you Carlo, the children and so forth. He is still sick but it goes better for him now.

How is Alfred? As soon as I become somewhat calmer, I shall write to him in Colorado and Hochfelds in Los Angeles to whom you please send my regards.

Everybody is surprised that I was able to accomplish to be employed by the Jewish Community office. Many people hold a grudge against me because of this. I surely have acknowledged Walter's long letter; the mail probably got crossed. He should send me a detailed report about his school. I hope to receive mail from you again soon and will write to you again in great detail. Have now little time since I don't sleep well at night.

Regards to all the loved ones, especially Alfred and Walter. And to you my most beloved Carlo, many, many regards and many kisses from your ever loving you and longing little wife,

Carla

There was much euphemism in this paragraph, a paraphrasing my mother incorporated into her letters. It was very revealing. In her letter of October 20, 1941, she wrote that we shall not get to go to where Edie was interned but to the other city. Originally, she thought they were going to be transported to a camp in France. By the other city, she undoubtedly meant that the latest information was transports to the East, perhaps Minsk, Russia or Riga, Latvia. This possibility also existed for Sine and son Werner, wife and son of Leo, and Lola, her sister-in-law and husband Joseph. Rumors were rampant and circulating among all the members of the families and friends. Witness the following letter from Lola Goldschmidt to my father in New York. .

From Lola Goldschmidt
Thomasiusstrasse 14
Berlin, Germany   Berlin, the 15th October 1941

My dear Hannah,

I was very pleased with your personal letter of 7th September which arrived at the beginning of October. In the meantime, you moved to your own place and I hope it was not too strenuous for you. I think so much about you because I always feel you are working too hard. Are your eyes so weak that you must wear glasses all the time? You probably waited too long as I did. The eye doctor was horrified when he saw that I have not had an examination for six years. Until sixty years, one should have an examination every two year; then every one year.

My hair, dear Hannah, is still quite dark as it always has been. It is only beginning to get gray at the temples despite all the worries one has. But that really does not always have something to do with it. In the meantime, all of you surely spent the Jewish New Year and Yom Kippur well.

It was so nice that you could be with Carlo and Walter. I am sure you cooked something special. I miss my little Walter with his ingratiating manners so much. He should remain a brave boy. What is it with his school? Does he like it? He should write about it soon. And how is he getting along with the English? It is too bad, dear Hannah, that you have such difficulties learning the language. I know you are working very hard. As you yourself say, "I am not twenty anymore." I feel it as well.

I have written Family Gourarys for an affidavit for us but, now, it is only possible if we had the opportunity to go by way of Cuba first. First, we want to see what will happen with Carla and the children. One hopes all the time that it will still work out. Mr. Loewenstein here believes that, indeed, her emigration will still materialize.

We had communication from Leo and Edie from the camps in France through the Red Cross. It pleases me to see Edie's handwriting again. Both their letters were from the 7th and 18th of August. Leo writes again about money. I beg you, dear Hannah, not to send him any for the time being because he receives some money from an acquaintance of mine out of Switzerland. In addition, he simply does not have to travel to Marseilles two times each week. Most people can not do the things anymore they would like to do. He has bought, as he wrote to Sine, quite a few things, like shirts, shoes, and so forth.

We can not go to the synagogue in the Levetzow Street anymore. The past holidays, we went to the Wilsnacker Street on the forth floor, a temporary synagogue, but only the men could attend.

It goes well for brother Siete and Friedel. probably because Friedel is not Jewish which classifies them as a mixed marriage. Do you remember Hertha? She is now at forced labor. Don't feed Walter Baer all the time; after all, he has some money. He should see to it that he can get his sister Sine and son Werner to Cuba. After all, he does have good connections.

Mrs. Feder now has to share our large dining room with another lady. Martha Markus has our other room. Not a pleasant situation. Betti has our living room, which she has to share with Miss Auerhahn, Aunt Eva has the little room and Mrs. Urmann the little room in the back. That leaves almost no room for Joseph and me.

Now my heartiest regards to you, dear Hannah, from your
Sister Lola

The beautiful apartment of my dear aunt and uncle had become overcrowded. It seemed that the consolidation of Jews into fewer and fewer lodgings had finally begun in Berlin, the genesis of preparations for the deportations.

With travel totally restricted now, the only means of communication was by letter and telephone. It seems, all the relatives left in Germany wrote more and more letters to each other. All of them suffered terribly and felt the heavy burden of complete isolation. Their world became smaller and smaller. Shortly after Aunt Lola's letter to Hannah in New York, she and Uncle Joseph wrote another letter addressed to me in the hospital in Denver.

October 21, 1941

From: Lola Goldschmidt
    Berlin, Germany
To: Alfred Koppel
National Jewish Hospital
Denver, Colorado

Dear Alfred,

You have surely received our last letter written to you in September. In the meantime, you have had a very nice birthday. One seems to spoil you in Denver. And you received such fine presents. Over the holidays, we thought much about you which we do all the time. Who is Mr. Levisohn who knew your grandfather? Maybe he could issue us an affidavit, which by now is very important. I hope you will write to us soon and in great detail. Most important, how are you health wise?

Miss Heymann and Martin had the lease on their apartment cancelled. They still do not know where to move. Siegmundshof (location of the synagogue) is over with for us. One has to pray now in the Wilsnackerstrasse on the forth floor. It's only for the men. Leo and Edie wrote us that they had received your cards, at that time from Portugal (she erred; I had sent card from Spain). Yesterday we had mail from them through the Red Cross. Werner and his mother Sine were recently in Steubenweg with Uncle Bernhard and Aunt Ulli. They wrote it was a very nice outing in the country. I am sure you already know that Uncle Bernhard and Ulli visited your mother and the four children in Munich and also Aunt Lene in Frankfurt.

Günther has to work very hard and has such along way to travel to work. He is unable to use his bicycle anymore! (All bicycles had been confiscated by the Nazis) That Uncle Nathan (Leipheimer, brother of my father's mother) visited you must have been nice for you. I am sure you were not too self-conscious. Did you converse with him? How goes it with the English? Undoubtedly, you are doing very well. I am unable to learn English. Well, I shall take lessons from you, I hope. I wish we were at that stage, being in America.

What do you do the entire day? What is being done to cure you? Write us all of it in detail because Dr. Dosmar here in Berlin is very interested in it as well. Can you send us a photo of yourself to us? Surely, someone there has a camera. Your Aunt Hannah gave you wonderful presents. I hope you will be able to pay her back some day for all the good things she has done for all of you. If it only works out for Mutti and the children! That is something we all hope for.

I want to write your father today as well. Did we write you that you had a postcard from the labor office in Berlin to report for forced labor here? It is too bad that one can not travel to Uncle Bernhard in Hamburg or Mutti in München anymore!

The weather here is still nice, actually better than in the summer. How time flies! Now you are already three months in America. Without a doubt, the food in Denver is surely extra good, yes? Enjoy it so that you gain good weight. I will also try to enclose a pre-paid letter envelope so that you can write to us again. For today, my dear Alfred, my very best regards to you from your thinking of you all the time,

Lola

Many regards, Uncle Joseph

Apparently, the pressure in Munich had become extreme. Günther had to give up his bicycle, which had been a great help for his mobility. Then, my aunt writes, that I (Alfred) had received a post card from the labor department to report for forced labor in Munich. I had just recently turned fifteen years old at that time. She also confirmed that travel on the *Reichsbahn*, the German Railroad, was now forbidden for Jews. Luckily, Uncle Bernhard and his wife had just recently visited my mother and the children. Lola's letters now were of greater importance. It seems correspondence was the thread giving each of the families the courage to go on living.

From: Lola Goldschmidt
Thomasiusstrasse 14   Berlin, the 27th October 1941
Berlin

To: Carl Koppel
233 Rogers Ave,
Brooklyn, New York, USA

Dear Hannah, dear Carlo,

Last week, Carla probably did not get a letter from you or else, I would already have heard from her. I am waiting today or until tomorrow for mail from Carla. She can not write so often anymore since she has reported for work.

By now, my mother had to report for some work. She attempted to get a job at the Jewish Community Organization in Munich where she could utilize her expertise what she had learned in business school. She was hired.

The main thing is that one remains healthy. Bernhard from Altona and Lene from Frankfurt now write more often than usual so that one always has news.

It is sad about the death of Mr. Reis. Mrs. Reis probably wrote that her boys overseas still know nothing about it that their father had died already in June. Now, there are many people in the neighborhood of Mrs. Reis or Selma Herz, as Rachel, Max Braunschweiger and other acquaintances. (This seems to be another "between the lines" announcement of the Jewish people being forced to move into and double up in the Jewish apartments resulting in terrible crowding). I hope you will have further good news about Alfred. I wrote him last week and enclosed a reply envelope so that he can write us directly. Walter, we hope, is industrious at school. I can imagine how proud he was when he earned his first money; he should save carefully so he can assist Uncle Joseph and Aunt Lola (Goldschmidt) later once they arrive in America. It is too bad that daughter Claire does not have the spirit anymore to complete the matter for her father and Lene, (Max Oettinger and his wife, my Aunt Lene in Frankfurt) whereby it is so necessary at this moment. Today, they will send another telegram to Claire. Additionally, if only the matter with Carla and children would come to fruition.

For us, I wrote to Family Gourarys in Cuba for affidavits; no response! Without such affidavits, the entry into Cuba is very, very expensive. I don't even know if Cuba would do it if we had affidavits. You may have to write and give them our birth dates. I was born July 14, 1887 and Uncle

Joseph on September 8, 1872, both in Altona. It is difficult to believe that people in America make things so difficult.

We had mail from France, from brothers Leo and Edie, through the Red Cross. I responded to them right away. Edie writes and Leo did earlier, that we should send them money through the local currency exchange but, regrettably, it is not possible. Can Leo and Edie actually meet in the two camps in France? Bernhard and Ulli were at the Steubenweg for an outing over the holidays in September and took Sine and Werner with them. Now, fall is coming and it is already very cool.

It is too bad that one can not travel to Bernhard in Altona anymore; after all, one has always something to discuss.

I am happy that all of you were together in Brooklyn over the holidays. That was particularly nice for you, dear Carlo, that Hannah did everything in the house, cleaning and cooking. Our Walter is then very happy; he likes to eat.

I probably wrote you already that the men now go to pray in the Wilsnacker Strasse. For the ladies it is not possible anymore.

So, the mail came without a letter from Carla. Her letter will probably arrive tomorrow morning. I wanted to write much the last days, but one's head is empty. That is happening to all the people. We now have changed our living room to be our dining room inasmuch as we had to "sell" the large dining room to some stranger!

On October 30, Aunt Lola continued the letter. This time it was hand written. All Jewish people finally must have had to give up their typewriters.

Now the letter is not sent yet; everything is hurried and each day brings something else. At any rate, there has been no mail from you here. Carla wrote nothing about a letter. Ulli and Bernhard wrote today. Bernhard who always had been so jovial, is now very, very nervous. The circle of acquaintances is getting ever smaller. Last evening, a married couple from our neighborhood here had to return from the railroad station. The wife is not yet 60 years old; no one between birth and 60 is allowed to leave Germany anymore. That is the newest.

Here, we already had the first snow and it is beginning to get cold. Have you, dear Hannah, bought yourself a new winter coat? Walter will probably still be able to wear his. One would like to write so much but, after all, don't know what or how.

Only you, please, write really soon. You, dear Carlo, see to it that you earn much money until we are able to come to America. When you write Leo and Edie, tell them, I will write to them also soon. Only I can not write so much anymore, only 25 words! Is Walter learning much and how goes it with the language? Are you saving the good bed sheets? Does Alfred have the opportunity to learn while he is in the hospital in Denver? Write about everything.

Heartiest regards from

Your Lola

From: Bernhard and Ulli Koppel   20th October 1941
Altona (Hamburg), Germany

To: Carlo Koppel
233 Rogers Avenue
Brooklyn, New York

My Dears (Carlo and Hannah),

We hear from Carla about you all the time and now, it is very pleasant to finally receive a letter from you directly. It is probably more than half a year now that you let us have a few lines. Will keep quiet though if you will let us know and help us regarding our own emigration. A while ago, you dear Hannah, wrote…concerning financial affidavits. Now it is "Ulli and Bernhard's" turn. Alas, that's where it remained. We have complete understanding that everything is very difficult and especially you, dear Brother, have enough to do with the matter of Carla and the children. But

I had begged to have the affidavit of sister Lene Oettinger extended in order to have something to show officials, but heard nothing about this. I have begged to make a connection with my friend Fritz Neuwahl again. I have heard nothing about this either, although it is now very important and will soon be too late. It is possible that Fritz will not respond, but one can at least attempt to contact him. Sons Hellmut in Israel and Kurt in Canada admittedly have not received a response in the meantime. Perhaps you can elicit a response. He would surely place $1,000 at our disposal to be able to obtain visas.

It will surely be very difficult to find people who have the confidence that, through the commitment of a loan only, they will receive their money back. But, something must be found in order to be allowed to journey into Cuba. Many people travel there at this time. For this, a sum of money must be out on deposit. One tells me in confidence that the Warburg Foundation in New York might give the necessary sum in Cuba against reimbursement in equivalent dollars. In addition, one would also need, of course, some advance money. This amount, Fritz would certainly cover. I have given our friends, the Dr. Borchardt's over there, all the information. They will contact you in New York. I am not certain if they have already landed there. In any case, they will certainly be in America by the time you receive this letter. Their address will be Dr. Curt Borchardt, c/o Wotinsky, 5036 Massachusetts Avenue, N.W., Washington, DC. I assume that Borchardts will spend some time in New York City inasmuch as he has many relatives there. In any case, I expect that you will earnestly make efforts on our behalf and not let a day pass because it is easily possible that the chance for Cuba will pass.

About the U.S.A., it is undoubtedly very difficult. If one can get to Spain or Portugal, then one can accomplish something more readily. But, this is totally useless to even try. A transit visa through Spain or Portugal will be given by those countries, after all, only if the American Consul in Spain or Portugal confirms that a visa will be issued by Washington. No matter where one turns to, nothing works out and no one wants to give financial help.

As already said, it is important to find somebody who is confident that he will be repaid the money from Fritz Neuwahl. Also, please try to speak with Katten in New York. Even with the possibility of not being able to meet with him right away, one could remain in his neighborhood for half a day and in this way find his office after a few hours.

Desperation, desperation to the highest degree from the former jovial and happy brother and desperation of all the brothers and sisters of this large family.

Also, for Ettingers in Cedar Rapids in America for example, it would be a small matter to put up such a deposit that will not be touched by us. In addition, an acquaintance of Hirsch, who just traveled to Ecuador, will support me. The address of Mr. Hirsch is in care of Senor Don Carlos Seminario, Quito, Ecuador, Calle Allmagro. This man will probably not be there before the middle of December. He promised to write to me from a stop over in Cuba; also was going to write to you too.

Dear Carlo, you told me at one time, it is a mistake on my part that you, (Carlo), rarely repeat yourself in your letters. I have to correct you about this inasmuch as you have written at least 'one hundred thirty five times' that the *Hilfsverein*, after all is guilty of omissions, that the *Hilfsverein* now has to do everything after they missed all matters concerning Carla, and so forth. You can naturally write this as often as you feel like it, but it will not accomplish anything. Indeed, if you convey such feelings of yours to your loyal and dear wife 'imprisoned' in Munich, you will help to destroy this heroic woman.

You surely want to have an accurate report about our recent visit to Munich. I can tell you that, since that visit in Munich, I have the feeling that you make Carla even more nervous when she repeatedly reads in your letters something that can not be changed, like the matter with the *Hilfsverein*. For that reason we stayed an extra two days with Carla and the children more than planned. It is, after all, very difficult with the visas for Spain and certainly not possible through you, Carlo.

Regrettably, we could not travel to Berlin anymore. I would have gone to Loewenstein for a conference with him about Karla and the children. But just today, I want to write about Carla's situation with the comment that I have convinced myself she is a heroic person. Maybe talking about it helps.

 With our visit there, I have to mention that I am wondering where such darling children came from. Did you have other co-workers, inasmuch as looking at your profile, they did not turn out like you and is, after all, very good for the children! The little one is like a little doll and so well behaved; one can hardly believe it. She sits on the toilet and never complains. The other little one, Ruth, is likewise a lovely child, so well behaved and smart. Your boy Hansi I find to be good looking, a finely chiseled head and very blond. He has a good appetite; can eat huge amounts. We took the children to an outing to the Tegernsee one day and they were well behaved. We had coffee and cake just like the grown up people. Only I am not used to go to the toilet with this size boy. Carla has undoubtedly reported everything. Also the room and board was good which I want to underscore. To be sure, we brought along some food, but the preparation was the important thing. All in all, we were happy to have been there because it was very pleasant and comfortable if one overlooks the lack of room.

I am begging you again to set everything in motion to achieve something for us. Couldn't one receive a guarantee from Fritz that he will contribute the sum of money a little later, if he can not do it right away? The letter from our son

Kurt we received from you with thanks and were as always very pleased with it. I will write him today but you could inform him since your letter to him in Canada will arrive there sooner than ours. I will ask him if his friend Krwiett could do something. I am not sure if wife Ulli can or has the time to add to this letter. After all, she must take care of her fingers. She has an inflammation on her right index finger, but it is almost well again. She is also getting very nervous and apprehensive. So now, I must close.

To all of you, my dear ones, heartiest regards and many thanks for your constant efforts for us.

Bernhard

In addition to my writing of yesterday, I have to say the following. I just read that one can immigrate to Ecuador as an in-between country. Regrettably, the legation is closed and it can only be managed through the *Hilfsverein*. That would be for us a roundabout way. I feel a direct handling will have quicker results. I am of the opinion, first to put up the deposit, and then the visas will be easier to obtain. Can one not find someone who would have some trust? The money will be returned when you immigrate hence, there is no risk for Fritz in America since he will have his money returned. There should be at least $1,000 made available to us. The man has a big practice with eighteen employees. He has money. Can't one send a telegram to him? Do you have his address? Otherwise, write Kurt at once to Canada. He can give his address to you, but you will have to get on it right away.

People who will be in Ecuador only temporarily in order for them to continue to the U.S.A. or a South American country have to bring evidence that there is $400 capital per family as well as $100 per person. The legation in Berlin requires as well that a monthly pension for an indeterminate time will be available for the immigrant. I assume there is an Ecuardorian Consulate in New York that has information concerning this. One has to submit all kinds of papers along with the money or perhaps the papers can be submitted later. I could not discern which. It says the application is to be prepared in Spanish and in duplicate. A Mr. Hirsch who recently left for Ecuador will be glad to follow through and do everything for us, but until he arrives there, it will be the middle of December. So there are a number of problems. Naturally, if the Cuba matter can be handled quickly, it would be best. You need to obtain advice and leave nothing unturned.

Despite your wife's misfortunes, one must not have our matter overlooked. I am writing sort of mixed up because I am not feeling quite well. In any case, a good number of people nowadays are traveling to Cuba. To be sure, we may still be able to achieve it. I know you will do everything in order to help us. There are so many people in New York who together can work on our matter, if not money-wise, then certainly in some manner. If anything is within the grasp of success, it should be telegraphed at once as to what is to be done and what the chances of success are.

We just had a letter from Lene and Max (Ettinger) from Frankfurt who writes that Mrs. Sonnenberger, Max's sister-in-law, received a telegram that their trip to Cuba has been sent in. Now, Lene hopes that Claire Weger will accomplish the same for her and Max. (Claire Weger was Max's daughter). There will be a great rush for applications to Cuba. I will add that one can take Sine and son Werner to Ecuador with the $400, only then in addition, extra money will have to be deposited. This, of course, complicates matters.

I hope to hear from you with the hope that this letter will be in your hands soon.

I wish all the very best and much blessings for the boys,

Bernhard

My father's brother Bernhard, who had been an easy going, fun loving person all of his life pulled no punches in his letter to my father. Indeed, it was almost an attack on my father that had to be occasioned by the extreme situation Jews found themselves in Germany. After Bernhard and wife Ulli visited my mother in Munich, having had long discussions about the terrible conditions with her, about the impossibility to pull together the necessary documents to emigrate, he chided my father for accusing the *Hilfsverein* (the Jewish Committee) again and again for not performing, and for not helping his family to be able to leave Germany.

I can not even begin to imagine the stress my father must have experienced. Here is this vituperative letter from his elder brother Bernhard from Hamburg. Brothers Leo and Edie were asking for help. Sisters Lene Oettinger and Lola Goldschmidt and husbands, while not directly inflicting pressures, must also have been constantly on his mind. It must have been a feeling of utter helplessness and despair.

On the same date Bernhard wrote his letter, my mother wrote another letter. She had become so unnerved that she failed to add the usual salutation to her dear husband.

> From: Carola Koppel
> Thierschstrasse 7/III
> Munich   the 24th October 1941
>
> I want to use the opportunity during my lunchtime in the office here, to begin a letter inasmuch as it goes faster with a typewriter. Today, I can confirm your dear letter of 26th September. I was so pleased and happy to receive it.
>
> Regrettably, I can not send you a confirmation about the departure for the children and me as you must know because there is an official prohibition for it. (Could this have to do with what Herman Judell wrote June 30, 1941, about a secret agreement of no more visas being issued?)
>
> The departure will be determined case by case and Loewenstein will surely take care of that and, because of the children, would add me, their mother, to a Spanish transport. The difficulty with my age does indeed exist. The problem is the age to obtain permission to be able to

be added to a Spanish transport. In any case, Loewenstein, is now very hopeful after I sent him the notarized photocopy of the Spanish Consulate. I hope you have, in the meantime, also received the copy of this letter and sent it on to Washington as an addendum to your visit there. I am debating if I should send another photocopy to the American Consulate in Barcelona, just as the American Consul should send in a confirmation. (see Herman Judell's letter of June 30: "Consulate confirmations are worthless in Washington")

I shall now compose a letter and then write it here at work on the typewriter. About Cuba, I will send you a copy later of the communication of Loewenstein. For obtaining of a tourist visa for Cuba, the following is required:

$ 2,000 deposit
$ 500 further deposit
$ 150 deposit for trip continuation
$ 275 expenses for obtaining visas

In order to obtain the visa based on the numbers above, one must get in contact with a reliable middleman company. Such companies can be mentioned without obligation.

Ignatz Rosenack, 233 Broadway, Woolworth Building, New York

Herbert Seeliger, c/o American Lloyd, Inc. 55 West 42nd Street, New York

Maybe you can make contact with these people in case you have heard nothing from Washington to date. It would have been much more prudent for you to meet with the Joint (Joint Distribution Committee) because, I assume, from the Reichvereinigung (the Federal Organization), Frau Professor Berliner has sent the photocopy of the letter to the Joint in order to assist you in your efforts. Maybe you can inquire about it New York.

The children are, thank God, well. I visited them last Sunday in the Antonienheim; they were very happy with my visit.

This Sunday, Günther will go to visit them. His visit helps, because when I visit them I must walk for three hours with my bad legs.

So, now I must close; will write more when I am home.

Now I am already home and will have to close right away since it is almost the beginning of the Sabbath. I will be off tomorrow, but then on Sunday I work from half past eight until half past twelve. Next week I will receive my identification card. I am glad about that; one can not know how one might be able to use it sometime. You do understand me!

I was not able to locate a second page, nor was there any signature on this letter. No one in Germany at this time seemed to know that the American State Department did not allow local Consulates, such as the one in Spain, to issue any American entry visas. Further, what did my mother mean by being happy to receive the identification card? Was this to identify the men, women and children in case of a transfer of all the Jews to the East such as Poland or Russia? In addition, why did she repeat the names and addresses of Seeliger and Rosenack as contacts? She had already written about these two in her letter of October 8, 1941. Was it hope, was it desperation, or was it utter confusion?

My mother had problems with swelling of her legs. Yet, she walked from her house to the Antonienheim for one and a half hours each way to be able to spend a little time with her little children. By edict from the Gestapo through Oberburgermeister Fiehler, use of public transportation by Jews was forbidden.

October 26, 1941

To The Representative of the Lieutenant-General
The Office for the Transfer & Conversion to Aryan Use
Widenmayerstreet 27
Munich

To The Lord Mayor of the 'Capital of the Movement'
München

Colonel General Karl Fiehler

Concerning: The Use of City Streetcars and Buses by Jews

Honored Mayor!

The Lieutenant-General and State Minister, Gauleiter Adolph WAGER has, in his capacity as commissioner of State defense, given the order yesterday for the maintenance of peace and order, that it is forbidden for Jews, effective immediately, to use city transportation vehicles.

I have advised the Jewish Community Administration to advise their members immediately of this ban.

I request acknowledgement of this.

Visit of Hellabrun Zoo by Jews

Additionally, among sections of the population, complaints have been lodged at the NSDAP (National Socialist German Worker's Party), that the Jews spend time Sundays, today as before, in the Hellabrun Zoo. In agreement with Major LEDERER may I please present to you that you advise the administration of Hellabrun Zoo to remove the Jews from the grounds of the zoo in the future.

> Heil Hitler!
> Signed Wegner
> WEGNER
> SA-Captain

(Source: Yad Vashem MRP-2/1)

The following letter was written by hand again (typewriters were expropriated some time ago).

München, the 30th October 1941

From: Carola Koppel
Thierschstrasse 7/III

My dear, dearest Carlo!

Today, I received your dear letter of the 10th of the month, No. 51, which made me very happy. First, I want to relate to you the following. I work with a Mr. Jonas and he told me today, during a casual conversation, that they are related to the bank Aufhäuser of the Loewengrube address here in Munich. Upon my surprised question as to where he learned of this, he said that some time ago he was Chief of the Secretary's office there. Incidentally, he speaks badly about them because they promised to help him with emigration, but did not keep their promise. In any case, he told me both brothers have been in New York for a long time and they are faring very well.

You must absolutely look them up right away because they, themselves, or through contacts would be in a position to help you or to finance the Cuba matter. I already wrote you in my last letter that the $2,000 could be dealt with through a bank guaranty. You can not let up with them and must tell them what kind of responsibility they would incur if they deny help. It is really now the very last moment so they can not afford to ignore this opportunity. A Mr. Brunnez in care of Gleichroeder Co., 30 Broad Street, New York will give their address to you. Mr. Brunnez is a cousin of Dr. Schaeler of the Jewish Community Administration here, very wealthy and circulates on a friendly basis with the Aufhäusers. Maybe Mr. Brunnez can advise his cousin Dr. Schaeler about this. It would not be too difficult to do this through Gleichroeder. You can refer to the names of Dr. Schaeler and Mr. Jonas; so please, do well.

Another matter is with the departure from here. Since yesterday, one can not leave between the ages of 0 and 60!

It is impossible to imagine this. I still hope that in my case an exception might be possible. You would have to make a request over there in America; one must think about this. It is the worst for so many people who were ready to emigrate and are now unable to leave. Among those many are also Dr. Schaeler and Mr. Gutmann.

Yesterday, I sent a certified letter with return envelope to the American Consulate in Barcelona with photocopy of the written confirmation of the American Consulate and the Spanish letter. You can see that I will not let up

The children are fine. I will visit them again Saturday or Sunday in the Antonienheim in the afternoon. Now it is almost half past eight and I must go to bed. I have to get up in the morning before six. That makes for a long and difficult day for me. Maybe I'll write again on Sunday.

Many regards and kisses for the boys and Hannah. And to you my beloved Carlo, unending, deepest regards and kisses,

Your much loving you little wife,
Carla

Vilnius, Lithuania

It's extraordinary how nothing ever dies
completely, even the evil that was Nazi
Germany's and which today is gaining ground
in this land.
　　　—Yehudi Menuhin, from interview of
　　　France's Le Figaro newspaper.

Our plane landed in Vilnius. Although the Vilnius airport was not very large, hundreds of people were milling around. It was utter turmoil. Somehow, Robert and I managed to retrieve our luggage and pass through customs. Pulling our wheeled luggage, we left the terminal and faced even more confusion among the hundreds of people trying to board buses and taxis. Men were shouting in Lithuanian. No one spoke any English.

It was cloudy and cold. We were tired and in no mood trying to maneuver via the public buses. We approached the taxi queue and tried to negotiate the fare into the city. This was quite difficult inasmuch as we did not know any Lithuanian and the driver knew no English or at least pretended not to know any English. He wrote on a piece of paper: 60 Litas. I had a Vilnius pocket guide that indicated the 5-kilometer trip should cost less than 40 Litas. Being very tired, we negotiated, as we learned later, at outrageous 50 Litas for the trip. It should have been no more than 30 Litas. One dollar was equal to four Litas, an easy to remember ratio.

The ride to the center of Vilnius took about fifteen minutes. The Hotel Zaliasis Tiltas, an old building on Vilniaus Street 2, was in the center of town. An ornate façade of the turn of the century style, this hotel had been the headquarters of the Russian government until their departure in 1991.

"*Laba diena*, good day," I said to the smiling receptionist. I had made it a point to memorize a few phrases in Lithuanian. We had our reservations and the check-in took only a few minutes. Keys in hand, Robert and I proceeded to the elevator. The hallway was dark. One had to turn on a timed switch to illuminate the way. I opened the door to my room with the giant heavy key and was greeted by a relatively small room with a single bed and a small bathroom in the corner. The plumbing was as old as the building. It had not been updated. The five-foot bathtub had a raised seat at one end. Consequently, one could not lie down. Instead, one had to sit in the tub to take a bath. But I did not come to Lithuania for a holiday experience. I had to overlook these types of inconveniences.

We decided to take a stroll and investigate the immediate area. Across from the hotel was a large concert hall. Beyond the concert hall were municipal and government buildings, both in the neo-classical style of the turn of the 19th to 20th century. We took a short walk to Gedimino Street, the main street in town. This led us past a park to the old cathedral and a museum. On the way back to the hotel we sat down on a bench in the park we had passed earlier and watched people strolling by. Old ones, young ones, girls and boys flirting with each other and young children playing catch the ball. A seemingly normal scene. The old men, many of them hunched over with age had the biggest impact on me. What did they do during the war, I asked myself? I had read horror stories and saw photos of the killing of hundreds of Jews by Lithuanian prisoners freed from prisons. In June 1941, they bludgeoned hundreds of Jews to death with steel rods. Visions of the dead lying in a sea of blood flooded my imagination. Were some of these old men participants in this bloodbath in Kovno? "Let's move on," I said to Robert, never letting on my about my horror images.

By now, it was evening, time to have a meal. We passed the Hotel Neringa on Gedimino Street. Their dining room looked inviting. We entered, sat down and looked around us. The dining room was bustling with many people. On the far wall was a mural depicting Soviet heroes, a relic from the time that Soviet Union was in control of the country. (In March 1990, the Supreme Council of Lithuania declared independence for the country from the USSR) So far, it had not been removed as with so many other Soviet statues and murals throughout the city. The meal was good and very inexpensive. For both of us the total bill, including taxes and tip came to 46 Litas or about eleven to twelve dollars. That night I slept the sleep of an exhausted and drained man.

The next day I telephoned Mrs. Rachel Kostanian of the Jewish State Museum of Lithuania. I arranged a meeting with her at the museum for that afternoon. The location of the museum, at Pamenkalnio Street 12, was within walking distance from the hotel. The museum, a green wooden clapboard building, was set back from the street about forty feet. Rachel Kostanian, a vivacious, articulate and outspoken woman, welcomed us. She had a deep commitment to the museum, its artifacts and documents depicting life of the Jewish people in Lithuania over many centuries. Permitted by the Soviet Lithuanian authorities, the museum opened on October 1, 1989 and has continued to collect additional materials ever since.

The walk through the small museum was a revelation. I had known very little about this Baltic country. Vilnius, its capital, was at one time the "bastion of Judaism and Jewish life." *(From the brochure: The Jewish State Museum of Lithuania 1996). Vilnius had, before the war, 102 synagogues and prayer houses, Jewish schools and libraries, medical, scientific and cultural institutions. In 1938, six daily newspapers were being published in Hebrew and Yiddish.

In 1940, the Soviet regime closed down nearly all of the Jewish organizations, the museums in Kovno and Vilnius, the Hebrew schools, and all but two newspapers. Complete destruction came with the Nazi occupation beginning in June 1941. Of approximately 225,000 Jews in Lithuania at the start of the war, only about 8,000 survived. (From the brochure: The Jewish State Museum 1996.) The museum exhibited pictures of large ghettos established by the Nazis in Vilnius, Kovno and other cities in Lithuania. Then the Nazis killed almost everyone in these ghettos. I was overwhelmed with emotion realizing that 96% of the pre-war Jewish population of Lithuania had been murdered.

We asked Rachel about our guide for the next two days. "I have made the arrangements with a nice young lady," she told us, "who speaks excellent English. You will also have a driver to take you to Kovno on the second day. Tomorrow morning, Regina Kopilevich will pick you up for a walking tour in Vilnius."

Robert and I were sitting in the lobby of the hotel when, promptly at nine o'clock, a young lady walked through the door. "My name is Regina Kopilevich," she greeted us, "and I will be your guide for the day." Smartly attired in ankle length skirt and matching jacket—it was cool and windy that day—this attractive young lady with dark brown hair combed back and held together with a barrette, indicated that she was ready to take us to all the interesting places in Vilnius.

I had read several books about Lithuania, and had learned that in late 1890s, Jews had made up 40% of the population of Vilnius. By 1916, it had increased to 43.5%. Seven years later it had dropped to one third of the total population, probably because of immigration to America, to approximately 55,000 out of a total population of 165,000. The city had produced many famous scholars, writers and artists, among them the famous violinist Jasha Heifetz, born in Vilnius in 1901.

Vilnius had two ghettos during the war. A small one and the large one, just a short distance from our hotel in, what is considered today, the Old Town. Winding narrow streets were faced with dilapidated buildings. Those twisting roads took us finally to both ghettos. Here and there, we found tablets affixed to a building commemorating people and events. One such plaque indicated that Jasha Heifetz, had attended this school of music from 1905 to 1909. Then there was a street named Gaono, after the famous Gaon (meaning genius), Rabbi Elijah ben Shlomo Zalman, the world-renowned rabbi of the eighteenth century. Another building had a plaque indicating that 1,200 Jews had been killed in this ghetto. I stopped at an archway with ornately carved wooden doors and walked into the courtyard of the building. Cracked walls and chipped plaster greeted me as I stood on the rough cobblestones. My mind raced. What had transpired behind those walls in the numerous apartments crowded with humanity? I imagined I could hear babies crying, a mother singing softly to her sick child, the sound of cooking utensils as the women prepared the evening meal.

On the way back to our hotel, we passed the large Opera and Ballet Theater. We asked Regina if she could join us for a ballet scheduled to be performed in a couple of days. As she accepted our invitation, she said, "Follow me to the other side of the building," starting to walk in that direction, and continued, "See these steps? Look closely and you will see that these steps are built up with gravestones from the Jewish cemetery." I bent over and could discern the faint imprints of Jewish writings, the names of the deceased. It was a disturbing ending to the day.

At the hotel, Regina told us to be ready early in the morning for the trip to Kovno. "Henrich Kostanian will be our driver," she informed us. "It should take about one hour to drive there."

That evening in Vilnius before our trip to Kovno the next day, I decided to read all the most recent letters and correspondence again concerning my family in 1941. I had brought a file folder full of copies of these documents, realizing I needed to prepare myself for this last leg of the journey into the past. I needed solitude for this and waited until Robert and I had finished dinner. Alone in my room, I pulled out this file and began to read.

Munich

The world is too dangerous to live in—not because of the people who do evil, but because of the people who sit and let it happen.

—*Albert Einstein*

München, 6 November 1941

From: Carola Koppel
Thierschstrasse 7/III
Munich

My dear, dearest Carlo!

Today, I can confirm to you your two letters, namely of 3rd and 10th October. The one from the 10th came even earlier than the other one. I am very disappointed about the news from Washington. Regrettably, I received today a similar communication from the American General Consul in Barcelona. They are only responsible for people in their own area, in Spain, and are not allowed to give me a confirmation that they would issue me a visa for America upon arrival in Barcelona. It can only be done upon an expressly issued advice from Washington. They don't see any way at this time to help and wrote that we would have to await a better situation in Europe. All very polite nothings and no help. The lack of understanding for our situation from all people is simply incomprehensible. When the help comes too late, then it is after all not necessary anymore.

I am at this time completely without hope for our emigration and believe it has no purpose that you even keep on working on it. You only spend money unnecessarily. At this time, emigration permission is impossible since all five of us fall within the blocked ages of years. Therefore, we have to wait first for a change of this. There would have to be a miracle for this to happen.

By the way, I hear it is also possible that another type of emigration will happen to us very soon. The trip route would be for a part the same as you made in your time when you left for the United States which is to the East and the Baltic States or maybe Poland. I don't know any details yet. Rachel Cohn, Braunschweigers, Miss Heymann, Mr. Less and acquaintances of Lene (my father's sister in Frankfurt) have now visited Magda Reis since they came to the same area. (These were people who seemed to have been crowded into a "Judenhaus," a Jewish house in Hamburg).

Also, Bernhard and Siete, both in Hamburg had an intention to flee over the border, but for the time, they decided against it. (Did she mean that the two brothers wanted to escape over the border or was it the order for transport to the east?) However, if and when they will decide to execute it, you will hear about it. By the way, did you receive both my certified letters? However, it is now without purpose.

I am working very hard at my job. I leave the house at seven in the morning and come back in the evening the earliest at half past seven. Then, I still have to do most of the necessary things for the household, wash dishes, sew, wash clothes and iron, write letters and so forth. Therefore, you should not be angry with me when I don't write as promptly as you are used to. I have, of course, far too little sleep and it is fortunate that the three little children are in the Antonienheim (the Jewish children's home). I couldn't handle the children on top of all this. Günther goes to bed in the evening already at eight since he is always so tired from his strenuous work. For me, the worst part is the long walk…after all, I have to walk two hours every day and you can surely imagine how my legs look.

Our Old Anna (the household help from years ago) lives now at Schwindstrasse 3; remember it! (We never learned if my mother left some valuable items with her for safekeeping).

At the moment, I am sorting my suitcases because I will not be able to take all of them along. If only I knew where to put the bed covers in case of emergency. Now I need the bed sacks which I gave along with Alfred and Walter for America. One does everything incorrectly.

You do have all our papers with you in New York, such as birth certificates, marriage certificate, engagement certificate, and so forth. Also the affidavits which you, if necessary, can photocopy and get notarized through the German Consulate there. That is very important. If we find ourselves in the same situation as Leo and Edie (the brothers of my father who fled Germany to France in 1939 without any papers and were interned there) it can not be helped if we then do not have all the documents. You will surely do everything correctly.

Have you found a new and nice apartment already? Advise me of a new address via a telegram so that, in case of emergency, I am not without your address. Now comes the most important date namely the congratulation for your birthday. This is the fourth birthday since we have been separated. I must not even think about this. In any case, I wish you from the depth of my heart all the imaginable good things. May all our longings and wishes materialize and, with God's help, we will be soon united again. That is what I pray for night and day.

By this time, my father had been In New York over a year and a half. The reason my mother talks about having been separated from each other for four birthdays, is that in the year of 1938, my father spent his birthday in the Dachau concentration camp. Similarly, in 1939 he was incarcerated in Stadelheim prison in Munich the next birthday. Birthdays three and four, of course, were 'celebrated' in New York inasmuch he had been forced to leave Munich in 1940.

The three little ones are, thank God, doing well in the Antonienheim with all the other children. They have acclimated themselves there quite well because now they are among many children there. Regrettably, I can visit them only very little since to walk to the home is a great distance and very strenuous. But, I know that they are well taken care of and telephone them on many occasions.

I am pleased with my work at the Jewish Community offices, but it is very hard work. Hechinger gave me a comparatively spacious work place, in the 'Statistics and Apartment Spaces' department, and I have very much to do. But I am pleased with it and I am happy when I don't have to think about things during the day. It is quite good there even when, at times, one does not feel like doing it.

Mr. Karse does honorary work here, in case you see two return names on the envelope; you don't have to worry about it. In the morning, when I leave the house, the post office is not open yet and in the evening, it is already closed. For that reason, if I can not get away sometimes during the day, I give the letter to someone, such as Mr. Karse, for mailing.

I hope you have good news from Denver about Alfred. Walter has not written in some time. Günther is all right, thank God. He is really tall and thin—no wonder. The care Alfred receives in Denver, Colorado would do Günther much good. At his age, the body needs quite a few extra nourishments that he is not able to receive.

Now, I must close the letter to you. I still want to write Lola, Bernhard and Lene so that one has mutual signs of life from the loved ones; otherwise, one becomes so scared. And now I must go to bed or else I won't be able to get up in the morning. So, regards for Alfred and Walter, Hannah and everybody else in New York.

To you, my dearest Carlo, always the deepest regards and many, many heartfelt kisses,

> Your unending loving little wife,
> Carla

PS The longing preys on me and only the thought that I must be here for the children keeps me going.

I could barely go on reading the next few letters after I had read of my mother's desperation and loneliness. She was crying out for help. She was clinging onto the letters with news from her brother-in-law and sisters-in-law. Although there was no chance of physical contact, or talking to one another, the letters seemed to give her some semblance of comfort. She knew the departure from her home was imminent, sorting her suitcases and getting ready for this "evacuation."

The day after my mother's last letter to her husband, the Munich branch office of the Reich Organization of the Jews in Germany, which was located at the Jewish Community Office, had sent out a notice to all the Jews in Munich about an evacuation.

ISRAELITISCHE KULTUSGEMEINDE
MUNICH
BRANCH OFFICE OF THE REICH
ORGANIZATION
OF JEWS IN GERMANY

Munich, the 7th November 1941

Lindwurmstrasse 125, Rückgebäude.
Mr/Mrs/Miss Carla Koppel
Thierschstrasse 7/III
Munich

Subject: EVACUATION

According to an order from the Secret Statepolice (GESTAPO)—Statepolice Headquarters—Munich, we must advise you that you and the below mentioned family members have been selected for an Evacuation Transport.

At the same time, you are herewith obligated, together with the below mentioned selected persons to the Transport—beginning: Tuesday, the 11th November 1941, to keep yourself ready at your current accommodations and not leave without special permission from the authority, not even temporarily.

Any attempt to oppose the resettlement or to circumvent it, is pointless and can lead to serious consequences for the persons concerned. In case older family members wish to join your transport voluntarily, it must be reported to us for forwarding to the authorities.

Completing the above order, we advise you additionally of the following:

Every Transport participant may take along luggage up to 50 kg (110 lbs), packed in either:

2 suitcases or 1 rucksack and 1 suitcase (it must be realized that the Transport participants, at times, must carry the luggage themselves).

In any case, to be taken along:

Warm outer and regular clothes, underclothes, shoes, a little wash basin, a pail for washing clothes, blankets, travel provisions, eating utensils (only plate, cup and spoons—no knives and forks), featherbeds (only for children).

An outline of the most important items of necessity is enclosed.

Every Transport participant is to take along RM50 (Reichsmark). Surplus money, securities, deposit slips, and other bank identifications are all to be taken along in an envelope which must have on it names and index of all the contents. In addition, the enclosed Wealth Register Form, as per order of 10th November 1941, must be filled out completely and brought along in a special unsealed envelope.

Personal documents of all sorts, emigration papers, identity cards and passports, food ration cards, are to be taken along as well.

Details will be conveyed to you either through us or the authorities.

The behavior of our members, as shown in the prescribed labor operations, have proven that through a community spirit, all the difficult obligations can be solved. We are, therefore, justified in the hope that on the occasion of the evacuation, the affected persons will face the ordered evacuation in an orderly manner.

> Carola Sarah Koppel–mother
> Günther Israel Koppel–son
> Hans Israel Koppel–son
> Ruth Sarah Koppel–daughter
> Judis Sarah Koppel–daughter

The following is a register of items to be considered for choosing to take along, considering the weight limitation and fact that it may be necessary to carry luggage yourself.

Items, which will be necessary during the journey and immediately after arrival, are to be packed in rucksack or in the second suitcase.

1. General

Bedsheets (possibly sleeping bag)

Hand towels

Dish clothes

Scouring cloths

Dust cloths

1 pillow Blankets (as many as owned)

Toilet items

Comb and brush

Clothes brush

Eyeglasses (reserve)

Writing paper, envelopes, pencils

Fountain pen, prayer book, etc.

Briefcase, money purse, chestbag

Card games

Important Papers

Birth certificates, wedding papers

Emigration papers

Identity cards–passports

1 piece of soap

Tooth brush and paste

Wash cloth

One wash powder

Shampoo

"Tempo" handkerchiefs (pocket tissue)

Nail file

Toilet paper

Shopping bag

Medication: none except

Frostbite salve

School reports

Address materials

Passport photos

Food ration cards

Handkerchiefs

Shawl

Laundry bag

Shoe laces

Ear muffs

Baldrian (valerian)

2. Women

Body powder

First aid dressing

Apron

Sewing Materials: (no scissors)

Thread and sewing yarn

Buttons

Safety pins

Rubber bands

House shoes

Cooking and Eating Utensils

Tumbler

Thermos

Travel cutlery

Bread box

Bread bag

Spirit stove with hard spirit

Cleaning rags

Dresses (winter and summer)

Occupational dresses

Pullover or knit jacket

Costume

Raincoat

Winter overcoat

Shoes or high shoes

Overshoes

Day shirts

Panties

Nightgowns or pajamas

Underclothes

Stockings, wool socks

Gloves

Girdle, garters

Brassieres

Sanitary napkins, cotton

Flashlight with reserve batteries

Hat, head scarf

Candles, matches, lighter

Insect powder

3. Men

Rope, leather strap	Suits
Pocket tools	Work pants
Haircutting machine	Overalls
Clock (alarm)	Work aprons
Pullover or knit jacket	Training suit
Winter overcoat	Raincoat or wind jacket
Shoes or high top shoes	House shoes
Hose or socks	Day shirts
Collar, ties	Undershirts
Undershorts	Nightgowns or pajamas
Winter gloves	Shaving brush and soap
Suspenders	Sock holders
Spats	Cap, hat
Collar buttons, etc.	

Deceptions, deceptions! Through the Jewish Community organization, the Gestapo tried to convey to the unsuspecting Jews that the "Evacuation" would be something quite ordinary hence, the long list of items to be taken along on this journey to the East. The evacuation to Riga, Latvia was a concentration camp destination, not a resettlement into houses in this strange land.

I felt the need to continue to read the letters in preparation for the trip to Kovno tomorrow. I was not sure how I would find the strength for this trip. The next letter from my mother was the most upsetting one. Apparently, she was confined to the apartment in Munich unable to walk to the post office to send a letter to her husband overseas in New York. Instead, she sent the following local letter to my aunt Lola in Berlin to be forwarded to my father in New York.

From: Carola Koppel
Munich

To: Hannah Koppel   10th November 1941
Brooklyn, New York
USA

My beloved Carlo and dear Hannah!

When I send this letter to Hannah's address in New York, instead of my husband's address in New York, you surely know that it signifies something special. This is the last letter that I can write from Munich since all of us will go on a journey tomorrow. I can not communicate any new address to you, but will do so as soon as it is possible. Lola from Berlin will obtain information here for you and keep you posted. You don't have to worry about me. At first, I was totally in despair, but now I have calmed down; one never receives more difficulties and burdens than one can bear. After all, I am in great company so that I can always receive help and support. There are, among others, the two children's teachers Kissingers (uncles of Dr. Henry Kissinger), also teachers Stern and Adler, the van Wiens, Adlers from the second floor in our apartment house and Miss Stiller, Miss Gutmann, Gertrude Schaeffer, Fritz Hermann, Abels and so forth.

I just received a post card from Bernhard in Hamburg. He and Ulli have, together with their friends Rachel Cohn, Sommers, Braunschweigers and others, departed Thursday also on a journey. My big wish would be that I will at least still receive mail from you. I have all my papers with me, also the passports. If necessary, you can have photocopies made in New York. Now, there simply must be finally ways and means because I have to be on top of everything.

I am unable to write Hochfelds in Los Angeles anymore; you are undoubtedly in communication with them. By the way, Mrs. Oberndorfer will also travel with us. She is very agitated since she still has no news from her daughter that her child had arrived overseas.

The children are, thank God, well and will help all of us pass the time. Now I will have to close since I have much work ahead of me. Always think about us. To all of you, heartiest regards and do what you can. Also regards for Hochfelds. For the boys many hearty regards. Hopefully, Alfred will soon be well again.

Now, my dear Carlo and also my dear Hannah, my deepest regards and many, many kisses from your loving you very much and having unending longing for you.

 Your little wife

Carla

PS Friedl and Lotte (wife of Siete and her sister from Hamburg) visited us today; you will get the mail as soon as it is possible and the opportunity allows.

Please write Hochfelds in Los Angeles. Günther is still on the go, shopping. I am so glad that I have him with me.

The Journey

Dr. Andreas Heusler of the city of Munich archives advised me that my mother and Günther were taken away from the apartment in the Thierschstrasse in a furniture wagon about the middle of November 1941. Undoubtedly the other tenants of the apartment house were transported at the same time to a camp called Milbertshofen located in the northern area of Munich. Alfred Hartmann, an eyewitness, reported late in 1941, during an investigative proceeding against Gestapo officials, as to what happened after the arrival of people in this camp called Milbertshofen:

> "After their arrival at the camp and shown to the barracks, the luggage was collected and examined by officials of the Gestapo for weapons, jewelry and the like. In addition, a physical examination was performed on them. During these examinations on all the people, there occurred at times ugly scenes, since things were arbitrarily taken from the existing luggage of the "emigrants" which, obviously, because of high value, were held back without cause during the search by the Gestapo officials. One could imagine where these articles disappeared to."

About one thousand Jews had arrived at Milbertshofen from various Jewish Houses from all over Munich. Gestapo officials not only supervised the arrivals as described in the eyewitness' report, but also bore down on this mass of intimidated humanity. Chaos must have reigned. My mother must have been frantic because there was no sign of her three little children from the Antonienheim, the children's home.

Other parents had their children with them, most of them crying, not understanding what was happening. After the humiliating searches, the shouting by the officials, the despairing men, women and children were assigned to various barracks.

Erwin Weil, another eyewitness, described the period leading up to the conversion of this collection camp Milbertshofen in the northern part of Munich:

> "There came an order that Jews had to give up their fur coats, overcoats, skis, cameras and so forth. We had to contact the older people with bicycle and hand wagon and deliver these items to the Kaulbachstrasse, to the old age home there in Munich, which was the collection point for these items. All these items were then picked up.

> "In the summer 1941, on order of SS *ObersturmFührer* (Lieutenant Colonel) Muckler stated that I had to report to Knorrstrasse 148 (location of camp Milbertshofen) with four companions. We saw there for the first time that a barrack camp had been built but had no idea for the purpose of it. We had to put insulation under the roofs of the barracks, which was difficult, because there was little room between the ceilings and the flat roofs.

> "Early November, we were sent by the Jewish Community Administration of Munich to the freight railroad station of Milbertshofen to load potatoes, vegetables and coal into railroad wagons. It was said it was for the Jews to be evacuated to Poland. Shortly thereafter, an order came from Muckler that five of us were to report to the Knorrstrasse, to the Milbertshofen camp, at seven in the morning. It was a dismal, overcast November day as we arrived at the barrier of the entrance to the camp. Just beyond the barrier were several SS men. The grassy place surrounded by the wooden barracks was empty. Then Muckler appeared with his band of Gestapo and shortly thereafter, the first freight trucks full with women, men and children, suitcases and other bags arrived. We had to help with the unloading and the delivery of suitcases into the barrack next to the entry

of the camp. In the middle of that barrack was a big room that contained a scale. The suitcases and bags were placed on the scale; I don't know how many kilograms were allowed but, at any rate, a chaotic and humiliating shouting and screaming went on. Everything, of course, was too heavy according to these beasts and with devilish smirks and obvious pleasure things were thrown out of the baggage without rhyme or reason. A huge mountain of dresses, suits, shoes and so forth piled up. They then had to go to the barracks with the rest of their belongings. The barracks were outfitted with double-deck wooden plank beds without mattresses or straw sacks. There came truck after truck. We recognized many people; in fact, there were some relatives of mine. We could still, under great danger, take out some letters, money and jewelry and bring these to the addresses given to us.

"On the third day at Milberthofen, we were not allowed to leave this collection camp.

"We lay down for a while until the SS men screamed, 'Everybody up and out.' One thousand people had to line up before the barracks on the muddy earth caused by heavy rains."

These two eyewitnesses gave the chilling accounts of what happened before and during the "evacuation" of the one thousand Munich Jews. Here is the continuation of the report of Mr. Hartmann.

"At the time of the removal to Riga (Latvia), especially sharp measures were employed in order to prevent attempts to flee. Two days before the removal to Riga, the usually permanent guards consisting of camp residents or camp laborers of the entrance to the camp, were now occupied by the SS. Until the removal to Riga, patrols were used inside and outside of the camp fence, partly through 'protection' guards, SS men, and partly through so-called supervising orderlies who were taken from the Jews who were not to be transported. These were in the camp for forced labor and whom the state police threatened with the strongest measures if any of the 'emigrants' were to flee because of their negligence.

"At four in the morning on November 20, 1941, after coffee had been prepared at two in the morning, the 'emigrants' were escorted in pouring rain under the cover of strongest military contingent, a full SS company, to march to the railroad station. All the luggage and boxes had already been taken to the waiting train by a special forced labor detail. After carrying out the loud commando 'load up,' the departure from the camp began. The site, usually blacked out by order, was exceptionally brightly lit by many searchlights. Under the accompaniment of the SS, they were marched to the freight railroad station at Milbertshofen twenty minutes away."

Weil continues:

"The masses of people had to march through streets blocked by the SS to the railroad freight terminal. We helped as best as we could, to help the old people, bent over, with the lugging of their suitcases. One old woman's shoe became stuck in the mud. In the same moment that I came to her to help her, she collapsed. She was dead. 'Go on, go on,' yelled the guards, 'let her lie here.'

"At the freight railroad station stood a train billowing steam into the air from its locomotive. We had to help to load the luggage and the people into the compartments, which soon was not possible because the compartments began to be crowded with twice as many people as they had seats.

"Slowly, it got lighter in the sky, and then, a terrible screaming by the sadists guards Muckler, Pfeiffer and others, 'Push the people in and throw the luggage out.' The people however insisted on keeping their luggage. A horrible chaotic scene played out in the compartments. The SS men pushed the doors shut with force. The tortured people screamed and cried, but we could do nothing for them.

"Then, a bus arrived with armed SS people who brought the little children from the Antonienheim. We had to put them up into the train. We attempted to ameliorate their fear—it was dreadful. I shall never forget this moment. I have never heard anything of the people on this transport to the east. Does anyone know what happened to them? And what actually happened with these beasts Muckler, Pfeiffer and so forth after the war?"

The next few weeks were a total void. No one knew what happened to my mother and the four children since my mother wrote her last letter dated November 10, 1941. My father's sister Lola in Berlin attempted a 'last resort' communication, always exuding a ray of hope.

From: Lola Goldschmidt
Thomasisusstrasse 14
Berlin   17th November 1941

To: Carlo, Hanna and Walter
233 Rogers Avenue
Brooklyn, New York

We are waiting in vain for the last three weeks for a letter from you. Surely, it is not your fault because we believe that you have written.

By the time this letter arrives in New York, you will probably already have a letter from Lene (Sister in Frankfurt) which will give you a foretaste of what is happening. Bernhard and Ulli were resettled to Minsk about fourteen days ago together with Hermann S., family, and many others. That caused a lot of work and it is too bad that one could not help them, exactly how one could not help Carla and the children. Günther had to work outside for some time and from the place where they were for several days (the Milbertshofen camp in Munich), they will then be transported further. As soon as we have an address, we will make it known to you and Carla will, of course, also write herself. The little children were last in the Antonienheim and they are all right. Carla is a smart and courageous woman. This week or next, Sine (wife of Leo Koppel from Hamburg) and son Werner will also be going away. When you write Kurt in Canada, tell him about his parents Bernhard and Ulli. I will write him and also Helmut (Kurt's brother) in Haifa. We have almost daily mail from Lene and Max. By the way, how is Alfred? Do you have good news from him? We shall write to him shortly.

What is happening at school in the big city of New York, dear Walter? Is it going somewhat better? And who do you think was here earlier? The Olm! (the former domestic help of Lola in Berlin). She needed a cooking pot and asked if I had a spare one. Well, and then she wanted to know much about all of you.

Dear Carlo, the main thing is that you have already a new apartment. Tell us immediately your new address. How is your business? Do work hard so that all of us later can live from that. Here, the weather turned to winter early. It is cold and uncomfortable.

I am now waiting for news from Carla which, to be sure, will take a lot of time. Do write to us very soon. I hope that all of you are well and it goes well for Hannah. We are still waiting for pictures.

Now for today, I don't know anything else to report. Anyhow, this letter became very difficult for me to write. Remain well, that is the most important thing, and for today, many hearty regards from

Your,

Lola

Many hearty regards to all of you,

Your Joseph.

Lola's letter apparently did not arrive in New York until sometime in December 1941.

Things were happening at a fast pace now. The only family members left in Germany in late November were Lola and Joseph Goldschmidt in Berlin, Lene and Max Oettinger in Frankfurt and Siete Koppel and his wife Friedl in Hamburg. The news of all of the deportations of family members had not yet made an impact on my father because of the slow mail deliveries. My father and others were still feverishly working to get his family out of the clutches of the Nazis.

Note that this following letter by Carl Koppel dated November 19, 1941 was sent to the State Department before the receipt of his sister Lola's letter from Berlin, dated November 17, 1941.

From: Carl Koppel
233 Rogers Avenue
Brooklyn, New York

To: Department of State   November 19, 1941
Visa Division
Washington, D.C.   Re: VD 811.11 Carl Koppel

Gentlemen,

I refer to the letter you have written to the Honorable Senator Richard B. Russell on September 23rd, 1941. I refer to certain sentences in your letter that reads as follows:

"The case should not be taken up with the Department, the Visa Division"

"...or had made actual travel arrangements, and in this connection, have assurances that they will be granted exit permits and transit visas to enable them to proceed to the country where they will apply for American visas"

I therefore inform you that I have received notice from my wife in Germany that definite travel arrangements have been made. She has a definite confirmation from the Spanish Consulate in Munich, as per enclosed letter, that her transit will be permitted through Spain if she can show some kind of confirmation from an American Consulate in Spain that her visa may be granted upon her appearance at that Consulate. I also enclose a letter from the American Embassy in Berlin suggesting that I may communicate with your Department in this case.

It appears to me now that all of your requirements have been met. Inasmuch as you know the very tragic situation of my case, I sincerely hope that something can be done now so that they can report to the American Consul in Barcelona or Madrid for the final examination. All I ask of your Department now is to instruct one of your Consulates in Spain to communicate with my wife in Munich, Germany and inform her that upon her appearance at that Consulate, her visa application will be taken up again. This would be sufficient for the Spanish Consulate in Munich to grant my wife and the children the transit visas.

I sincerely hope, Gentlemen, that this favor can be granted to me in order to enable me to receive my wife and the children in the United States. May I also point out that steamship tickets have been bought and paid for and reservations that had been cancelled were renewed again.

Awaiting your favorable reply, I am

Sincerely Yours,

Carl Koppel

The State Department obviously was not about to convey any instructions to issue visas to the consulates in Spain. Mr. Judell had already alluded and commented about this in his letter to my father after he tried to petition the State Department on June 30, 1941. At that time, he had learned about the secret agreement with Germany.

My father in Brooklyn as well as his uncle in California and others in the USA had no inkling as to what was happening in Germany, as evidenced by the following letter.

From: Siegfried Hochfeld
4417 Santa Monica Blvd.
Los Angeles, California   30 November 1941

Dear Carlo!

I am writing this in bed. I have a very painful inflammation in my back for several days, but am somewhat better today.

Just now, Mr. Newmark (a friend in California) was here and brought us the letter, which I have enclosed for you. I answered that letter today. Please go immediately to Mrs. Zamkin at the National Refugee Service in New York personally with this letter and don't let them intimidate you as happened before. We have to be grateful that someone like Newmark worries about this matter and gets involved. I know from experience that one must always go on and speak up.

In a hurry, with regards to all of you,

Your Uncle (Siegfried)

Will write Carla tomorrow

This is a continuation of the letter from my uncle Siegfried Hochfeld in Los Angeles to the National Refugee Service in New York.

National Refugee Service
Migration Department
New York, NY
Attention: Mrs. F. A. Zamkin
National Refugee Service

Dear Mrs. Zamkin

Mr. Newmark brought me your kind letter you sent to him, and asked me to give you an answer.

Mr. Koppel's wife is the only child of my wife's late sister (Selma Wagner). Her father died when she was one and a half years old and we took her mother (Selma Wagner) and child (Carla Koppel) to us. She grew up with our only child, son Rolf, like a brother and sister. You can imagine that we can not be really happy until that time when this niece of ours and her sweet children have arrived in the U.S.A.

We are so happy to know that this case is in your and Mr. Newmark's hands and are thankful for your assistance to Mr. Koppel.

The name and address of Mr. Koppel is as follows:

Carl Koppel 233 Rogers Avenue, Brooklyn, New York

The following family members of Mr. Koppel are stuck in Munich

Carola Koppel   born May 18, 1903 Munich
Günther Koppel born March 6, 1924 Munich
Hans Koppel   born January 9, 1936 Munich
Ruth Koppel   born August 11, 1937 Munich
Judis Koppel   born August 18, 1939 Munich

Carla and the four children are all still living in Munich, Germany. Carla and Günther were living in the building designated as a "Jewish building" at the Thierschstrasse 7 address. The three youngest ones, Hans, Ruth and Judis, had been put into the Jewish children's home called the Antonian Home. Both are locations within Munich

I sent your letter of November 26 to Mr. Koppel in Brooklyn and he will see you as soon as possible. We arrived here fifteen months ago, so we are newcomers and you will kindly excuse mistakes in this letter.

Best regards,
Sincerely yours,
Siegfried Hochfeld

The following letter from my brother Walter living at home wirh his father in Brooklyn must have been the first inkling my father had that something terrible must have happened. Walter wrote to our mother in Munich on December 2, 1941. His letter was returned many weeks later as undeliverable.

From: Walter Koppel
233 Rogers Avenue
Brooklyn, New York   New York, December 2, 1941

To: Carla Koppel and the four Brothers and Sisters
Thierschstrasse 7
Munich, Germany

All my Dears,

In order to write again, I must take some time. It's classy writing this on our typewriter (What irony! Here, Walter innocently mentions using his typewriter just when my mother's typewriter had been confiscated a short time ago).

I always have much to write about, but when I sit down to write, I don't know anything anymore. I like school very much. Also, I speak English quite well. In fact, I can hardly speak German anymore. I <u>even</u> receive good grades. I am in class 7-A which is pretty advanced. You probably thought I was going to be in Kindergarten. There is much homework to be done. For me, that's, of course, very difficult. I already read English books. I always thought that I would never be able to learn English, but it goes better than one thinks. I eat a lot here! (This was another innocent sentence on the part of Walter. Little did he realize how much that last five word sentence must have hurt!).

The enclosed was letter received from Aunt Lola in Berlin. She asks Walter how is it going with your school in Brooklyn?

And how about my friend Sänger in Munich; show him all my letters. He could write to me sometime. Are all my things gone? What do your sub-renters do?

Now, Mutti, how are the little ones and how goes it with your job? We have not had any mail from you for a long time. Have you received all my letters? Write to me often…I just love to receive mail.

Today, there is a big exception—no homework! Did I leave anything out from my trip report? Please reply to everything. Regrettably, Papa is not here right now but he will add onto this letter later. I have started to save money in our school bank. Have now one dollar in it. I go to movies now and then; nice movies. Regrettably, I can't go too often.

Tomorrow, Aunt Hanna is coming to us and maybe she will add to this letter. Günther probably has very little time to write.

Now I have written a lot. This page is already full and I don't know any more, only nonsense which is of no interest to you.

Just now, I was at the barber for a haircut. It always costs so much money—40 cents! Now I really know almost nothing more.

So, many regards and kisses.

Your loving son,
Walter

The return of Walter's letter by the post office was a very ominous sign for my father who continued to attempt to get his family out of Germany. His only accomplishments were setback after setback.

From Department of State
Visa Division
Washington, D.C.   December 3, 1941
 In reply refer to VD 811.111 Koppel, Carl

To: Mr. Carl Koppel
233 Rogers Avenue
Brooklyn, New York

Dear Mr. Koppel:

With reference to you letter of November 19, 1941 regarding the visa cases of your wife and children, now in Germany, it appears that their entry into Spain is contingent upon the assurance that they will receive immigration visas at an American Consulate in Spain.

In this connection, you are advised that no assurance may be given that an alien will receive a visa at an American Consular office until he appears in person and is found upon examination to qualify in all respects under our immigration laws.

I regret my inability to furnish you more favorable information at this time but I shall be glad to advise you regarding the further procedure to be followed in presenting their cases if you will inform me subsequently where your wife and children will apply for visas in the event definite arrangements are made for their departure from Germany and their entry into Spain or some other country.

Sincerely yours,
M. Warren
   Chief, Visa Division

Mr. Warren's letter was *Chutzpah*—shameless audacity to the nth degree. The State Department was not about to hand out any visas. No assurance for a visa maybe given until they appear in person at an American Consulate in Spain, he stated. How was she going to appear in Spain when the Spanish authorities required evidence of an entry visa to America first prior to issuing a Spanish transit visa? The Spanish government would allow entry into their country through a transit visa only if they had absolute assurance of an American entry visa that would permit a continuation to the United States. And an entry visa from Washington could not be issued unless one appeared in person at the foreign American consulate!

Mr. Warren magnanimously explained he would be glad to advise my mother when he learns where my mother would apply for visas for definite arrangements for departure from Germany. He failed to state that all American Consulates had been closed since July 1, 1941. All dealings, documents and so on had to be handled by the State Department in Washington. He further failed to state that the Visa Department had quit issuing entry visas since July 1, 1941. This was already indicated in Herman Judell's letter to my father as far back as in June 30, 1941.

My father's next letter to his wife was dated December 8, 1941 and postmarked December 10. Even at this date, he had no inkling of the horrendous situation that had developed in Munich. This letter was returned to him four months later with the remark: "Service suspended. Return to sender." No one was able to explain to my father what was going on in Germany with his family.

From Carl Koppel
233 Rogers Avenue
Brooklyn, New York   December 8, 1941

My dear little Carla:

Now the fifth week begins already and there is no mail from you. This upsets me very much inasmuch as I don't know the reason. I fervently hope that something arrives from you tomorrow and I shall then add the confirmation of arrival to this letter. I hope that you received my several letters and I long for your reply to them. Mr. Kochenthaler had already a letter from Munich of November 11. Your last letter was dated October 24 and our own Uncle Siegfried had a letter from Munich dated as late as October 30. I will try to pull together the money for Cuba and can hope that I will be able to accomplish this, because it is the only way.

Also today, nothing arrived and I really don't know what to make of it. My thoughts are with all of you day and night and have no interest for anything anymore. The newest developments did nothing to improve my mood. Alfred writes often and is, thank God, quite well. The doctor is very satisfied. Alfred has new wishes all the times which I fulfill contingent upon the size of my billfold.

Enclosed are letters for Bernhard and Lola.

How do you like your job and can you stand it? What are the little ones doing? What are Günther's times for his job? One does not know what will happen with Cuba. At this time, I have only one third of the money. I hope it will not be too late. I would love to have a good picture of you but, in all probability, this is not possible. The only diversion for me is the cinema; otherwise, I do not go anywhere. I spoke with Dr. Levison, our pediatrician from Altona; he will visit me sometime.

Now, I am nearly one and a half years away from you; the loneliness is overwhelming. Walter has grown a lot and is still the big "Schmoozer." (the affectionate and ingratiating type talker). Alfred is already nearly five months in Denver in the hospital. How time flies! How are you health wise? I miss you so much and without you I can not begin anything of substance because I don't know if I will remain in New York or, because of Alfred is out west in Colorado, may migrate to the West.

We always eat at six in the evening. Mornings and evenings I prepare myself and at lunchtime, we eat at Max's. Our apartment is being admired by all, but the furniture is missing. What we do not have now, we may have in the future. To buy anything now has no purpose when one does not know for sure if we shall stay here in New York—aside from the money problem. I have a very difficult time writing because of my restlessness and can only write in detail when I receive mail from you again. I am sending this letter right away. Should I receive mail from you tomorrow or the next few days, I will write again. So, my dearest Carla, please carry on with corresponding so that I will always know what is happening with you.

To the children and you my most affectionate regards and kisses.

To you, with great longing and much love and always thinking of you and living for you,

Carlo

Just now, your mail of October 30 and November 6 arrived and I am so relieved to have a sign of life from you. The possibility to leave via Cuba I have to doubt. The next few days will probably clear things up. You can imagine my mood relating to this. I will write to you again the end of the week contingent upon that things will still work out which I very much hope they will.

So, for today, again regards and kisses

Your

Carlo

I am so happy to have finally received mail from you!

Mail service from Germany became even slower in late 1941. It took four and five weeks for my mother's letters to arrive in New York. Much had happened in those four to five weeks and no one in America really knew yet the earth-shaking events that were developing in Germany.

Finally, some of the news leaked out. One of the earlier ones was a letter from an engineer named Wolfer in Switzerland to my mother's aunt Else Hochfeld in Los Angeles.

From Ing. R. Wolfer
Beethovenstrasse 45
Zurich Switzerland Zurich, the 15th December 1941

Representation for Firma C. Rompel, Munich
and Traugott Golde in Gera
Ray and Electro-medical Apparatuses

To: Mrs. Elsa Hochfeld
4417 Santa Monica Boulevard
Los Angeles, California

Dear Mrs. Hochfeld,

I am only now able to get to reply to your letter of the 10th of October 1941 and, regrettably, have to report to you, after I had the opportunity to speak with our mutual friends, the following:

Maybe you already heard of the last events, if not, I report that Mrs. Koppel, as well as the children, are not in Munich anymore. On November 11, they, with 1,000 people departed Munich. Until now, one does not know the destination. One speaks of Riga, mentions also Litzmannstadt (Lodz, Poland) or Lemberg. That these are not ideal places to live, is self-evident.

The matter would be different after, as you write, support is at hand through Washington. As said before, one does not know where your relatives are today.

Your acquaintances have surely done everything themselves that was within their power, but against this matter they were powerless. Besides, it was very dangerous for them. At this moment, it is not possible to establish any remittance even from here or else I would have been glad to come up with some for Mrs. Koppel

The conditions in your former homeland have, through these events, changed very much. My relatives are glad that they and their loved ones got away in time, even with great struggle. I hope that things will change in the world and peace will come.

With my best regards, also for your relatives,

Yours,

R. Wolfer

Lithuania

*A wise man once said, All that is
necessary for the triumph of evil is for
enough good men to do nothing.
—Unknown*

In 1995, I had sent a letter to the Lord Mayor of Munich asking for help in my research regarding the destiny of my family. A response came from a Dr. Heusler of the Munich City Archive, who sent me the following letter which I had brought with me to Lithuania.

From: 27. June 1995
Landeshauptstadt München
Dr. Andreas Heusler
Stadtarchiv München
Winzerstrasse 68
München

To:
Mr. Alfred Koppel
1219 Ticonderoga Drive
Fort Collins, Colorado 80525
USA

Research into the History of the Koppel Family

Dear Mr. Koppel,

Your letter to the Lord Mayor was forwarded to our organization. Based on your information we were able to determine further information regarding the destiny of your family. We are terribly sorry to convey to you today that there exists a high probability your mother, brothers and sisters were deported to the East and during the transport, were murdered. Our records show that the transport left Munich on the 20th of November 1941 with approximately 1,000 men, women and children from Munich to Riga. However, the transport did not arrive in Riga. On the 25th of November 1941 all these 1,000 people were murdered by machine guns by members of *Einsatzgruppe* A (special Action Group A) in Kaunas (Kovno), Lithuania. Nothing is known of any survivors.

We also feel that a reconstruction of individual destinies is necessary in order to attempt to picture the unbelievable dimension of the Holocaust. We want to support you with your effort to write the story of your family. So long as it is possible, we shall be pleased to answer any questions you may have and help you with any problems.

Enclosed is a copy of the Deportation list of 15th November 1941 (a portion of it) and also information about your parents, brothers and sisters, as the City Archive could ascertain it).

With friendly regards,
Dr. Andreas Heusler

Attachments:
The List of deportees
The information about my family

MUNICH, the 15th NOVEMBER 1941
GESTAPO
EVACUATION OF JEWS TO
RIGA, LATVIA OUT OF MUNICH

No.	Name, First	Occupation	Date of Birth	Domicile
270	Koppel, Carola S.	Business	18 May 1903	Thierschstr. 7
271	Koppel, Günther I.	Carpenter	6 March 1924	Thierschstr. 7
272	Koppel, Hans I.	No Occup.	9 January 1936	Antonienstr.7
273	Koppel, Ruth S.	No Occup.	11 August 1937	Antonienstr.7
274	Koppel, Judis S.	No Occup.	25 August 1939	Antonienstr.7

The letter had devastated me when I had first received it, and again, as I read it that night before traveling to Kovno. Tears welled up in my eyes. I could barely read the list of the deportation of my loved ones, my mother and my brothers and sisters.

> *The past is not dead. It's not even past.*
> —*William Faulkner*

I tossed and turned all night, worrying, being apprehensive about my trip to Kovno. Finally, light entered the window. Morning had arrived. It was Friday, April 26, 1996, a gloomy day, matching my state of mind. The sky was heavily overcast. I rang Robert's room to see if he was ready for the day.

We met at the breakfast room of the hotel at half past seven. For some reason, the waitress was extra cheerful and helpful this morning. She brought us more marmalade and another cup of coffee, usually rationed at one portion each morning. *Aciu*—Thank you," both of us extended to the cheerful young lady.

Promptly at eight, Regina Kopilevich showed up in the lobby. From the serious look on her face, I could tell we would have a very difficult day ahead of us. "Are you ready," she asked

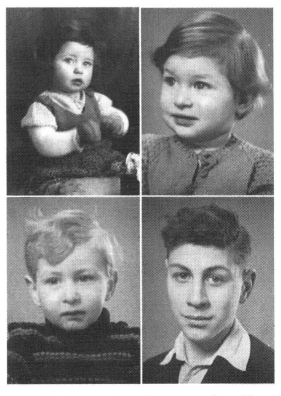

My two brothers and two sisters, together with their mother were "evacuated" from Munch to Rigor, Latvia on November 14, 1941 - per Dr. Andreas Heusler of the Stadtarchiv in Munich.

and continued, "Henrich Kostanian is waiting by the car around the corner." Henrich, or Henry, was the husband of Rachel Kostanian of the Jewish Museum in Vilnius.

Robert and I hurried back to our rooms to retrieve our cameras. Ten minutes later the three of us left the hotel to walk around the corner where Henrich was waiting by his car which, I believe, was a Russian-made Lada. I sat in the front seat because of my long legs; Robert and Regina were in the back seat.

Henrich maneuvered through the heavy morning traffic until we reached a highway leading out of the city on the way to Kovno. Angry clouds billowed up on the horizon. Rain began to fall which soon became a downpour. Oh, how I wished we had a friendly sunny day for this difficult journey.

About thirty minutes out of Vilnius we decided to stop for some refreshments. All of us started to get out of the car to walk to a refreshment stand except for Henrich. He explained later that he had to remain with the car to protect the side view mirrors and windshield wipers that were often stolen if the car were left unguarded.

All of a sudden, as I stood up, I felt sweaty and became dizzy. I was so stressed that things began to whirl around and I felt I was going to faint. Quickly I bent over and pretended to tie my shoes so the others would not notice my distress. Slowly, as I was regaining my balance, I walked over to the store and obtained what may have been a Coca-Cola.

Al praying for his family at the 9th Fort in Kovno, Lithuania at the huge memorial.

The rest of the trip to Kovno proved to be uneventful. The downpour had stopped, but the sky remained dark and threatening. It rained intermittently. I braced myself for the arrival at the Ninth Fort. Regina told us during the drive to Kovno that Russia in the 19th century decided to fortify its western borders against Germany. All roads and railways connecting Germany and Russia had to pass through Kovno. For that reason, Tsar Alexander II authorized the creation of strongholds around Kovno. The building of the nine massive fortresses surrounding the city began in 1882 and continued until the outbreak of World War I. The Ninth Fort was built in 1909.

Way in the distance, up on a hill, I saw the jagged edges of what looked like a huge carving of granite. As we approached the Ninth Fort itself, I could see that these huge coarse looking stones reached about eighty feet into the sky next to the Ninth Fort. Then I discerned the agonizing faces and tightly clenched fists hewn out of the rocks. It was an overwhelming and distressing memorial built, as I would later learn, by the Russian sculptor A. Ambraziunas to memorialize the 75,000 victims of slaughter at this Ninth Fort. To the right of this monument, stood the gruesome looking fortress itself, the infamous Ninth Fort.

We parked by the administrative office to visit the Director of the Ninth Fort Museum whom Regina had contacted earlier. Zita Nekrosyte, the Director, was an attractive young lady, with blue eyes and auburn hair. Sitting in her office at the museum, Zita told me, "You are the first German relative of the Jews shipped here to visit this site." Apparently, few people by 1996 had even

The huge memorial made of granite by A. Ambraziunas is approximately 80 feet tall.

heard of this killing ground. I briefly told her the story of my family and showed her pictures of my mother and the four children. "Could we have these pictures for an exhibit about the German Jews sent here?" she inquired. I readily assented for I had more copies of these photos. She then described the museum built next to the fort and wanted to know if she should come along with us. Regina replied that she had been here a number of times and could give us a proper tour.

The museum was a short walk from the office. Inside it was dark and gloomy matching the state of my mind. Alongside one wall were several illuminated windows exhibiting various paraphernalia. One window showed piles of shoes of the murdered Jews. It sadly reminded me of a poem I saw at a school in Wales while giving a presentation to those students about the Holocaust.

Shoes

In a museum of Resistance and Nazi memorabilia at Kovno, Lithuania:

Way-worn by Oslo
one Sunday afternoon
our feet sought out
a museum's gentler pace:

a museum of shoes,
regiments and regiments
in row upon neat row
of children's shoes,
removed and set down in an orderly manner
before the little ones were gassed in an afternoon.

So bereft of meaning are shoes without feet.

Stout little shoes,
shoes with laces tied and hardly worn–
unsplashed through puddles,
unscuffed against bark,
not a toecap grazed to bewail a fall,
no leather creased into durable smiles
by the deft percussion of tiny soles;
shoes hinting of
just-beginning-to-walk.

And that's how
there erupted this blister–
through bearing witness
one Sunday afternoon
to a people and the manner
they met their end
so noiselessly
in their stocking feet.

Menna Elfyn, Wales

Translated by Nigel Jenkins
Pont Books

We approached the next window holding a variety of items that had been dug up. I saw a comb, a shoehorn, and a fork and then … it hit me! I was in a state of shock. There, in front of me lay a half dozen children's eye glasses. I immediately recalled my mother's letter from October 1941 where, word for word in which she wrote to my father in New York: "I was at the eye doctor with Muschi (Ruth) this

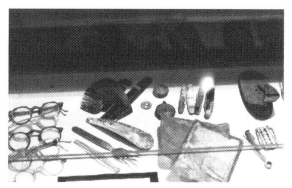

In the museum at the 9th Fort are items dug up. Note the children's eye glasses - one could be from my sister Ruth.

week. She has something on both corneas, was born with it and it is nothing to worry about. She has poor vision because of her squinting. Next week I will have to go again for a more thorough examination and she will probably get eyeglasses." Here in front of me was possibly a sign, a record of my little sister. One of these glasses could very well have been hers, a connection with my little Sister Ruth. The last time I saw her had been about seventy years ago–a little baby. I trembled.

It was a short walk to the high wall surrounding the buildings of the fort towering behind. On top of the wall, barbed wire was strung the entire perimeter, interrupted only by guard towers that undoubtedly had contained guards manning machine guns. All this had a chilling effect on us. We entered through the gate beside the guardhouse and found ourselves in a courtyard. I had seen pictures of prisoners arriving at a prison such as this, huddling in the courtyard of such a monstrous edifice, men, women and children. My stomach churned at the sight of the ugly two-story gray building in front of us. Acid tasting juices were rising in my throat. This evil place had been the final destination of my family.

When the train arrived at the railroad station in Kovno, the one thousand Jews from Munich were told that they would walk to a labor camp. The walk took them along the edge of the Ghetto in the city of Kovno where they saw a huddled mass of people behind barbed wire. "Is this the Ghetto?" some of the German Jews asked the figures in rags behind the barbed wire. (*Heroism & Bravery,* Alex Faitelson, Gefen Publishing) Undoubtedly, they felt great compassion for these imprisoned Jews, while they themselves would be resettled into new areas for work details.

The winding ascent of the Zemaiciu Road out of Kovno led to the Ninth Fort. It was a long walk. The distance from the railroad station to the fort was six kilometers (3.6 miles), all uphill.

Al with local guide Regina Kopilevich approaching the 9th Fort of Kovno, Lithuania.

Luggage had to be left behind, to be collected and de-livered later. I tried to visualize how my mother and the four children walked this long, uphill way to the fortress. Did my mother carry baby Judith in her arms?

Upon entering at the wall stood the grim looking fortress.

Did Günther, at seventeen and the male head of this family, carry little four year old Ruth? Surely, Hansi, who was five and a half year old had to be brave and walk all by himself.

The date was November 23, 1941 when this column of 1,000 Jews from Munich arrived at the top of the hill. All of a sudden, the forbid-ding fortress was staring them in their faces. This did not look like a resettlement place. By this time, many more Gestapo people showed up together with Lithuanian militia to herd this mass of Munich Jews into the courtyard of the fortress, the same one we just had entered. In

1996, I experienced a sense of impending doom. What did my mother, my two brothers and two sisters, the thousand men, women and children feel when they were herded into this enclosure?

I had to force myself to go on. The entrance to the building was in a corner. I started to shiver immediately as I entered. For us visiting the Fort in late April it was cold and moist everywhere. Undoubtedly in

The entrance of the 9th Fort in the corner.

November 1941, the cold and moisture must have been overwhelming. I could see my mother holding her children tightly, wrapping their overcoats carefully against the bitter cold.

Each floor had many large cells behind heavy iron bars. The walls were dripping with moisture, weeping for the victims who had occupied the cells. Double deck wooden bunks the length of the cells served as hard beds for the prisoners. The railroad cars that had brought them here had been so terribly overcrowded that many people had been forced to stand during the journey to Kovno. These cells also would have been bursting with this mass of humanity. There were inscriptions on the walls of the cells. I desperately looked for some signs of my family but only saw signatures like Levy-France; E. B. Marcel, Vendenheim, Nov. from Monaco via Drancy and Paris to Kaunas; Hayat Isaac de Marseille arive le 15/5/44 scratched into the faces of the walls. The condemned leaving a final sign of their fate. So it was, in cell after cell, the sad history of Jews of Europe.

For two days, the Jews from Munich were incarcerated in this prison. On November 25th, 1941, in groups of fifty, they were led to a ravine nearby and machine gunned to death by the German *Wehrmacht Einsatzgruppe* 3-A.

Had the adults, had my mother an inkling of what was in store for them as they were herded toward the ravine? Or, had the horror man-

ifested itself only when they were forced against the granite rocks and faced the machineguns in front of them? By this time, the children must have been terrified and screaming, "Mutti,

The inscription: "At this wall they shot people and burned the corpses."

Mutti, what is happening here? I am so afraid!" as the staccato of the machine gun fire reverberated at the ravine, killing the one thousand Jews from Munich on this freezing winter morning.

The people shot were piled in the excavation before they were burned.

Their blood flowed like water...
and no one was there to bury them.

—The 79th Psalm

From Gestapo SS StandartenFührer—Colonel Karl Jaeger of Einsatzgruppe—Action Group 3-A, letter of December 1, 1941, reporting to his Berlin SS headquarter:

> Out of a total of 133,346 Jews killed at the Ninth Fort Kovno, Lithuania, 10,000 Jews were shipped here from Germany to be killed. Among these were the 1,000 Jews from Munich murdered on November 25, 1941. Colonel Jaeger committed suicide in prison in Hohenasaperg on July 22, 1959.

All this was racing through my mind as I walked out of the last cell on the second floor. I was shivering... my chest tightened up. I could barely breathe. I had to get out of this horrible place.

"Regina, Robert," I shouted, "I can not stand this any longer. I must get out of here." As we walked downstairs toward the entrance door, I added, "It is time for me to say *Kadish* (the memorial prayer for the dead) for my family. I want to do this at the memorial."

I stood before a huge meadow next to the giant monument. This was the killing field. My mother, who was only thirty eight years old at the time of her murder, together with Günther, seventeen, Hansi, five and a half, Ruth, four, and Judis, two years old were ashes scattered somewhere in this vast expanse of grass. There were no gravestones for them, nothing to remember them by, not even some flowers—just the barren open space in this far away foreign land.

Epilogue

The Babylonian captivity of the Jews, which dates back two and a half thousand years, is always still in the consciousness of the world. And Auschwitz (the Holocaust) will remain at least as long in the consciousness of the world.

—Helmut Schmidt, Chancellor of Germany, 1974–1982 (from a conversation with Der Spiegel, 24/2001)

This conversation was published in the German magazine *Der Spiegel* by the former Chancellor Schmidt (born December 23, 1918) of the Social Democratic Party. He was a very capable and popular chancellor who won the esteem of many of the West German citizens and was one of the most respected and influential leaders of Western Europe.

The pronouncement of this popular former chancellor must be remembered in view of the tragedy that emanated from within Germany affecting millions of people in Europe and the East, men, women and, above all, the 1,500,000 innocent children who were murdered during the Holocaust.

The 1996 trip to Europe left me devastated with grief. I was looking for answers but found none. Why then did I spend those four weeks in Europe, searching for memories, traveling to my several former homes in the cities of Hamburg, Munich and Berlin?

This question marked the beginning, the genesis of a need to write about the murder of my family. It would be a difficult task. Where should I start? How does one develop such a difficult subject? I was struggling.

While many survivors have told their stories, there are still many of them living who have not. Most of them are unable to communicate their grief into a document or a book. Why would another memoir, the story of my family, contribute any more to this ghastly time in history? Why would I want to relive the agonizing tragedy of my family unless it was for a purpose?

I had blocked from memory the murder of my mother and my four siblings for more sixty five years. Was the purpose in writing this book to effect a closure of this terrible pain? Was I spared the fate of my family to be able to make a difference, to convey our story to new generations to keep the memory alive, to prevent a future occurrence?

The more I delved into this heart-wrenching moral dilemma, the more I realized that there could not be a closure for me. Instead of closure, there will be a long healing period enabling me to grieve about my loss and the loss of millions, many who have no one to grieve for them anymore.

Indeed, there exists a parallel situation within the populace of Germany. Closure essentially equates to shutting off all memories and so it is with German population. Many Germans want closure after more than five decades, preferring to be analytical, to evaluate, to put into historical perspective, rather than become emotionally involved with this terrible loss of fellow citizens.

While much has been written about the Holocaust from a statistical approach, of events, pertinent data in schoolbooks, memorials and plaques have been erected in many cities, the emotional and ethical aspects of that period are largely missing. Today, it seems less important to know all the details about the Holocaust, the murders of so many including the one and a half million children. Of far greater importance is for today's generation, especially the younger generations, to reflect, to be able to grieve about the losses of so many, men, women and children, those million and a half children, who did not get to live and grow up and become productive citizens.

How many future schoolteachers, doctors, writers, artists and musicians died in the Holocaust. How many potential Nobel Prize winners such as Albert Einstein, Physics, Gustav Hertz, Atom Physics and so many more, were to perish in the Holocaust?

To compound my problems, my dear wife of fifty years died in May 1997. I was in despair. I was unable to accomplish anything. Another year and a half passed before I was able to pull myself together.

In the months and years after my long search in 1996, the reasons for this task began to crystallize. Indeed, it dawned on me that I had several reasons to write this difficult book. Among them the need to keep the memory of the Holocaust alive for a warning to future generations. Further, to beseech the churches in Germany to expiate their sins of omission during the Nazi period. And finally, to alert the younger generations of the potential dangers of a recurrence, possibly in their lifetime.

In 1998, and later in the year 2000, I found some answers. In 1998, I began to give lectures on the subject of the Holocaust to the new generations, to students in Germany. I was aware that German law dictated that the subject of the Nazis and the Holocaust was to be taught in all schools. Still, I felt a presentation of the destiny of one family, my own family, might put those terrible events into a proper perspective. After all, how can the mind absorb the killing, the murder of six million human beings? So why write another memoir, this story of one family, my own family? No matter how much one reads about this subject in history books, such monstrous numbers become abstract, something almost impossible for the mind to absorb.

Early in 1998, I had an interesting, indeed, a challenging experience right in my own hometown in America. I was able to interview an exchange student from Berlin. Upon questioning her how the subject of the Holocaust was taught in her school, she replied quite diplomatically, "It all depends on how the teacher presents this subject."

Her answer was quite unsettling. Despite the fact that the subject was government mandated to be taught in German schools, many students did not receive a meaningful understanding as to what happened during the twelve years of Nazi oppression. Much of the reason for this is the general lack of communication from their parents as well as the lessening to focus on this period in the schools. Indeed, recent public opinion polls indicate that "Two thirds of all 14 to 18 year old Germans can not begin to understand the concept of the Holocaust.

But whoever has seen the eyeglasses and suitcases from Auschwitz, has read the farewell letters (of the victims) and observed the photos of the firing squads, can not forget." (Der Spiegel magazine, 3/2002)

I decided to make my presentations to the youth in *Gymnasien*, the high schools, *Hochschulen* and similar schools in Germany. Most students' parents had never talked about the Holocaust to their children, the students I now addressed, ranging from about sixteen to nineteen years of age. Why? Because most of the parents rarely discussed the war period with their children. Therefore, the students are learning about this dark period of German history from books. Some of the teachers presenting this dark period of German history are very dedicated. Others will only briefly touch the events of the Holocaust as shown in the history books and then, quickly go on to the next chapter.

In 1998, I gave fourteen presentations in German Gymnasien in a number of cities. Among them were schools in the cities of Düsseldorf, Munich, Duisburg, Gladenbach, Alsenz, Bad Kreuznach. It was an amazing experience. Most of the students were hanging onto every word I uttered. Although they were taught about the Holocaust in their schools, someone talking about his personal experiences seemed to have an overwhelming impact upon them. While such programs have a positive impact on the student population, it is important to point out that survivors making such presentations are slowly dying out necessitating new approaches to teaching this important subject.

School directors usually allotted two periods to my speeches, the equivalent of one and half-hours. I ended every presentation with a question and answer period and was generally bombarded with many questions.

One of the students, I do not remember from which city, protested that his grandfather never had anything to do with the Holocaust. He went on to tell us that his grandfather was at the Russian front and lost a leg in a battle. This, after I put the "grandfather generation" collectively into the "perpetrator generation." Obviously, his grandfather, in terms of age, matched that description. I finally answered him that I was not attacking his grandfather as one of the perpetrators, but merely used this expression to pinpoint an age group.

Then I turned the tables on him. I addressed this young man, probably about eighteen years of age, by asking him, "After hearing about the fate of my family, all the horrendous events that befell the Jewish population during the Hitler years, do you think something like the Holocaust could happen again in Germany?" I added that we should assume that Germany might have high unemployment and high inflation at some time in the future, something similar to what enabled Hitler's rise in the late 20's and early 30's."

Dead silence ensued in the auditorium. The young man was earnestly digesting my question. Finally, after a minute or two, he replied. "Given the right circumstances," he said, "I believe the Holocaust could happen again in Germany."

I was speechless. By law, school systems in Germany are required to teach the subject of the murder of six million Jews. Yet, in many schools, despite the fact that the subject of the Holocaust must be taught as part of the schools regular curriculum, is regrettably, only glossed over. Here was this young man earnestly thinking about a potential situation whereby something like a Holocaust could happen again. He was quite sincere about it. I was shocked!

The public opinion poll quoted from a German magazine underscores the importance, the need of survivors' of the Holocaust to talk in as many schools as possible about their experiences. However, the number of survivors is dwindling rapidly with time. By 2020, there will not be any survivors alive anymore. Indeed, I have an uneasy feeling that much of the population in Germany is eagerly awaiting the demise of these last survivor to eliminate the remembrance of the *Scham und Schande*—the shame and disgrace of their country some sixty years ago. It was certainly expressed forcefully by Martin Walser, an important German writer in a speech upon receiving the Peace Prize from the German book trade organization in 1998. He said: "... *dass sich in mir etwas gegen die Dauerrepräsentation der deutschen Schande wehrt*,"—"that something in me is against the enduring representation of the German shame." Further, Walser exclaimed, "*Eine Routine der Beschuldigung sei entstanden. Auschwitz werde zum 'Einschüchterungsmittel', zur 'Moralkeule' oder auch nur 'Pflichtübung.'*"—"A routine of accusation has arisen. Auschwitz becomes a medium of intimidation, a moral club or an exercise of duty." Walser, 75 years old in 2002, belongs to the "older generation who wonders, that 50–60 years after, the past is still so present." (From *Sueddeutsche Zeitung*, 9 November 1998.) The *Sueddeutsche Zeitung* and *Die Zeit*, two important German newspapers have printed *Leserbriefe*— Letters to the Editor, echoing Mr. Walser's sentiment, expressing an *Enthemmung*—a loss of inhibition of much of the population when discussing the Holocaust years. An example: "*Martin Walser hat ausge-sprochen , was ich empfinde. Dafür danke ich ihm.*"—"Martin Walser has said what I feel. For this, I thank him."

One of the more successful schools I had visited was the *Freiherr-vom-Stein Schule*, an *Europaschule* in Gladenbach near Marburg.

In 1997, I had visited Israel. I had found that most people living in that country as well as visitors were happy to enter into conversations with me. One day, as I was heading for breakfast in my hotel, taking the elevator down to the dining room, I heard two men speak German. My ears perked up; I was listening intently to their conversation as I realized that they came from a school in Germany. Before we reached the main floor, I addressed them, asking them to grant me an hour for a conversation. A Mr. Niemeyer said he would be happy to meet with me in the hotel lobby the next evening.

That next evening I learned that Mr. Niemeyer, a teacher, and his school director Mr. Seyler from the *Freiherr-vom-Stein Schule*, a *Europaschule*, were visiting Jerusalem to find a Jewish sister school. The purpose was to exchange information and arrange for a visit of the Gladenbach students to Jerusalem and students from the Jerusalem school to Gladenbach.

Mr. Niemeyer explained further that they had studied a number of events about the Holocaust. One such subject was the internment camp of Gurs in France. This camp had been located near Pau in the Pyrenees in southern France. Two my uncles from Hamburg had fled from Germany and were interned at that camp. Eventually, they were sent to the East where they were killed.

Mr. Niemeyer explained that the class studied the history of "Gurs" in preparation for a trip to this internment camp.

After an hour's conversation with Mr. Niemeyer, he invited me to come to Gladenbach to his school for a presentation to his students. I readily accepted. In fact, during my trip to Germany in 1998 I spoke to two large and attentive groups of students at this progressive school.

I was impressed, while visiting Gladenbach, to learn about their Gurs project. Some of the student's comments were insightful. Anja S. stated, "The problem is forgetting. It is important to learn about the past, especially for us! Only in this manner can we be cognizant about our great responsibility." Simone D. expressed her thoughts, "I hope that such activities will occur often (for example, with other schools) and that they will be dealt with in a positive manner."

It is so easy to let events of history evaporate into thin air. I learned during a subsequent trip to Germany in the year 2000 that most of the middle-aged generation, the parent generation and certainly the grand-parent segment did not want to talk about the Holocaust anymore. Indeed, this sentiment was underscored during my visits to the school in Gladenbach that had a great many photographs exhibited of a sister school in Jerusalem. A mother, upon seeing this exhibit commemorating a happy interchange between the children of both schools, their views and ideas, growled, *"Könnt ihr nicht etwas vernünftiger machen?"*— 'Can't you put on something more sensible?"

During my journey through Germany in May that year, I noticed the mood of many Germans since 1996 had changed toward the Holocaust. An example of this happened on my flight from Denver to Munich, Germany. A young lady in her thirties, obviously a professional person, sat next to me on the plane. We talked. I learned that she worked for Siemens, the giant German electric manufacturer. She wanted to know why I was visiting Germany. I briefly summarized my reason for the trip. Her response to the Holocaust subject was, "I must tell you, we are a new generation," and continued, "the subject is fading. It becomes weaker and weaker. It is only political now, reported in newspapers and magazines which, mostly, are read by people with a yawn."

Two years later I began to perceive a slide into apathy, indifference, a lack of interest by the general population about the Holocaust. In fact, it began to spill over into the school system. While schools such as the Freiherr-vom-Stein school are still deeply involved disseminating the subject of tolerance, of not forgetting the terrible past, many others are doing a perfunctory presentation of this subject. Who, in fact, is teaching the teachers? Who will make certain that more than about one third of the student population who know little or nothing about Auschwitz, will be taught about it. Who will tell the young population that "He who forgets history is doomed to repeat it." (Georg Santayana)

Most history books in Germany and other countries present the twelve years of horror through the use of Auschwitz as an icon for the Holocaust. Indeed, Auschwitz is the best-known extermination camp. Dachau, near Munich was first concentration camp in Germany. Others, Treblinka, Sobibor, Belzec in Poland, the Warsaw Ghetto are also relatively well known. But little is mentioned about the hundreds of smaller, lesser-known killing sites. The Ninth Fort in Lithuania, the killing field of my family, is one of those lesser or almost unknown sites where so many of the murders took place.

The German magazine, *Der Spiegel*—The Mirror, an important weekly magazine, had an article early in 2001 that a large number of Germans are sick of being confronted with the nation's past. The article further stated that sixty percent (of the population) feel neither guilty nor responsible for the Holocaust. Asked whether one should "not always poke around old wounds" of the Nazi era, sixty-one percent flatly said they were fed up hearing about terror of the Third Reich. There is also a feeling that almost sixty years since the end of the war, the time has come for ending discussion of the Holocaust and the erection of memorials.

While it is true that nearly sixty years have passed, the subject of the Holocaust did not become known in a significant way until twenty to twenty-five years after the end of the war. During the first twenty to twenty-five years after 1945, this was a subject rarely talked about or discussed in a meaningful way. Then, in the nineteen-seventies, the writings about this subject exploded. An ever-increasing number of books appeared year after year, especially with the appearance of new evidence and the thousands of documents released by Russia.

During those three decades, the German government has attempted to memorialize the Holocaust in a number of ways. Parliament established a national Holocaust Memorial Day on January 27, 1996. Most cities observe this as a solemn day. City leaders, bishops, priests and ministers would read the names of the murdered Jews during that day.

Parliament, for more than a dozen years, has been discussing the erection of a national monument to the victims of the Holocaust. I had followed the debates about this memorial very closely. Indeed, in 1996 I had even debated this before several *Abgeordnete*, members of the Berlin parliament during a *Meinungsaustausch*—an exchange of thoughts. While it is true that this will be a somber memorial, a warning not to forget this period of oppression and murder, a period of twelve years Germany would just as soon like to forget, it is so important to keep the memory of six million murdered Jews alive to prevent the repeat of such a horror. The words of the Gymnasium student at one of my lectures remain vividly in my mind. "Yes, something like the Holocaust could happen again in Germany." After many years, parliament finally gave the go ahead to have it built in a prominent place in Berlin.

Most of the "perpetrator generation" is now dying out. So the feeling that it is time to make a *Schlusstrich*—a bottom line to the Nazi period, and forgive and forget is being reinforced with their passing

But only the victims can forgive and they are dead. Today's generation, in high schools and universities do not need to be forgiven. They were not responsible for the Holocaust.

Yet, to forget would be reprehensible and inexcusable. It is a matter of remembrance. Remembrance never to forget that something like the Holocaust can happen again.

Could such conditions happen again?

Yes, they could under the right circumstances.

It took only one decade for Hitler to come into power after the *Hitler Putsch* (coup) of 1923. The seeds of discontent, high unemployment and huge inflation had germinated.

Today, there is a revival of Jewish life in Germany. Many synagogues have been built and more are on the drawing board. The 90,000 to 100,000 Jewish people residing in Germany in the year 2002 have freedom, and can practice their religion. Many of its Jewish citizens have, by and large, had adapted themselves into the German society.

However, clouds are appearing on the horizon. Skinheads, the neo-Nazis and others could one day explode into a force to be reckoned with. The German government is watching and staying on top of this potential menace.

While in Munich, I visited the liberal synagogue, *Beth Shalom.* During a lively discussion with a member of this synagogue, a, statement made by Steven made a deep impression on me. When I asked about the integration of the Jewish population into the German fabric, he replied that it would take at least two more generations for Jews to become integrated into the German society.

This sentiment was repeated a couple of days later, only far more negatively. A Jewish official who had survived the Holocaust stated, "When the survivors are gone, including myself, the subject of the Holocaust will recede into history." When I told a person that I had heard it would take at least two more generations before Jews will be integrated into German society, the response was, "Never!" Jews were not integrated in the1900s during the democracy. They were only accepted!"

The problem is the *Gesellschaft,* the society, of people of the middle-aged generation who still have deeply ingrained misconceptions about the Jews. That makes it a generational problem. Only the next generation would be capable of overcoming the ghosts of the past. Indeed, one lady in her '50's told me that her mother, as late as 1948, told her that you can not trust the Jews, that they have kinky hair and crooked noses and that they cheat you.

Consequently, that 'middle generation' did not impart much knowledge about the Holocaust to their children who are now of high school and college ages. Many of these children have a great desire of wanting to know what happened during those war years. Yet, here too, is a diminishing interest. Public opinion polls show that two thirds of 14 to 18 year old German youth can not deal with or understand the concept of the Holocaust. (*Der Spiegel,* 3/2002)

Most Jewish buildings, synagogues, schools, and offices have a police presence in front of them. The old *Knabenschule,* the former boys' school in the Grosse Hamburger Street in Berlin, and today a Jewish high school, is protected against vandalism or worse with an eight foot tall metal fence all around it. During my visit to Germany in 2000, I spoke to the policeman and two other men guarding the school at the entry gate and learned that the two men in civilian clothes were Israelis. They were stationed there helping the police to protect the children in the school. One of the men telephoned the Director of the school advising him that I wanted to visit with him.

The Director's office was on the second floor. An earnest looking man, the Director granted me about half an hour of his valuable time. Discussing the extreme protection at this school, he told me there is no such police protection at any of the city's mosques or churches. He concurred with my view that the Jewish population in this city seems like 'an isolated island situated in the ocean of the German population.'

Upon leaving the school I was dumbfounded when I saw a prominent sign at the front door stating: "*Aufenthalt der Schüler vor der Schule auf Sicherheitsgründen verboten!*"—'It is forbidden to congregate in front of the school because of safety issues."

My visit to the school was unnerving. That same day, I engaged the proprietor, a man about forty years old, of a store near the school in a conversation. Upon asking him how he was getting along living in Berlin, he gave a reply that had an immense impact on me, "*Es ist ein unnatürlices Leben hier*"—"The living here is unnatural."

An official of the *Zentralrat der Juden in Deutschland* told me anecdotally speaking, that he is now even more negative about the situation in Germany. He exclaimed, " When survivors finally die out, what then? Today, more than 30% of the children do not know anything about Auschwitz. After the survivors are gone, the percentage may go up to 50%." He agreed that the children need Holocaust education, but first, the teachers need to be trained to be able to teach this challenging subject properly. He worried about the *Gehörsamkeit*, the discipline of the Germans to follow orders, one of the attributes of the population, a trait that enabled the rise of Hitler. I had to agree with these comments for I recalled an instance trying to cross a wide street with Robert, my Welsh companion. It was rather late in the evening. The traffic light was red and displayed the message, "Do not walk." Despite the fact that no traffic was visible in either direction, no one dared to step off the curb to get a head start crossing the street.

This discipline culminated into the ultimate discipline during the Nazi period of *Befehl ist Befehl*—orders are orders, as evidenced by the many Nazis when interrogated in court as to why they executed the many anti-Jewish policies and, eventually, murdered so many Jews.

In May 2000, I met with Professor Dr. Rita Suessmuth, member of the German Bundestag (Parliament) and formerly the President of that body. A lovely lady and energetic lady, she granted me an hour interview. She is deeply involved in the fight against intolerance such as the National Association called, 'Never Again.' She is one of the many top government officials deeply involved furthering an interaction between Jews and Christians.

May 2000 also was the month during which the German government founded, countrywide, the "Alliance for Tolerance," emphasizing non-violence and fighting extremism and force against minorities. (*Tagesblatt*, May 24, 2000) Minister of the Interior Otto Schily stated that the alliance is directed against power and violence from both the Right and the Left. The principle stated that one should not exist and live only next to each other but with each other. Minorities belong into the German society and are not to be merely tolerated. A noble and worthwhile project of the German government, much like laws against the denial of the Holocaust, and the policies regarding the protection of all the Jewish synagogues and schools, demonstrates that the government and its leaders have been and are doing all the right things for the Jewish minority.

One has to wonder how the theme of tolerance, the living with each other, filters down to the German population. One further has to wonder what would happen if the population experiences pressure similar to those of the Weimar Republic.

Two institutions in Germany are destined to lead the country, countervailing the pressures of a potential repetition of a Holocaust. The schools must rejuvenate its standard of teaching ethics and morality as related to the frightful period of the Holocaust years.

Further, the churches, despite a percentage loss of membership over the years, must be deeply involved with the teaching of ethics and morality. In absolute numbers, both the Catholic and Evangelical Churches still constitute a large membership. (54 million members out of 82 million population–1998. Statistical Report from yearly books of the German Bureau of Statistics)

After all, it was the church, which had contributed so much to the rise of anti-Semitism. It was the church that promulgated anti-Semitism throughout centuries, indeed even millennia, all the way into the twentieth century.

Afterword

I started this very difficult biography about my family some seven to eight years ago. My intention was to describe and share with my immediate family the years of heartaches and deep emotions buried deeply in my mind. Getting up in age I felt I needed to bare my innermost feelings buried for so many years in the recesses of my tortuous mind. As I began to write this story, something happened in one of the major cities of Germany that prompted me to bare my innermost pain and sorrows of so many years ago.

I was born in Hamburg, Germany in the earlier 1926. My father decided to move to Munich, the capital of Bavaria in the early 1930s, the third largest city in Germany with a population of 1,185,400. Munich is a beautiful city not far from the southern mountains, the Alps. Over the last ten plus years I had made annual visits to Munich primarily as part of my world-wide business travel as an executive of the well known Samsonite Corporation.

This type of travel was fascinating and interesting and at times adventurous although quite exhausting. During these many visits to Munich, I had made many friends, both Jewish and non-Jewish, that included *Mittagessen*—lunches—and fascinating conversations with Mrs. Charlotte Knobloch, a lovely and interesting person and the head of the Jewish community in Munich. I still remember that very early on I learned she was in favor of the placement of the so-called *Stolpersteine*—stumbling stones, the memorial brass plaques—that depicted the Jewish tragedy and horror of the men, women and children who were deported in 1941 and in subsequent years were killed.

Mrs. Knobloch generally invited me to a lunch in the dining room of the Jewish office building, always having interesting conversations with each other. The only disconcerting experiences of those early visits with Mrs. Knobloch was the fact that four policemen would always accompany us to the dining room of the Jewish office building. In fact, Mrs. Knobloch was continuously accompanied by these four policemen wherever she went. This resulted into a weird and strange feeling during those visits.

At the outset of writing this AFTERWORD I mentioned that the book-length biography would be the private life story of my immediate family. I soon had to change my mind regarding the privacy statement for a number of reasons.

There are two protagonists, the principal persons of this human drama in this major city of Bavaria, namely the *Oberbürgermeister*—Chief Mayor—Christian Ude and Mrs. Charlotte Knobloch, the head of their respective domains.

Munich had been deeply involved with the ascent of the *Führer*—the leader—in the early 1920s. Hitler used to live in those early times within a city block or two in an apartment in the Thierschstrasse—Thiersch Street—where our family was later forced to move into the over crowded building in 1939 into, what was called, a *Judenhaus*—a Jew House. This happened after the removal of my family from our beautiful apartment house on the prestigious *Maximilianstrasse*—Maximilian Street—into the tiny third floor apartment on Thiersch Street. In the late 1930s, all German cities designated a number of apartment houses specifically to house only Jews to enable the government to keep track of all the Jews.

Fast forward of this historical story. As of July 2009 more than 455 cities and towns commemorated the murder of the German Jews with placements more than 20,000 of what are called *Stolpersteine*. *Stolpersteine* translates into Stumbling Stones which are 4 inch x 4 inch brass plates containing the following inscriptions: Here lived–name of the murdered Jew, date of birth and place of murder such as Auschwitz or Kaunas, Lithuania and the date of death. These solid brass plates have been placed at the entrances of buildings from which families were taken and shipped to the various places for extermination. Auschwitz was the most notorious and evil extermination camps. About 1,500,000

Jews were killed in this killing center. But beyond Auschwitz, there were many other death camps in Poland as for example Treblinka, Sobibor, Chelmo, Belzec and more. Jews – men, women and children were singled out for *Sonderbehandlung*—special treatment. This entailed a methodically killing of Jewish children, women and men with poisonous gas.

The major concentration camps in Germany were located in Buchenwald, Neugamme, Bergen-Belsen, Stutthof, Ravensbruck Theresienstadt, Sachsenhausen, near Berlin (my uncle Bernhard was imprisoned there in 1938), Dachau near Munich (my father was imprisoned there in November through December 1938). In 1940 he was again incarcerated in the Stadelheim prison in Munich. He never talked about this probably because of threats made by officials.

While these lists of horrors were only pertaining to locations in Germany and Poland, I am not listing here the many places of killings and starvations in other areas of Europe during the years of 1938 to 1945.

The spread of terror among the Jews was the murders of six million Jewish men, women, and among them were one and a half million children. Focusing now on only the killing of the Jewish population in Germany during the seven years between 1938 and 1945, were 160,000 to 170,000 men, women and children. Further, relating it only to the city of Munich, 2,500 to 3,000 Jewish people were unable to escape and were killed by late 1941 and afterwards. Among them were my mother Karla, 38 years old, my elder brother Guenther, 17 years old, a brother Hans, 5½ years old, my younger sister Ruth, 4 years old, and my little sister Judith, 2 years old.

I made eleven visits to Munich during which time I began to chronicle the horrors of the latter years of the 1930s and 1940s. I began to memorialize my Munich memories.

Munich's immense main synagogue, a liberal house of worship, was built in 1887 and was torn down in June 1938 by an edict from Hitler. This beautiful synagogue lasted only 51 years. The other synagogue built in 1892 was in the Herzog-Rudolf-Strasse and was called Ohel Jakob, set on fire in the night of November 9th to 10th in 1938 during the *Reichskristallnacht*—the crystal night—so called because all the Jewish businesses and most of the Jewish homes' windows were smashed by the Nazi mob. This synagogue lasted only 46 years before being totally destroyed.

The third synagogue located in the Reichenbach Strasse in Munich was completely devastated through fire set in the interior of the synagogue.

Today, most of the cities and towns in Germany have been memorializing the murders of the Jewish people. Fourteen of the major cities in Germany with a population of about 500,000 inhabitants or higher are displaying these Stolpersteine as memorials on the sidewalks of the buildings where Jewish people used to live. All the largest cities in Germany are participating except one. They are:

City	Population
Berlin	3,275,000
Hamburg	1,686,000
Cologne	965,000
Frankfurt	648,000
Essen	588,000
Dortmund	587,600
Stuttgart	581,100
Düsseldorf	568,900
Bremen	527,900
Hannover	516,399
Duisburg	513,400
Nuremberg	486,700
Leipzig	486,100
Dresden	473,300

Please note that the third largest city is missing from this list. Munich, with a population of 1,185,400 decided, at a major meeting of the City Council hurriedly called together by the *Oberbürgermeister* Christian Ude for June 16, 2004, not to place these 4 inch x 4 inch brass *Stolpersteine* in front of the homes from where deported Jews used to live.

This was a hurriedly called meeting of all 80 of the *Stadträte*—council members—and was prompted by pressure exerted on all the *Stadträte* by the *Oberbürgermeister*. The pressure on the council members had mounted after the publicity of several letters from the mayor. The following was an early letter, a *Serienbrief*—serial letter—of pressure by the mayor in late 2003 exhorting council not to support the *Stolpersteine*. Excerpts of this early serial letter are shown here:

First Rundbrief (a major circular) from *Oberbürgermeister* Ude issued late 2003 ...

Stolpersteine   No date shown–delivered late 2003

Sehr geehrte Frau ...   (Honored Ms.)

Sehr geehrter Herr ...   (Honored Sir)

First of all may I cite the *Erinnerungsarbeit*—work about memory—about Munich and its impact on me personally. In the last ten years of duty as mayor, the work of the mayor was extraordinarily important… it is, of course, that Munich in its historical responsibility has built, in the center of the city, a synagogue, an office building, a Kindergarten, school and a kosher restaurant. In addition, a Jewish Museum is operated by the city staff, (not the Jewish community).

The next question is, if it is an inflation of memorials that leads to of an expansion of memory work. I (as the mayor) as well as all the members of the *Ältestenrat*—a small number of senior advising city council members—advising the 80 members of the city council have considerable doubt.

Initially, years ago, the mayor of Munich circulated a number of letters to the population along the vein of the above. Then, the mayor ceased to be directly involved with such letters. Instead, Mrs. Charlotte Knobloch head of the Jewish community in Munich took up such letter writing and comments to the newspapers against the placement of the *Stolpersteine* in Munich. One must assume her stance against the *Stolpersteine* may be in appreciation and gratitude for the mayor's help in building such a beautiful synagogue and another large building. One needs to point out, however, that the cost of the 40 million Euros center is probably somewhat comparable to the former huge and magnificent synagogue that was destroyed in 1938 on the order of Hitler.

Additionally, according the mayor, the *Stadträte* want to make certain that these small brass memorials do not hurt the feelings of the Jewish citizens. Per the mayor's office, it is known that many Jewish people feel it is an inappropriate acknowledgement of these forms of memories. Really! How do the *Stadträte*, the mayor and the head of the *Israelitische Kultusgemeinde* know this? Did they poll the thousands of the Jewish citizens about this? Were the approximately 9,000 Jewish citizens interviewed and questioned about this? This is ludicrous. Actually the opposite is true. Most of the Jewish citizens of Munich, indeed of all of Germany, consider the placement of the *Stolpersteine* as the only dignified memorial where one can stand and remain a while and think about the victims—the parents and children who were torn out of their apartments and then murdered.

Stolpersteine have a higher worth than the memory plaques in both the old and the new *Rathaus* (city halls). Indeed, the main *Rathaus* gets locked up every evening and the two days on the weekends. And the old *Rathaus* is locked up almost the entire year. Consequently, both city halls have little opportunity to view the plaques.

To summarize, these five solid brass Stolpersteine plates (4 inches by 4 inches) shown above, are commemorating the murder on November 25, 1941 of the five members of the Koppel family. They are being held privately in Munich until their placement will finally be allowed by the city of Munich. The Stolpersteine are to be placed in front of the apartment house on the Maximilianstrasse where the Koppel family lived from 1935 until 1939. These family members were then displaced from this beautiful apartment building into a tiny apartment in a "Jewish Building" until the eventual murder took place on November 25, 1941.

It is hoped that the city of Munich, having been so deeply involved in the Nazi era, will finally come to the conclusion, that through the placement of these five Stolpersteine, my murdered family from Munich will finally be recognized and honored as has been done in more than 450 other German cities and towns.

The artist, Gunther Demmig, has created by far the largest decentralized Holocaust Memorial in the world.

A new generation has made an entry to the Koppel and Wolff families. Al Koppel, the great-grandfather is holding his precious and lovely great-granddaughter Hallie—

A new generation.

A new beginning.

Al with his one year old great-granddaughter Hallie.

Addendum

Of my father's family, eight siblings, only three survived the Holocaust. My father, his brother Siete and sister Hannah. Murdered were the following five siblings:

Sister Lene and husband Max Oettinger from Frankfurt to location unknown.

Brother Bernhard and wife Ulli from Altona (Hamburg) were deported to Minsk, Russia August 11, 1941.[1]

Sister Lola and husband Joseph Goldschmidt from Berlin were deported to the East in 1942.

Brother Leo from Altona (Hamburg), who had been interned in France, was relocated to Theresienstadt on July 19, 1942 and on to Minsk, Russia on September 26, 1942. Leo's wife Sine and son Werner were deported to the concentration camp at Riga, Latvia and perished there in late 1941[1].

Brother Edie from Altona (Hamburg) was also interred in France and shipped to Auschwitz, December 17, 1942.[1]

Bibliography

Baker, Leonard. *Days of Sorrow and Pain*. New York: Macmillan Publishing Company.

Bauer, Yehuda. *A History of the Holocaust*. New York: F. Watts, 1982.

Benz, Wolfgang. *Legenden, Lügen, Vorurteile*. Munchen: 1992.

Bergen, Doris L. *Twisted Cross*. Chapel Hill, North Carolina and London: The University of North Carolina Press, 1996.

Birnbaum, Halina. *Hope is the Last to Die*. New York: Harper & Row, 1961.

Blumenthal, W. Michael. *The Invisible Wall*. Washington, D.C.: Counterpoint, 1998.

Bokovoy, Douglas und Meining, Stefan, Herausgeber. *Verasgte Heimat* Munchen: Verlag, Dr. Peter Glas.

Cahnman, Werner. *Die Juden in Munchen 1918 – 1943*. Munchen: Zeitschrift fur bayrische Landesgeschichte, Band 42, Heft 2, 1979.

Carlebach, Miriam Gillis. *Jedes Kind ist mein Einziges*. Hamburg: Doellig und Galitz Verlag, 1993.

Charlesworth, James H., editor. *Jews and Christians*. New York: Crossroad Publishing Company, 1990.

Cornwell, John. *Hitler's Pope*. New York, NY: Viking, 1999.

Dawidowicz, Lucy S. *The War Against the Jews 1933 - 1945*. New York: Holt, Rinehart & Winston.

Dwork, Deborah. *Children with a Star*. New Haven: Yale University Press, 1979.

Dobroszycki, Lucjan & Gurock, Jeffrey S. *The Holocaust in the Soviet Union*. Armonk, N.Y. & London: M. E. Sharpe.

Eisenberg, Azriel, editor. *The Lost Generation, Children of the Holocaust*. Pilgrim Press, 1982.

Esh, Shaul. *The Establishment of the Reichsvereinigung der Juden Deutschland and its Main Activities*. YVS vol. 7,19 - 38, 1968.

Ehrenburg, Ilya and Grossman, Vasily. *The Black Book*. New York: Holocaust Library.

Faitelson, A. *Heroism and Bravery in Lithuania*. Jerusalem: Gefen, 1996.

Flannery, Edward H. *The Anguish of the Jews*. New York: The Macmillan Co., 1969.

Fremont, Helen. *After Long Silence*. New York: Delacorte Press, 1979.

Friedlander, Henry. *The Origins of Nazi Genocide*. University of N. Carolina Press, 1995.

Fraud, Anne. *The Diary of a Young Girl*. New York: Anchor Book/ Double Day, 1996.

Frankl, Victor Emil. *Man's Search for Meaning*. Boston: Beacon Press, 1992.

Friedman, Saul S. *Holocaust Literature*. Westport, CT, London: Greenwood Press, 1993.

Gay, Ruth. *Safe Among the Germans*. New Haven and London: Yale University Press, 2002.

Gerlach, Wolfgang. *And the Witnesses Were Silent*. Lincoln and London: University of Nebraska Press, 2000.

Goerlitz, Erich. *Taschenbuch zur Geschichte*. Paderborn, Germany: Schoeningh-Schrodel, 1979.

Goldhagen, Daniel. *Hitler's Willing Executioners*. New York: Vintage Books (Div. of Random House), 1997.

Goodwin, Doris Kearns. *No Ordinary Time*. New York: Simon & Schuster, 1994.

Gordon, Harry. *The Shadow of Death; The Holocaust in Lithuania*. Lexington, Kentucky: The University Press of Kentucky, 1992.

Graupe, Heinz Mosche *Die Statuten der drei Gemeinden Altona, Hamburg und Wandsbeck*. Hamburg: Hans Christian Verlag, 1973.

von der Gruen, Max. *Howl Like The Wolves*. New York: William Morrow & Co., 1980.

Gutman, Israel, et al. *Encyclopedia Judaica*. New York: Macmillan Publ. Co., 1990.

Gutteridge, Richard *The German Evangelical Church and the Jews 1879 – 1950*. New York: Harper & Row Publishers, Inc., 1976.

Hanke, Peter. *Zur Geschichte der Juden in Munchen zwischen 1933 und 1945* .Stadtarchiv Munchen, 1967.

Heinloth, Bernhard. *Geschichte fur Gymnasien*. Munchen: R. Oldenbourg Verlag, 1994.

Heusler, Andreas und Weger, Tobias. *Kristallnacht* Munchen: Buchendorfer Verlag, 1998.

Heumann und Hirschgraben. *Geschichte fur Morgen*. Frankfurt am Main: Hirschgraben Verlag, 1987.

Hilberg, Raul. *The Destruction of the European Jews*. New York and London: Holmes & Meier, 1985.

Hofer, Walther. *Der Nationalsozialismus, Dokumente 1933 - 1945*. Fischer Buecherei.

Isenberg, Sheila. *A Hero of Our Own*. New York: Random House, 2001.

Kertzer, David I. *The Popes Against the Jews*. New York: Alfred Knopf, 2001.

Klarsfeld, Beate. *Wherever They May Be!* New York: Vanguard Press, 1975.

Klemperer, Victor. *I Will Bear Witness: The Diaries of Victor Klemperer*. USA: Random House.

Krausnick, Helmut. *Anatomie des SS-Staates*. Olten und Freiburg, 1965.

Krondorfer, Bjoern. *Remembrance and Reconciliation*. New Haven and London: Yale University Press, 1995.

Lamm, Hans. *Von Juden in Munchen.* Munchen: Ner-Tamid Verlag, 1958.

Landeshauptstadt Munchen, publisher. *Judisches Leben in Munchen*. Munchen: Buchendorfer Verlag, 1995.

Lankos, Baltos. *The Days of Memory.* Lithuanian State Museum, 1993.

Leverton, Bertha & Lowensohn, Shmuel. *I Came Alone*. Sussex England: The Book Guild, 1996.

Levi, Primo. *The Drowned and the Saved*. New York: Summit Books, 1988.

Lindsey, Hal. *The Road to Holocaust*. New York, Toronto, London: Bantam Books, 1989.

Loftus, John. *The Secret War Against the Jews*. New York: St. Martin's Press, 1994.

Lorenz, Ina. *Identitat und Assimilation*. Hamburg: Hans Christians Verlag, 1989.

Martin, Gilbert. *Atlas of Jewish History*. New York: William Morrow & Co., 1993.

Martin, Gilbert. *The Holocaust*. New York: Henry Holt & Co., 1987.

Miller, Judith. *One by One by One*. New York: Touchstone Book (Simon & Schuster), 1990.

Mishell, William. *Kadish for Kovno*. Chicago: Review Press.

Mitscherlich, Alexander and Margarete. *The Inability to Mourn*. New York: Grove Press, 1975.

Neiman, Susan. *Sloe Fire; Jewish Notes from Berlin*. New York: Pantheon Books, Div. of Random House, Inc., 1992.

Nicholls, William. *Christian Antisemitism*. Northvale, New Jersey, London: Jason Aronson, Inc. 1993.

Phayer, Michael. *The Catholic Church and the Holocaust*. Bloomington and Indianapolis: Indiana University Press, 2000.

Pinsker, Sanford and Fischel, Jack, edited. *Holocaust Studies Annual, Vol 3*. Greenwood, Florida: The Penkevill Publishing Co.

Rabinowitz, Dorothy. *New Lives: Survivors of the Holocaust Living in America*. New York: Alfred Knopf, 1976.

Rapaport, Lynn. *Jews in Germany after the Holocaust*. Cambridge, UK: Cambridge University Press, 1997.

Rhodes, Richard. *Masters of Death*. New York: Alfred Knopf, 2002.

Rosenfeld, Else R. *Behrend-Ich stand nicht allein*. Hamburg, (ISBN 3406329020 <18.80>, 1950.

Rosenfeld, Gavriel D. *Munich and Memory; Architecture, Monuments, and the Legacy of the Third Reich*. Berkley, Los Angeles, London: University of California Press.

Rosenfeld, Harvey & Zborowski, Eli. A Legacy Recorded. New York: Martyrdom & Resistance, 1994.

Rossel, Seymour. *The Holocaust*. West Orange, New Jersey: Behrman House, Inc. 1992.

Ruerup, Reinhard, ed. *Topography of Terror*. Berlin: Verlag Willmuth Arenhoevel, 1995.

Schlant, Ernestine. *The Language of Silence*. New York, London: Routledge, 1999.

Schneider, Gertrude. *Muted Voices*. New York: Philosophical Library, 1987.

Schneider, Richard Chaim. *Zwischen Welten*. Munchen: Verlag Kindler, 1994.

Selig, Wolfram. *Synagogen und judische Friedhofe in Munchen*. Munchen: Aries Verlag, 1988.

Selig, Wolfram. *Richard Seligmann*. Munchen: Stadtarchiv Munchen, 1983.

Schoenberner, Gerhard. *Der Gelbe Stern*. Gutersloh, Germany: Bertelsmann, 1978.

Schoenberner, Gerhard. *Wir haben es gesehen*. Hamburg: Ruetten & Loening Verlag.

Stern, Susan, ed. *Speaking Out*. Chicago, Berlin, Tokyo, Moscow: Edition q, 1995.

Tory, Avraham. *Surviving the Holocaust*. Cambridge, Massachusetts: Harvard University Press, 1990.

Wandinger, Lorenz. *Das Lehel*. Munchen: Buchendorfer Verlag, 1994.

Wiesel, Elie. *All Rivers Run to the Sea*. New York: Alfred A. Knopf, 1995.

Wiesel, Elie. *The Night Trilogy*. New York: Hill & Wang, 1987.

Wiesenthal, Simon. *Every Day Remembrance Day*. New York: Henry Holt, 1987.

Wiesenthal, Simon. *The Sunflower*. New York: Schocken Books, 1997.

Wistrich, Robert, S. *Hitler and the Holocaust.* New York: Pantheon Books, 1991.

Wolffsohn, Michael. *Eternal Guilt?* New York: Columbia University Press, 1993.

Wollenberg, Joerg. *Niemandwar dabei und keiner hat's gewusst.* Muenchen: R. Piper GmbH, 1989 Engl. translation: Atlantic Highlands, New Jersey: Humanities Press International, 1996.

Wyman, David. *The Abandonment of the Jews: America and the Holocaust.* New York: Pantheon Books, 1984.

Zingeris, Emanuelis, ed. Lankos, Baltos, transl. *The Days of Memory.* Vilnius, Lithuania: Spausdino AB, 1995.

References

Leo Baeck Institute, New York, N.Y.

Institute fur Zeitgeschichte, Munchen, Germany.

Stadtarchiv Hamburg, Hamburg, Germany.

Stadtarchiv Munchen, Munchen, Germany

Yad Vashem, Jerusalem, Israel.

YIVO Institute, New York, N.Y.

About the Author

Alfred Koppel is a survivor of the years of hell in the land of his birth. Horror reigned in Germany in the 1930s and 1940s. The author witnessed the rise of the hordes in the black and brown uniforms, the SS and SA, who spread terror among the Jews of Germany.